WILDFLOWERS
of the
SOUTHERN INTERIOR
of
BRITISH COLUMBIA
and Adjacent Parts of

WASHINGTON
IDAHO AND MONTANA

WILDFLOWERS

of the

SOUTHERN INTERIOR

of

BRITISH COLUMBIA

and Adjacent Parts of

WASHINGTON

IDAHO AND MONTANA

by

JOAN BURBRIDGE

UNIVERSITY OF BRITISH COLUMBIA PRESS
VANCOUVER
1989

Canadian Cataloguing in Publication Data
Burbridge, Joan, 1919–
Wildflowers of the Southern Interior of
British Columbia

Bibliography: p.
Includes index.
ISBN 0-7748-0320-7 (bound)
0-7748-0325-8 (pbk.)

1. Wild flowers – British Columbia –
Identification. 2. Wild flowers – Washington
(State) – Identification. 3. Wild flowers –
Idaho – Identification. 4. Wild flowers –
Montana – Identification. I. Title.

QK203.B7B87   1989   582.13′097114   C89-091081-2

This book has been published with the help of grants from the Canada Council, Central Okanagan Foundation, MacMillan Bloedel Limited, Miss. B. E. Adams, Miss Joan Adams, Bridget Duckworth, Mrs. R. B. Moss, and Dr. P. Jones

© THE UNIVERSITY OF BRITISH COLUMBIA PRESS 1989
All rights reserved
Designed by Robin Ward
Typeset in Garamond #3 by The Typeworks, Vancouver
Printed in Canada by Friesen Printers, Manitoba
ISBN 0-7748-0320-7 (cloth) 0-7748-0325-8 (paper)

DEDICATED TO JIM
WHOSE PATIENCE AND ENCOURAGEMENT
HAVE GIVEN ME MORAL SUPPORT
OVER THE YEARS

ACKNOWLEDGMENTS

My grateful thanks are extended to all contributors, without whose co-operation this field guide would never have been possible. Dr. Katherine I. Beamish, Professor Emerata of Botany, University of British Columbia, gave advice and helped identify plants; Dr. Fred R. Ganders, Botany Department, UBC, provided an initial favourable review, slide identification, and invaluable advice; Mary Lou Tapson-Jones and the late Jim Grant assisted in plant identification. I am greatly indebted to Carol E. Thompson, plant ecologist, not only for plant identification but also for many hours checking slide identification, for many constructive suggestions, and for partially editing the manuscript. Special appreciation goes to Wayne Wilson, Kelowna Centennial Museum, who volunteered his personal time to prepare the illustrations and study area map. Thanks are due Gusta Holland, for preliminary typing of the manuscript, to Charles and Margaret Hayes who prepared the first draft, and to the Kelowna Centennial Museum, which provided access to its herbarium.

Joan Burbridge, Kelowna, B.C.

CONTENTS

9/11
INTRODUCTION

12/13
STUDY AREA MAP

14/15
HOW TO USE THIS FIELD GUIDE

16/73
PINK AND RED FLOWERS

74/147
PURPLE AND BLUE FLOWERS

148/237
YELLOW AND ORANGE FLOWERS

238/358
WHITE, GREEN, AND BROWN FLOWERS

359/361
PLANTS IN MORE THAN ONE COLOUR

362/366
GLOSSARY

367/375
FLOWER PARTS AND LEAF TERMINOLOGY

376/377
REFERENCES

379/398
**INDEX OF COMMON AND
SCIENTIFIC NAMES**

IDAHO LOOKOUT AREA, WEST KOOTENAYS

INTRODUCTION

An increasing number of people are interested in the outdoors. Many of these new enthusiasts have developed a keen appreciation for the great variety of wildflowers encountered on their sojourns. This conveniently sized field guide has been prepared to help naturalists, hikers, campers, and botanists recognize some of the numerous wildflowers seen on the trails, back roads, and parks in the south-central Pacific Northwest.

The field guide covers a region broadly known as the Southern Interior (see map on pages 12/13). It stretches from the Cascade Mountains in the west to the Alberta border in the east; from the Trans-Canada Highway in the north to roughly the 45th parallel (through Washington, Idaho, and Montana) in the south. Within this region a myriad of wildflowers colour the meadows, hillsides, and woodlands.

The Southern Interior region is geographically diverse and, accordingly, the area's flora varies dramatically with changes in climate, soils, topography, and elevation. These factors separate the vegetation into zones representing elevational bands across the mountain sides and valleys. Seven zones have been described for the Southern Interior.

At lower elevations in the drier areas the Bunchgrass, Ponderosa Pine, and Interior Douglas fir zones predominate. The Montane Spruce zone occurs on upland slopes at mid-elevations. At higher elevations, occupying the forested areas, is the Englemann Spruce-Subalpine fir zone. The Alpine Tundra zone is found above the treeline. In moister areas, at lower elevations, the Interior Cedar Hemlock zone is evident.

A starting point for the amateur enthusiast would be to learn to recognize tree species which aid in determining the zone. Usually specific plant communities are associated with different zones. For example, *Arrow-leaved Balsamroot* and *Big Basin Sagebrush* are characteristic plants of the Bunchgrass zone, whereas the herbs *Sitka Valerian* and *Simple-Stemmed Twistedstalk* are found at higher elevations in the Englemann Spruce-Subalpine fir zone. Therefore, understanding the relationships between zones and vegetation will aid in finding new flowers as well as in learning to recognize unfamiliar ones.

The field guide describes 335 species, each with an accompanying colour photograph for quick and easy identification. The wildflowers identified and described include: (a) the most showy, familiar or common plants encountered in the region; (b) alien and "weedy" plants that have become well established in the area. The enthusiast is thus provided with the knowledge to identify a wide range of flowers and to note where man has changed the look of the wilderness landscape. Included in the flowering plants are a few smaller flowering shrubs. Trees, ferns, grasses, horsetails, sedges, and rushes have not been described.

Enjoyment of wilderness landscapes is based on aesthetic appreciation and factual information. This field guide will augment the former and strengthen the latter. Enjoy these beautiful flowers.

Carol E. Thompson

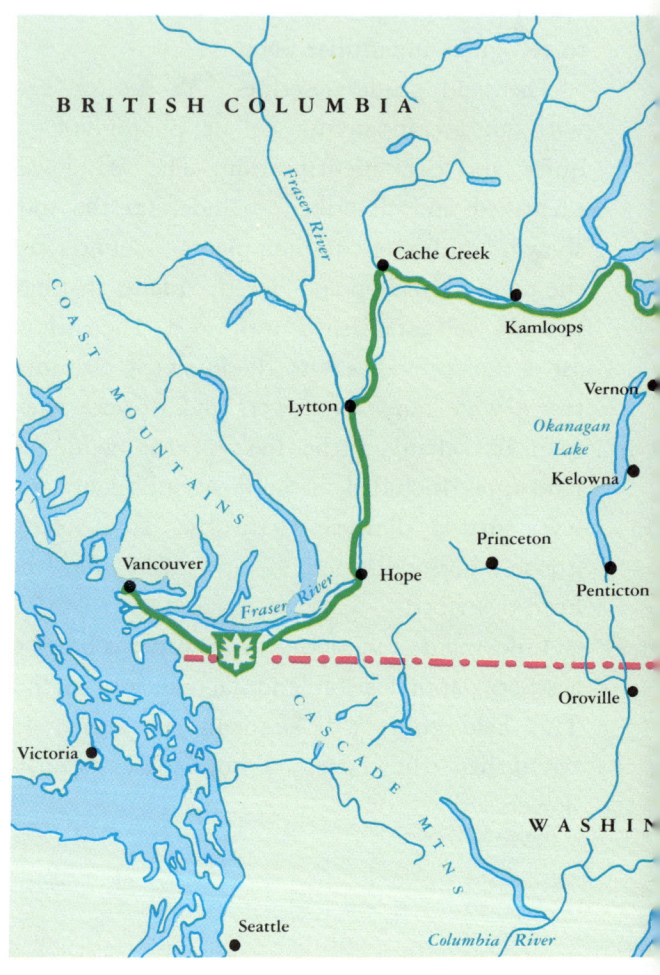

HOW TO USE THIS FIELD GUIDE

COLOUR is the first thing we notice about a flower. This field guide has been arranged in colour sections: (a) PINK AND RED; (b) PURPLE AND BLUE; (c) YELLOW AND ORANGE; and (d) WHITE, GREEN AND BROWN. Occasionally, a flower will have more than one colour. If this is true for the plant you are trying to identify, refer to the list of plants with more than one colour beginning on page 359. In this book a plant is only included once. Within each colour-coded section plant families are in alphabetical order according to scientific name.

Colour photographs of each plant are presented with simple, yet fairly detailed, descriptions which contain as few botanical terms as possible. However, a glossary is provided for those scientific terms used, followed by illustrations of flower structures and leaf terminology.

It is not uncommon for a flower to have several common names. The main common names used in this field guide are from a standard reference.* Botanists use a universal language, Latin, to classify plants. They are divided into familes, and within each family there may be from one to several groups or genuses and one to several species within each genus, thus giving each plant basically two names (e.g., Family = Asteraceae = Daisy Family; genus and species Aster conspicuous = Showy Aster). In this guide, if a family name, genus, or species has been changed, the old names are given in brackets.

The detailed description is provided for each flower for those wishing additional information. The parts of the plant such as (1) flowers (arrangement of the flowers on the plant); (2) each flower (description of a single flower); (3) leaves; (4) stems are described plus facts on colour, height, time of flowering, and the preferred habitat. Notes have been added (where applicable) referring to poison status to humans and to special habits such as parasitic or saprophytic. As it is often rewarding to visit an old haunt expecting to see familiar plants, the duration of growth (annual, biennial, and perennial) has also been included.

*R.L. TAYLOR AND B. MACBRYDE. *Vascular Plants of British Columbia: A Descriptive Resource Inventory.* Vancouver: University of British Columbia Press 1977

PINK *and* RED FLOWERS

SPREADING DOGBANE
Apocynum androsaemifolium

DOGBANE FAMILY
Apocynaceae
Perennial

COLOUR: Pink
HEIGHT: 20–50 cm (8–20″)
FLOWERS: In clusters at end of branched stems
EACH FLOWER: 5–7 mm (¼″) across, bell-shaped with 5 pointed lobes, recurved outwards; 5 stamens, grouped into cone shape inside base of bell; calyx pinkish with 5 small, pointed lobes
LEAVES: Opposite, usually drooping, short-stemmed oval leaves with pointed tips
STEMS: Smooth, round, branched; usually reddish
BLOOMING PERIOD: June–September
HABITAT: Dry ground from valleys to middle elevations
NOTE: Leaves and stems exude sticky, milky juice when injured
NOTE: Poisonous

SHOWY MILKWEED
Asclepias speciosa

MILKWEED FAMILY
Asclepiadaceae
Perennial

OTHER NAMES: Common Milkweed, Silkweed
COLOUR: Mauve-pink
HEIGHT: 40 cm–1.2 m (16″–4′)
FLOWERS: Small, heavily-scented flowers on downy umbrella-stems forming large globular head
EACH FLOWER: 2 cm (¾″) across with 5 pinkish to brownish-purple, pointed, down-curved petals, joined near base to form short tube; inside petals are 5 mauve-pink, erect, horn-shaped structures called hoods, longer than petals; inside hood purple anthers curve over pistil; 5 green sepals, often reddish-tinged at tips and down-curved
LEAVES: Opposite, lance-shaped, 10–20 cm (4–8″) long, up to 10 cm (4″) broad with pinkish mid-rib and pale almost transverse veins; blades softly hairy, downy beneath with short, stout stalks
STEMS: Woody, green, round, slightly downy, hollow
BLOOMING PERIOD: June–August
HABITAT: Moister sandy or gravelly open areas, especially near ditches and streams, also along roadsides. Found at lower elevations
NOTE: Injured stems and leaves exude sticky, milky juice

ROSY PUSSYTOES
Antennaria microphylla
(Antennaria rosea)

ASTER FAMILY
Asteraceae (Compositae)
Perennial

OTHER NAMES: Ladies-tobacco, Cat's-paws, Pink Pussytoes
COLOUR: Deep to pale rose
HEIGHT: 5–40 cm (2–16″)
FLOWERS: Tight clusters of cushiony flowers at tops of stems; often drooping
EACH FLOWER: 5–7 mm (³⁄₁₆–¼″) across; deep to pale rose papery bracts surround compact mass of downy hairs, giving effect of a cat's paw; below are greenish bracts
LEAVES: Many basal, downy, spatula-shaped leaves 8–30 mm (⅜–1¼″) long, forming a rosette. Stem-leaves, alternate, stalkless, narrow, up to 2.5 cm (1″) long
STEMS: Unbranched, erect, greyish with downy hairs
BLOOMING PERIOD: May–August
HABITAT: Open to sparsely wooded, dry areas from low to middle elevations

WAVY-LEAVED THISTLE
Cirsium undulatum

ASTER FAMILY
Asteraceae (Compositae)
Perennial

OTHER NAMES: Woolly Thistle, Prairie Thistle
COLOUR: Purplish-pink or lavender-rose
HEIGHT: 30 cm–1.2 m (1–4′)
FLOWERS: Several single flowers at ends of branches
EACH FLOWER: May be up to 7.5 cm (3″) across with many disk flowers forming large, spreading tuft; involucre fairly squat, round, bracts in tight spiral, outer bracts with sticky ridge, hairy margins and spiny tips
LEAVES: Divided into deeply toothed, spine-tipped lobes; lower leaves have flattened, spine-margined stalks, younger leaves whitish, hairy
STEMS: Downy, branching into flower-stems
BLOOMING PERIOD: May–September
HABITAT: Drier open valleys

PHILADELPHIA FLEABANE
Erigeron philadelphicus

ASTER FAMILY
Asteraceae (Compositae)
Biennial

OTHER NAMES: Daisy Fleabane, Common Fleabane, Skevish
COLOUR: Pink to white
HEIGHT: 20–70 cm (8–28")
FLOWERS: A few to numerous daisy flowers at ends of flower-stem branches
EACH FLOWER: Up to 2.5 cm (1") across with 100–400 very narrow ray petals, giving fringe appearance and surrounding yellow centre of disk-flowers; involucre has many, very narrow, hairy bracts
LEAVES: Basal leaves, inverted lance-shaped or spatula-shaped, narrowing towards base into flattened stalks; stem leaves alternate and clasping; blades slightly toothed, downy, especially on undersides of mid-ribs
STEMS: Slender, slightly downy, branching above into flower-stems
BLOOMING PERIOD: May–July
HABITAT: Mostly in moist, lush, grassy banks, meadows, but variable in habitat

NARROW-LEAVED SKELETONWEED
Stephanomeria tenuifolia

ASTER FAMILY
Asteraceae (Compositae)
Perennial

COLOUR: Pale pink
HEIGHT: 20–70 cm (8–28")
FLOWERS: Single at ends of multi-branched stems
EACH FLOWER: 5 tiny ray-flowers giving appearance of 5 petals with finely-toothed tips; involucre 7–11 mm (¼") high with 5 main bracts and a few smaller ones
LEAVES: Alternate, almost thread-like leaves up to 8 cm (3") long and 3 mm (⅛") broad, upper leaves reduced becoming almost scale-like
STEMS: Several branching near base
BLOOMING PERIOD: June–September
HABITAT: Dry, gravelly, or rocky open places from dry bunchgrass plains to moderate elevations
NOTE: Whole plant exudes milky juice when injured

POLICEMAN'S HELMET
Impatiens glandulifera

BALSAM FAMILY
Balsaminaceae
Annual

OTHER NAMES: Large Touch-me-not
COLOUR: Pink
HEIGHT: 60 cm–1.2 m (2–4′)
FLOWERS: Several in clusters at upper part of stem, from leaf-axils
EACH FLOWER: Large and showy, of complicated structure; large lower sepal 2-lobed, often purple-spotted, extending backwards into sac-shape, terminating in short, recurved spur
LEAVES: Usually opposite, may be whorled, blades pointed-elliptic, finely serrated with pinkish veins; stout, smooth, reddish stalks 2–5 cm (¾–2″) long
STEMS: Flower-stems and main stem, smooth, reddish
BLOOMING PERIOD: July–September
HABITAT: Moist to wet places along roadside ditches, and streams

BEE SPIDERFLOWER
Cleome serrulata

CAPER FAMILY
Capparaceae (Capparidaceae)
Annual

OTHER NAMES: Pink Cleome, Rocky Mountain Bee Plant
COLOUR: Pink
HEIGHT: 60 cm–1.5 m (2–5')
FLOWERS: Fuzzy clusters at ends of branched stems
EACH FLOWER: 4 lance-shaped petals up to 1.3 cm (½") long, narrowing towards base to form tube; 6 stamens protrude well beyond petals giving fuzzy appearance; 4 pointed, green sepals
LEAVES: Alternate with long stalks terminating in 3 narrow, lance-shaped leaflets 1.5–7 cm (⅝–2¾") long
STEMS: Branched, more or less smooth, often reddish
BLOOMING PERIOD: June–August
HABITAT: Prairies, roadsides, and waste land to lower mountainous elevations
NOTE: Poisonous

NORTHERN TWINFLOWER
Linnaea borealis

HONEYSUCKLE FAMILY
Caprifoliaceae
Perennial shrub

OTHER NAMES: American Twinflower
COLOUR: Pink
HEIGHT: 3–10 cm (1–4″)
FLOWERS: 2 nodding, fragrant, bell-shaped flowers
EACH FLOWER: 9–16 mm (½″) long, narrow, bell-shaped with 5 distinct lobes; petals hairy within; 4 stamens, 2 long and 2 short, surround a longer style
LEAVES: 11 mm–2 cm (¾″) long, opposite, small, rounded, leathery, slightly toothed above the middle on either side
STEMS: Trailing, often 1 m (3.3′) long, forming loose mats with short, erect, leafy branches, forked at top to bear "twin flowers"
BLOOMING PERIOD: June–September
HABITAT: Open to dense forests from low to upper elevations

DEPTFORD PINK
Dianthus armeria

PINK FAMILY
Caryophyllaceae
Annual

OTHER NAMES: Grass Pink
COLOUR: Bright pink
HEIGHT: 20–60 cm (8–24″)
FLOWERS: A few small clusters at end of branched stems
EACH FLOWER: 2–2.5 cm (1″) long, 5 petals, shallowly-toothed and white-spotted, 10 stamens, joined to petals; calyx acutely 5-pointed and hairy, surrounded by narrow, hairy, pointed bracts
LEAVES: 4–10 cm (1½–4″) long, opposite, and linear-shaped (almost grass-like)
STEMS: Single or simply branched, always hairy
BLOOMING PERIOD: May–August
HABITAT: Dry, gravelly, grassy banks, open places
NOTE: Flowers only open briefly at midday

MOSS CAMPION
Silene acaulis
subsp. subacaulescens

PINK FAMILY
Caryophyllaceae
Perennial

OTHER NAMES: Moss Pink, Cushion Pink, Dwarf Silene
COLOUR: Bright to pale pink to lavender (rarely white)
HEIGHT: 3–6 cm (1–2½″) and extending in tight cushions for nearly a metre
FLOWERS: Many small single flowers at ends of branches
EACH FLOWER: 8–10 mm (up to ½″) across, 5 notched flat petals join to form a tube; 10 stamens protrude slightly beyond petals; 5-pointed calyx encloses tubular flower
LEAVES: Mostly basal, short, needle-like leaves, crowded together to form bright green cushion (resembling patches of moss)
STEMS: Very short single flower-stem
BLOOMING PERIOD: June–August
HABITAT: Rock crevices, open exposed ridges on stony ground at high elevations above timberline

RED SAND SPURREY
Spergularia rubra

PINK FAMILY
Caryophyllaceae
Annual

COLOUR: Pink
HEIGHT: Up to 30 cm (12″) usually spreading in mats
FLOWERS: Several, from leaf-axils
EACH FLOWER: Up to 7 mm (¼″) across; 5 rounded petals, shorter than sepals; usually 10 stamens surrounding fat ovary with 3 styles; calyx 5-pointed, brownish, almost transparent margins
LEAVES: Very narrow, 5–15 mm (½″) long, arranged in bunches along stem
STEMS: Many, mostly forming mats
BLOOMING PERIOD: April–October
HABITAT: Dry, waste places

STRAWBERRY-BLITE GOOSEFOOT
Chenopodium capitatum

GOOSEFOOT FAMILY
Chenopodiaceae
Annual

COLOUR: Bright crimson
HEIGHT: 20–80 cm (8–32″)
FLOWERS: In dense strawberry-like, globular, stemless clusters, especially at top of stem, lower clusters in leaf-axils
EACH FLOWER: Minute with 3–5 lobes becoming bright-crimson after maturity; innumerable flowers form globular, strawberry-like, fleshy cluster, about 1.3 cm (½″) across
LEAVES: Alternate, triangular with base-angles extenuated, almost fleshy, up to 10 cm (4″) long with wavy margins; reducing in size up stem; stalks shorter than blades
STEMS: Smooth, green and branching
BLOOMING PERIOD: June–August; red at end of August–September
HABITAT: Waste places and roadsides

RED EUROPEAN GLASSWORT *Salicornia europaea subsp. rubra (Salicornia rubra)*

GOOSEFOOT FAMILY
Chenopodiaceae
Annual

OTHER NAMES: Samphire, Saltwort
COLOUR: Red
HEIGHT: 10–25 cm (4–10″)
FLOWERS: Extremely small, in 3's, scarcely visible, sunken just above scales that serve as leaves
LEAVES: Opposite, scale-like
STEMS: Main stem branches into reddish, thin, finger-like, jointed stems, on the whole more slender than *Salicornia europaea subsp. europaea*
BLOOMING PERIOD: July–September
HABITAT: Moist to dry alkaline soils around sloughs

KINNIKINNICK
Arctostaphylos uva-ursi

HEATH FAMILY
Ericaceae
Perennial shrub

OTHER NAMES: Bearberry, Sandberry, Hog Cranberry
COLOUR: Pale pink, red
HEIGHT: 5–10 cm (2–4″) mostly trailing
FLOWERS: Several in drooping clusters
EACH FLOWER: About 5 mm (¼″) long; urn-shaped with slightly 5-lobed petals; 10 stamens
LEAVES: Oblong spatula-shaped; 1.5–3 cm (⅝–1¼″) long; entire, dark green and shiny on top; alternate with short stalks
STEMS: Brown to reddish, trailing, often forming mats up to several metres broad
BLOOMING PERIOD: March–August
HABITAT: Sea level to just below timberline, moist to dry forests, open sandy areas

WESTERN SWAMP KALMIA
*Kalmia microphylla
subsp. occidentalis
(Kalmia polifolia)*

HEATH FAMILY
Ericaceae
Perennial shrub

OTHER NAMES: Swamplaurel, Mountain Laurel, Pale Laurel
COLOUR: Pink
HEIGHT: 10–40 cm (4–16″)
FLOWERS: Several in loose clusters at ends of stems
EACH FLOWER: 1–2 cm (¾″) across; petals form a 5-pointed, shallow saucer-shaped flower with crinkly appearance; 10 stamens, shorter than petals, about same length as pistil. 5 narrow, brownish-pink sepals 2–3 mm (⅛″) long form greenish ring where they join stem
LEAVES: Opposite, short-stalked leaves, narrow, oblong, oval-pointed, 1–4 cm (½–1½″) long, 7 mm (¼″) broad; upper surface dark green, shiny; under surface greyish and dull; edges rolled under
STEMS: Flower-stems deep purple-red, up to 2.5 cm (1″) long; lower ⅔ of main stem bare and woody
BLOOMING PERIOD: May–September
HABITAT: Bogs at lower elevations and wet mountain meadows

RED MOUNTAIN-HEATHER
Phyllodoce empetriformis

HEATH FAMILY
Ericaceae
Perennial shrub

OTHER NAMES: False Heather, Pink Mountain-heather
COLOUR: Pink to deep rose
HEIGHT: 10–40 cm (4–16")
FLOWERS: In short umbrella-stemmed clusters at ends of stems
EACH FLOWER: Up to 7 mm (¼") long, urn-shaped with 5 lobes and tips rolled under; 5-pointed calyx lobes; stamens 10; style protrudes just beyond petals
LEAVES: Numerous narrow, smooth, evergreen leaves 8–16 mm (1½") long and grooved on lower surface
STEMS: Woody, branched, forming large mats, young stems hairy and with glands
BLOOMING PERIOD: June–August
HABITAT: Mountain slopes and meadows from sub-alpine to alpine elevations

NORTHERN HEDYSARUM
Hedysarum boreale

PEA FAMILY
Fabaceae (Leguminosae)
Perennial

OTHER NAMES: Sweet Vetch
COLOUR: Bright purple-red to whitish
HEIGHT: 20–60 cm (8"–2')
FLOWERS: Numerous in loose, short, spike-like clusters on long stems
EACH FLOWER: 18–20 mm (1") long; standard erect with sides curved backwards; keel longer than lateral wings either side of it; all petals faintly veined; calyx 6 mm (5/16") long; 5 lobes, narrow and pointed, upper 2 lobes shorter
LEAVES: 9–13 leaflets, oblong-shaped or wider, no tendrils
STEMS: Square, often reddish
BLOOMING PERIOD: June–July
HABITAT: Dry, shrubby slopes and woodland

COMMON SAINFOIN
Onobrychis viciifolia

PEA FAMILY
Fabaceae (Leguminosae)
Perennial

OTHER NAMES: Holy Clover, Sandfain
COLOUR: Deep pink to lavender
HEIGHT: 20–40 cm (8–16″)
FLOWERS: Numerous small flowers in axillary and terminal spike-like cluster
EACH FLOWER: 10–12 mm (½″) long, wings shorter than standard and keel. Petals conspicuously finely-striped with deep purplish pink veins; calyx bell-shaped with long slender teeth; 10 stamens, joined together
LEAVES: Alternate with opposite pairs of narrow, oblong leaflets about 2 cm (¾″) long; reddish-brown pointed stipules
STEMS: Sparsely hairy with long flower-stems from leaf-axils
BLOOMING PERIOD: May–July
HABITAT: Open meadows, roadsides
LOCATION: Scattered throughout Dry Interior
NOTE: Grown for agricultural purposes

RED CLOVER
Trifolium pratense

PEA FAMILY
Fabaceae (Leguminosae)
Perennial

COLOUR: Deep red-purple red
HEIGHT: 30 cm–1 m (12–39¼")
FLOWERS: In terminal, globular head 2.5–3 cm (1–1¼") across, composed of many tiny pea-like flowers
EACH FLOWER: 13–20 mm (½") long; slightly recurved standard above with 2 wings below enclosing an upcurved keel; 10 stamens, joined together in 2 groups; calyx 5-toothed, green and hairy
LEAVES: 3 leaflets up to 6 cm (2⅜") long, lance-egg-shaped, on long stalks with stipules at base (this leaf is characteristic of most clovers)
STEMS: Softly hairy, branching from base
BLOOMING PERIOD: April–October
HABITAT: Lush meadows, roadsides

PACIFIC BLEEDINGHEART
Dicentra formosa

FUMITORY FAMILY
Fumariaceae
Perennial

COLOUR: Pinkish-purple
HEIGHT: 15–45 cm (6–18″)
FLOWERS: Several flowers droop in small, branched clusters at ends of long erect stems
EACH FLOWER: 2 cm (¾″) long, heart-shaped; 4 petals, in 2 pairs, outer 2 with pouch at broad base, narrow at the tip where they are pinched together, joined and out-turned, inner 2 smaller with wavy crest; flower has flattened appearance; 6 stamens in 2 sets; slender style terminating in 2-lobed stigma; 2 scale-like sepals that drop off
LEAVES: On long basal stalks 22–50 cm (9–20″), divided into 3 branches with fern-like leaf blades
STEMS: Smooth
BLOOMING PERIOD: May–August
HABITAT: Moist, shady woods from low to moderate elevations
NOTE: May cause dermatitis

COMMON STORK'S-BILL
Erodium cicutarium

GERANIUM FAMILY
Geraniaceae
Annual

OTHER NAMES: Crane's-bill, Filaree, Clocks
COLOUR: Pink
HEIGHT: 7.5–50 cm (3–20″)
FLOWERS: A few flowers on upright umbrella-stems at ends of simply branched stems
EACH FLOWER: 9 mm–1.3 cm (⅜–½″) across with 5 elliptical petals; 10 stamens, 5 shorter and almost scale-like, the other 5 with anthers; small sepals bristled at tips; fruit resembles stork's bill
LEAVES: Lower leaves have hairy, reddish stalks, oppositely lobed dissected leaflets; 1 or 2 pairs of opposite stem-leaves
STEMS: Rigid, hairy, reddish, opposite branching with small swelling and stipules where they branch
BLOOMING PERIOD: April–July
HABITAT: Open, drier ground

STICKY PURPLE CRANE'S-BILL
Geranium viscosissimum

Geranium Family
Geraniaceae
Perennial

Other Names: Pink Geranium
Colour: Pale to deep rose-pink
Height: 40–90 cm (16–35")
Flowers: Up to 3 (usually 2) large flowers at top of stems
Each Flower: 2.5 cm (1") across, 5 broad, rounded petals with fine, dark veins; 10 stamens surrounding a column-like pistil
Leaves: Mostly basal, 5–12 cm (2–5") wide, deeply cleft into 5 or more sharply-toothed lobes, covered with sticky hairs
Stems: Flower stems thick, hairy, sticky, and branched
Blooming Period: May–August
Habitat: Moist meadows and open woods. Scattered throughout Dry Interior

PURPLE BLUE-EYED GRASS
Sisyrinchium inflatum

IRIS FAMILY
Iridaceae
Perennial

OTHER NAMES: Grass Widows, Satinflower
COLOUR: Pale lavender-pink (occasionally deep purple)
HEIGHT: 10–30 cm (4–12")
FLOWERS: 1–3 delicate, almost nodding flowers at top of single stems
EACH FLOWER: 4 cm (1½") across on thin stem, backed by 2 pointed, ribbed bracts of unequal length; 6 petals, darker veined, oval and pointed; 3 stamens, partially joined with yellow anthers; pistil with 3-lobed styles
LEAVES: 2 or 3 smaller sheath-like leaves at base, longer grass-like leaves up to 10 cm (4") long wrap stem
STEMS: Dark green, ribbed, slightly flattened, unbranched
BLOOMING PERIOD: March–June
HABITAT: Moist bunchgrass-sagebrush or drier sagebrush-juniper communities and in open Ponderosa pine forests

WILD BERGAMOT
Monarda fistulosa

MINT FAMILY
Lamiaceae (Labiatae)
Perennial

OTHER NAMES: Horse Mint
COLOUR: Purple-pink
HEIGHT: 30–60 cm (1–2′)
FLOWERS: In clusters at ends of single stems, leafy bracts below clusters
EACH FLOWER: 2.5–3.5 cm (1–1½″) long, tubular with 2 petals, upper lip narrow and hairy, lower lip 3-lobed; 2 stamens, extending beyond tubular flower; calyx with 5 pointed teeth
LEAVES: Opposite, lance-shaped, 2.5–8 cm (1–3″) long, dull green; aromatic when crushed
STEMS: Square, unbranched, covered with fine, short hairs
BLOOMING PERIOD: June–August
HABITAT: Open, moist places from low to middle elevations. Sparsely scattered in Dry Interior

NODDING ONION
Allium cernuum

LILY FAMILY
Liliaceae
Perennial

OTHER NAMES: Wild Garlic, Leek
COLOUR: Mauve-pink or white
HEIGHT: 25–50 cm (10–20″)
FLOWERS: Nodding in cluster on pendulous, unequal length umbrella-stems
EACH FLOWER: 7 mm (¼″) across, 3, broad, pointed petal-like sepals and 3 darker, narrow petals inside; 6 stamens twice as long as petals; remains of papery sheath persist at hub of umbrella-stems
LEAVES: Several grass-like basal leaves, 30 cm (1′) or more long, margins curled in to give rounded appearance
STEMS: Single, leafless, round, green, covered with a bloom
BLOOMING PERIOD: June–July
HABITAT: Dry to moist wooded or open areas, from valleys to high elevations

WOOD LILY
Lilium philadelphicum var. andinum

LILY FAMILY
Liliaceae
Perennial

OTHER NAMES: Red Lily, Philadelphia Lily, Chalice-cup Lily
COLOUR: Orange-red
HEIGHT: 30–90 cm (1–3')
FLOWERS: 1–3 to single stem
EACH FLOWER: 7.5–10 cm (3–4") across, chalice-shaped with 6 broad, pointed, out-curved tepals, tapered at base, black-spotted inside; 6 long stamens with blackish anthers protrude almost beyond tepals and surround dark-tipped style
LEAVES: Alternate below, whorled at flower-stems; narrow lance-shaped, 5–10 cm (2–4") long 3–9 mm (⅛–⅜") broad, dull green above, shiny beneath with central rib
STEMS: Unbranched, dull green, smooth, round, rigid
BLOOMING PERIOD: June–August
HABITAT: Moist, open, often deciduous wooded areas, grassy meadows

SIMPLE-STEMMED TWISTEDSTALK
Streptopus roseus var. curvipes

LILY FAMILY
Liliaceae
Perennial

OTHER NAMES: Pink Mandarin
COLOUR: Pink to purplish-pink
HEIGHT: 30–80 cm (12–32")
FLOWERS: Several single flowers on single, thin, hairy stems hanging beneath leaves, slightly twisted flower-stems originate on main stem at leaf-axils
EACH FLOWER: Small bell-shaped, up to 5 mm (3/16") long with 6 tepals, flared whitish tips; 6 short stamens from base of each tepal
LEAVES: Alternate, pointed-oval, prominently veined longitudinally with hairy margins, almost clasping the stem
STEM: Unbranched, smooth, ribbed
BLOOMING PERIOD: June–July
HABITAT: Moist, shady woods at higher elevations

MOUNTAIN HOLLYHOCK
Iliamna rivularis

MALLOW FAMILY
Malvaceae
Perennial

OTHER NAMES: Wild Hollyhock, Globe Mallow
COLOUR: Pale pink to deep rose-pink
HEIGHT: 90 cm–1.8 m (3–6′)
FLOWERS: In loose spikes in upper leaf-axils
EACH FLOWER: Short-stemmed, up to 5 cm (2″) across with 5 petals broadening towards slightly notched outer margins; many fuzzy stamens, united below, surround a sturdy pistil with club-shaped stigma; calyx shortly 5-pointed
LEAVES: Alternate; large maple-leaf blades 15–20 cm (6–8″) long and 10–25 cm (4–10″) broad; maple-like leaf stalks about ⅓ as long as blades
STEMS: Green, woody, ridged; rough with main flower-stems from leaf-axils
BLOOMING PERIOD: June–August
HABITAT: Moist, grassy roadsides, streambanks from foothills to mountainous elevations

PINK FAIRIES
Clarkia pulchella

EVENING PRIMROSE FAMILY
Onagraceae
Annual

OTHER NAMES: Ragged Robin
COLOUR: Purplish-rose
HEIGHT: 15–46 cm (6–18″)
FLOWERS: In loose cluster at upper portion of stem
EACH FLOWER: 1.3–4 cm (½–1½″) across with 4 petals borne on a long, green ovary, each petal narrow at base with two tiny arms then broadening into 3 deep, rounded lobes which give a ragged appearance; 4 stamens with pinkish-white anthers; long, thin style terminates in a 4-lobed white stigma; pinkish sepals joined to form pointed sheath at right-angles to flower-stem
LEAVES: 2.5–4 cm (1–1½″) long, strap-like, grooved down middle
STEMS: Rigid, smooth, brownish-red and branched above
BLOOMING PERIOD: Late May to late July
HABITAT: Dryish, sunny banks

FIREWEED
Epilobium
angustifolium

EVENING PRIMROSE FAMILY
Onagraceae
Perennial

OTHER NAMES: Willow Weed, Great Willowherb
COLOUR: Purple-rose
HEIGHT: 30 cm–2 m (1–7′)
FLOWERS: In loose, pointed pyramidal spike
EACH FLOWER: Up to 2.5 cm (1″) across with 4 egg-shaped petals, broad end outermost; 8 stamens, shorter than pistil which terminates in 4-lobed crook-like stigma; 4 narrow, pointed sepals almost same colour as petals, flower borne on long, tubular pinkish ovary; lower flowers may be in seed as upper ones bloom
LEAVES: Many, long, narrow, willow-like, up to 5 cm (2″), arranged haphazardly up stem
STEMS: Strong, usually unbranched
BLOOMING PERIOD: June–August
HABITAT: Waste places, burns, roadsides, in less dry areas at most elevations to sub-alpine

PURPLE-LEAVED WILLOWHERB
Epilobium ciliatum
(Epilobium watsonii)

EVENING PRIMROSE FAMILY
Onagraceae
Perennial

OTHER NAMES: Watson's Epilobium
COLOUR: Pale to deep pink
HEIGHT: 30–90 cm (1–3′)
FLOWERS: Several small flowers from upper leaf-axils
EACH FLOWER: 4 deeply-notched petals 3–7 mm (⅛–¼″) long; narrow, pointed, purplish sepals; ovary below flower may be over 4 cm (1½″) long, slightly hairy
LEAVES: Lance-shaped, finely serrated, very short-stalked or stalkless above
STEMS: Green, slightly hairy
BLOOMING PERIOD: June–August
HABITAT: Wet, grassy areas

BROAD-LEAVED FIREWEED
Epilobium latifolium

EVENING PRIMROSE FAMILY
Onagraceae
Perennial

COLOUR: Deep rose to rose-purple
HEIGHT: 10–50 cm (4–20″)
FLOWERS: A few in open clusters at tops of stems
EACH FLOWER: 4 broad, rounded petals; 4 narrow, pointed sepals of similar colour; 8 stamens; longer than style with 4-lobed stigma, flower borne on long rose-purple ovary
LEAVES: Mostly opposite especially below, blue-green, fleshy, very short-stalked with lance-shaped blades, covered with whitish bloom
STEMS: Many branched stems; smooth and green
BLOOMING PERIOD: June–September
HABITAT: Mostly at alpine and sub-alpine elevations in moist places, streambanks, wet rocky areas, and gravel bars

ROUND-LEAVED ORCHIS
Amerorchis rotundifolia
(Orchis rotundifolia)

ORCHID FAMILY
Orchidaceae
Perennial

OTHER NAMES: Spotted Kirtle-pink
COLOUR: Pale purple-pink to white
HEIGHT: 10–30 cm (4–12″)
FLOWERS: In loose, short spike-like cluster at upper end of single stem
EACH FLOWER: 1.3 cm (½″) or more long, upper 2 petals hood-like and purple-veined inside; behind is a longer, paler petal-like sepal; 2 narrow, lateral wing-like sepals may be almost white, 3-lobed, about 1.3 cm (½″) long, spreading, with middle lobe elongated, notched, usually pale pink and dark purplish-spotted or sometimes with 2 blotchy, dark purplish stripes, elongated ovary, usually purplish with green, pointed bract below
LEAVES: Single broad, pointed egg-shaped leaf at base, 4–5 cm (1½–2″) long and 2.5–3 cm (1–1¼″) broad with central vein
STEMS: Rigid, round, smooth, may be reddish
HABITAT: Boggy, swampy, open wooded areas up to mountainous elevations in isolated areas

FAIRYSLIPPER
Calypso bulbosa

ORCHID FAMILY
Orchidaceae
Perennial

OTHER NAMES: Venus-slipper, Dear-head Orchid
COLOUR: Purplish-rose
HEIGHT: 10–25 cm (4–10″)
FLOWERS: A solitary nodding flower to a single stem; often grows in masses
EACH FLOWER: 2.5–4 cm (1–1½″) across with 9 mm–2 cm (⅜–¾″) long, narrow lance-shaped, purplish-pink sepals and petals, all alike, 9 mm–2.5 cm (⅜–1″) long, one is actually the third petal, pale pink and purple-spotted, sac-like, slipper-shaped with 2 small, spur-like projections at its tip; inside hairy, sac-like part brownish-purple
LEAVES: Single, dark green, pointed egg-shaped 2.5–6 cm (1–2¼″) long, ribbed, lower half narrows into stalk about same length as blade
STEMS: Flower-stem slender, pale biscuit to pale purplish, 1 or 2 brownish, sheath-like bracts
BLOOMING PERIOD: March–June
HABITAT: Cool, moist, mossy forest floors and banks

GIANT HELLEBORINE
Epipactis gigantea

ORCHID FAMILY
Orchidaceae
Perennial

OTHER NAMES: Stream Orchis, Chatterbox
COLOUR: Purplish-rose
HEIGHT: 30 cm–1m (1'–40")
FLOWERS: In very loose almost one-sided spike of 3–15 flowers
EACH FLOWER: 4 cm (1½") across consisting of 3 greenish-yellow, sometimes pinkish-tinged, pointed sepals, often green-veined on back; side ones 2 cm (¾") long, 7 mm (¼") broad, top one shorter and narrower, upper 2 petals, more pinkish-tinged, strongly purple-veined inside; purple-rose lip, pouched and 3-lobed, middle lobe protruding, appears hinged; ovary about 1.5 cm (⅝") long, green, ribbed, tapering below into very short stem arising from leaf-axils at upper ¼ of stem
LEAVES: Narrow lance-shaped from 15–20 cm (6–8") long, 2.5–5 cm (1–2") broad, softly hairy, ribbed, diminishing into bracts up stem which they sheathe
STEMS: Unbranched, green, smooth, rigid
HABITAT: Very moist stream-banks, lake edges, and marshes

LARGE-FLOWERED COLLOMIA
Collomia grandiflora

PHLOX FAMILY
Polemoniaceae
Annual

OTHER NAMES: Salmon-coloured Collomia
COLOUR: Pale salmon-pink to orange
HEIGHT: 15–60 cm (6"–2')
FLOWERS: Small tubular flowers in close cluster at top of single stems
EACH FLOWER: About 2 cm (¾") long with long, narrow tube opening into 5 elliptic petals; 5 stamens of unequal length; style equal in length to longest ones; calyx 5-pointed and slightly sticky as are 1.5 cm (⅝") bracts surrounding it
LEAVES: Alternate, stalkless, lance-shaped, up to 5 cm (2") long with deep central vein; lower leaves often wither early
STEMS: Rigid, almost smooth, often reddish
BLOOMING PERIOD: May–August
HABITAT: Dry, open areas

SCARLET SKYROCKET
Ipomopsis aggregata
subsp. aggregata
(Gilia aggregata)

PHLOX FAMILY
Polemoniaceae
Biennial

OTHER NAMES: Foxfire, Polecat Plant, Scarlet Gilia
COLOUR: Bright scarlet
HEIGHT: 20 cm–1.3 m (8″–3½′)
FLOWERS: In often one-sided, loose spike-like cluster on single stem
EACH FLOWER: Long trumpet-shaped up to 2.5 cm (1″) long, 2 cm (¾″) across; long, narrow tube opens out into 5 narrow, pointed, often white-mottled petals giving star effect; protruding just beyond petals are 5 yellowish stamens; calyx 7 mm (¼″) long with 5 narrow, pointed teeth; flower-stems may be over 1.3 cm (½″) long with bracts on main stem
LEAVES: May be up length of stem, lower ones 4 cm (1½″) long and dissected into several narrow, finger-like, opposite leaflets which are downy on upper surfaces; leaves become progressively smaller up stem
STEMS: Rigid, green and reddish towards base
BLOOMING PERIOD: May–August
HABITAT: Open, dry, gravelly banks and sparsely wooded areas and sagebrush country from low to higher elevations
NOTE: Poisonous

PINK MICROSTERIS
Microsteris gracilis
subsp. humilis
(var. humilior)

PHLOX FAMILY
Polemoniaceae
Annual

COLOUR: Pink
HEIGHT: Up to 2.5–6.5 cm (1–2½")
FLOWERS: Tiny flowers at ends of single or branched stems
EACH FLOWER: Tubular and 3 mm (⅛") across with 5 petals and 5 pointed, hairy sepals about length of tube
LEAVES: Opposite, elliptical, stalkless stem-leaves, 7 mm (¼") long, 3 mm (⅛") broad, hairy, especially beneath, lower leaves become reddish
STEMS: Slightly hairy, branched above
BLOOMING PERIOD: March–June
HABITAT: Dry to moist open places at lower elevations

LONG-LEAVED PHLOX
Phlox longifolia

PHLOX FAMILY
Polemoniaceae
Perennial

COLOUR: Pink to white
HEIGHT: 10–40 cm (4–16″)
FLOWERS: In loose cluster at ends of branched stems
EACH FLOWER: 2–2.5 cm (¾–1″) across; 5 petals, joined below into narrow tube 1.3 cm (½″) long, 5 green, pointed sepals as long as the tube
LEAVES: Opposite, up entire length of stem, thin, grass-like up to 4 cm (1½″) long
STEM: Woody and branched mainly near base
BLOOMING PERIOD: April–July
HABITAT: Arid to dry sagebrush slopes in rocky or gravelly ground to moderate elevations

WATER SMARTWEED
Polygonum amphibium

BUCKWHEAT FAMILY
Polygonaceae
Perennial

OTHER NAMES: Lady's Thumb
COLOUR: Rose pink
HEIGHT: Up to 80 cm (32″)
FLOWERS: Many tiny flowers in short, dense, spike-like, tight cluster 1–3 cm (½–1¼″) long at ends of erect flowering branches
EACH FLOWER: 4–5 mm (⅛–³⁄₁₆″) long; perianth 5-parted; 8 stamens, longer than perianth; 2 styles
LEAVES: Usually floating, elliptic, up to 15 cm (6″) long with conspicuous midribs; aerial stem-leaves if present, stalked, with stipules, alternate, blades larger and more pointed than floating leaves
STEMS: Prostrate when aquatic habitat and erect in streambank habitat. Flower stems always erect
BLOOMING PERIOD: June–September
HABITAT: Water or wet places, stream and pool banks

ALPINE LEWISIA
Lewisia pygmaea
var. pygmaea

PURSLANE FAMILY
Portulacaceae
Perennial

OTHER NAMES: Dwarf Lewisia
COLOUR: Pink to white
HEIGHT: 1.3–7.5 cm (½–3")
FLOWERS: 1 flower to a stem; there may be several stems from one root
EACH FLOWER: 5–9 pale pink to white, reddish-veined petals 7 mm–1.3 cm (¼–½") long forming a tiny saucer-shape; the 5–6 branched style is surrounded by 5–12 stamens; 2 shiny, greenish, oval, pointed sepals may be joined ⅔ of the way down
LEAVES: Several basal, fleshy, strap-like leaves, 6.5–13 cm (2½–5") long and 3 mm–1.3 cm (⅛–½") broad, tapering toward base and slightly warty on both sides
STEMS: Several flower-stems from fleshy root, green, fleshy with a pair of opposite bracts part way up
BLOOMING PERIOD: End of May–August
HABITAT: Drier open areas at high elevations from just below to above timberline

BITTERROOT LEWISIA
Lewisia rediviva

PURSLANE FAMILY
Portulacaceae
Perennial

OTHER NAMES: Rock Rose, Spatlum, Sandhill Rose
COLOUR: Rose to white
HEIGHT: 2–7.5 cm (¾–3")
FLOWERS: Large single flower to a stem; may be several stems to one fleshy root
EACH FLOWER: 5–7.5 cm (2–3") across when fully open, with 10–18 slightly-pointed petals from 2.5 cm–4 cm (1–1½") long which together with 6–8 creamy-pink sepals form a shallow saucer; style with 4–8 branched stigma surrounded by numerous stamens
LEAVES: Several long, narrow fleshy leaves, round in cross-section, usually withered before flower appears
STEMS: Flower-stems 2.5–7.5 cm (1–3") long, reddish with whorl of 5–6 bracts
BLOOMING PERIOD: May–July
HABITAT: Dry to arid gravelly or rocky slopes in sagebrush areas

SMALL-LEAVED MONTIA
Montia parvifolia

PURSLANE FAMILY
Portulacaceae
Perennial

COLOUR: Pale pink
HEIGHT: Up to 60 cm (2')
FLOWERS: 1 to several at ends of slender stems
EACH FLOWER: 5 rounded petals 7 mm–1.3 cm (¼–½")
long, darker-veined; 5 stamens; 2 sepals of unequal length
LEAVES: Basal leaves inverted egg-shaped from 1.5–2.5
cm (⅝–1") long in a rosette; stem-leaves alternate, much
smaller
STEMS: May be several flowering stems radiating from
base, often reddish
BLOOMING PERIOD: May–August
HABITAT: Moist areas

FEW-FLOWERED SHOOTINGSTAR

PRIMULA FAMILY
Primulaceae
Perennial

Dodecatheon pulchellum subsp. pulchellum
(Dodecatheon pauciflorum)

OTHER NAMES: Peacock, Birdbills, American Cowslip
COLOUR: Purple-rose
HEIGHT: 7.5–25 cm (3–10″)
FLOWERS: 1 to several to a single stem
EACH FLOWER: 1.3–1.5 cm (½–⅝″) across with 5 narrow, pointed, recurved petals, centre of which appear as a yellow circle centred by a point, formed by dark stamens, which enclose thin style; greenish, pointed sepals hidden by recurved petals
LEAVES: Basal, pointed paddle-shaped, 6.5–9 cm (2½–3½″) long 1.3–1.5 cm (½–⅝″) broad and reddish; reddish, softly hairy main stem, branches above into flowering stems
BLOOMING PERIOD: April–August
HABITAT: Moist grassy areas from low elevations to above timberline

MEALY PRIMROSE
Primula incana

PRIMROSE FAMILY
Primulaceae
Perennial

COLOUR: Pink
HEIGHT: 5–36 cm (2–14")
FLOWERS: Small flowers on umbrella-stems at top of single stems
EACH FLOWER: 3–7 mm (⅛–¼") across with 5 flat, deeply-notched petals; middle of flower appears as "yellow eye"; calyx has 5 lobes covered with mealy down
LEAVES: All at base, almost spatula-shaped, roundly toothed; covered with mealy down underneath, giving whitish appearance
STEMS: Single, wiry, covered with mealy down
BLOOMING PERIOD: May–July
HABITAT: Moist, mossy streambanks, meadows at moderate elevations

COMMON WESTERN PIPSISSEWA
Chimaphila umbellata subsp. occidentalis

WINTERGREEN FAMILY
Pyrolaceae (Ericaceae)
Perennial shrub

OTHER NAMES: Waxflower, Prince's Pine
COLOUR: Pink to white
HEIGHT: 10–30 cm (4–12")
FLOWERS: Several, often nodding, in loose cluster at top of mostly single stems
EACH FLOWER: 7 mm (¼") across with 5 rounded, waxy, pink petals, recurved to show circle of 10 short stamens with purple anthers, surrounding a stout style with a round 5-lobed very sticky stigma; sepals have jagged margins; flower-stems usually curved, about 7 mm (¼") long
LEAVES: Dark green, leathery, shiny, up to 7.5 cm (3") long, 2.5 cm (1") broad with sharply serrated margins; stalkless
STEMS: Green, rough and woody
BLOOMING PERIOD: June–August
HABITAT: Mostly coniferous woods

**COMMON PINK
PYROLA**
Pyrola asarifolia

WINTERGREEN FAMILY
Pyrolaceae (Ericaceae)
Perennial

OTHER NAME: Bog Pyrola, Oregon Wintergreen
COLOUR: Pale to deep pink
HEIGHT: 13–46 cm (5–18″)
FLOWERS: Several waxy, pink flowers in long, loose spike-like arrangement
EACH FLOWER: 1.3–1.5 cm (½–⅝″) across with 5, rounded petals; 10 reddish stamens bunched together under top middle petal; long, curved, beak-like style protrudes well beyond petals; 5 yellowish-green sepals
LEAVES: Several basal leaves up to 7.5 cm (3″) in diameter, round to kidney-shaped or elliptic, shiny, dark green above, dull beneath, often pink-tinged with slightly wavy margins and network of veins giving almost leathery appearance; stalks up to 9 cm (3½″) long and triangular in cross-section
STEMS: Smooth, often reddish, almost square with 2 or 3 small scale-like bracts
BLOOMING PERIOD: June–September
HABITAT: Moist shady or often open areas, and bogs

OLD MAN'S WHISKERS
Geum triflorum

ROSE FAMILY
Rosaceae
Perennial

OTHER NAMES: Lion's Beard, Plumed Avens
COLOUR: Purplish-pink or yellow
HEIGHT: 15–46 cm (6–18″)
FLOWERS: 1–9 in loose cluster at end of stem, often nodding
EACH FLOWER: 2 cm long; calyx cone-shaped with narrow bracts longer than the sepals; 5 petals, pinkish or purplish to yellow, sometimes hidden by bracts; lower portion of style feathery; numerous stamens
LEAVES: Basal, 5–15 cm (2–6″) long, downy; leaf appears feathery, leaf segments deeply cleft
STEMS: Flower-stems up to 30 cm (1′) long, hairy, pinkish above; pair of small, cleft leaves with pinkish stipules halfway up stem
BLOOMING PERIOD: April–July
HABITAT: Moister open banks, often in sagebrush areas and up to higher altitudes

MARSH CINQUEFOIL
Potentilla palustris

ROSE FAMILY
Rosaceae
Perennial

OTHER NAMES: Marsh Fivefinger
COLOUR: Wine-red
HEIGHT: Up to 1 m (39¼")
FLOWERS: In loose few-flowered clusters
EACH FLOWER: 2.2 cm (⅞") across with 5 small, shiny, wine-red, pointed petals, 5 longer, sharply pointed sepals, hairy at tips on the outside, greenish on outside, brownish-red on inside. 5 tiny recurved bracts alternate with sepals. In centre of flower up to 25 wine-red stamens surround cone of wine-red styles
LEAVES: Have stalks up to 7.5 cm (3") long sheathing stem. Three or 4 pairs of opposite, elliptic, toothed leaflets and 1 terminal leaflet. Upper surface green, under-surface almost greyish
STEMS: Woody, hollow, may be creeping or erect, green, slightly hairy above, reddish towards base
BLOOMING PERIOD: June–August
HABITAT: Lake edges, bogs, wet meadows, and streambanks. Scattered throughout the area

HARDHACK
Spiraea douglasii

ROSE FAMILY
Rosaceae
Perennial

OTHER NAMES: Steeple Bush
COLOUR: Deep pink
HEIGHT: 90 cm–1.8 m (3–6′)
FLOWERS: Many tiny flowers in dense, fluffy, close spikes forming one large spike
EACH FLOWER: Up to 3 mm (⅛″) across with long stamens giving fluffy appearance
LEAVES: 4–20 cm (1½–8″) long, oblong, toothed, round at tip, dark green above, paler beneath
STEMS: Rigid, brownish
BLOOMING PERIOD: June–August
HABITAT: Swamps, lake margins, wet meadows

COMMON RED INDIAN PAINTBRUSH
Castilleja miniata

FIGWORT FAMILY
Scrophulariaceae
Perennial

OTHER NAMES: Painted Cup
COLOUR: Red
HEIGHT: 20–80 cm (8–32″)
FLOWERS: In clusters at ends of stems
EACH FLOWER: Tubular, hairy 2–4 cm (¾–1½″) long; upper long, hood-like lip, red; lower short, 3-toothed lip, dark green; calyx unequally toothed, again toothed; silky-haired, red bracts practically conceal flower
LEAVES: Alternate, lance-shaped, covered with very short hairs; upper smaller leaves may be reddish-tipped
STEMS: Square, covered with short fine hairs
BLOOMING PERIOD: May–September
HABITAT: Lower to middle mountainous elevations in meadows

BREWER'S MONKEYFLOWER
Mimulus breweri

FIGWORT FAMILY
Scrophulariaceae
Annual

COLOUR: Pinkish to reddish
HEIGHT: Up to 15 cm (6″)
FLOWERS: Usually in pairs, 1 from each opposite leaf-axil
EACH FLOWER: 5–9 mm (3/16–3/8″) long, tubular, opening into 2 indistinct lobed lips; inside of throat often blotched with yellow; 5-pointed pale green calyx
LEAVES: Opposite, narrow, from 9 mm–2 cm (3/8–3/4″) long, 2–3 mm (1/16–1/8″) broad with very short stalks
STEMS: Usually unbranched
BLOOMING PERIOD: June–August
HABITAT: Dry to moist open areas, mountain slopes to middle elevations

LEWIS'S MONKEYFLOWER
Mimulus lewisii

FIGWORT FAMILY
Scrophulariaceae
Perennial

OTHER NAMES: Red Monkeyflower
COLOUR: Rose-red
HEIGHT: 30–60 cm (1–2′)
FLOWERS: Loose, paired clusters on long stems from leaf-axils
EACH FLOWER: Snapdragon-like trumpet shape, 2.5–5 cm (1–2″) long, opening into 2 lips; upper lip has 2 notched lobes with darker rose-red vein down middle; lower lip has 3 notched lobes, yellow hairs at throat; 4 stamens, 2 long and 2 short
LEAVES: Opposite, stalkless, broad lance-shaped, ribbed, sticky-haired, 3 cm (1¼″) long, 1.3 cm (½″) broad, halfway up stem smaller above and below
STEMS: Flower-stems in opposite pairs 2.5–4 cm (1–1½″) long; main stem green, sticky-haired
BLOOMING PERIOD: June–August
HABITAT: Wet places from sub-alpine to alpine

ELEPHANT'S-HEAD LOUSEWORT
Pedicularis groenlandica

Figwort Family
Scrophulariaceae
Perennial

Other Names: Little Red Elephant
Colour: Purplish-red
Height: 20–46 cm (8–18″)
Flowers: Compact spike at upper end of stem
Each Flower: Shape of an elephant's trunk, 1.3 cm (½″) long excluding trunk; upper hood extends into long trunk-like projection at least 1.3 cm (½″) long, curled up at end; 3 broad, short petals, 2 wings and a lip, calyx with 5 pointed, purple sepals 7 mm (¼″) long; 4 stamens enclosed in base of trunk with long style extending through trunk and just visible at end; deeply cut green bract at base of each flower
Leaves: Mainly basal, 5–25 cm (2–10″) long with many fine, serrated leaflets; smaller leaves scattered up stem
Stem: Green, succulent, purplish towards top
Blooming Period: End of July through August
Habitat: Open, marshy, boggy places at high elevations, from just below to just above timberline

RICHARDSON'S PENSTEMON
Penstemon richardsonii

FIGWORT FAMILY
Scrophulariaceae
Perennial

COLOUR: Pink to bright lavender
HEIGHT: 20–80 cm (8–32")
FLOWERS: Several flowers may be loose-clustered towards top of stem or more spaced down upper part of stem; many stems branching from base
EACH FLOWER: Broadly-tubular, hairy on outside 2 cm (¾") to over 2.5 cm (1") long with 2 lips; upper lip 2-lobed, lower lip 3-lobed; true stamens and 1 hairy sterile stamen, the "beard-tongue"; calyx short and 5-pointed
LEAVES: Opposite up stem, usually stalkless, from 3–5 cm (1¼–2") long, pointed, and deeply cleft or serrated
STEMS: Slender, woody, brittle; may be reddish towards base
BLOOMING PERIOD: May–August
HABITAT: Dry areas, in rock cracks and cliff crevices at lower elevations

PURPLE *and* BLUE FLOWERS

FERN-LEAVED LOMATIUM
Lomatium dissectum

PARSLEY FAMILY
Apiaceae (Umbelliferae)
Perennial

OTHER NAMES: Chocolate Tips, Carrotleaf
COLOUR: Deep purple or yellowish
HEIGHT: 30 cm–1.5 m (1–5′)
FLOWERS: Many small flowers in tight, flat-topped clusters on short umbrella-stems, which terminate several longer umbrella-stems
EACH FLOWER: 2 mm (1/10″) across with 5 outcurved petals, purple stamens with anthers becoming white in maturity
LEAVES: Arise from broad, papery, ribbed sheaths, becoming rigid and divided into 3 stalks; each again divided bearing finely dissected leaflets; leaves from base have long, ribbed stalks
STEMS: Main stem tough, ribbed, hollow, purplish at base, as are main flower stems
BLOOMING PERIOD: April–June
HABITAT: Open rocky slopes, dry meadows, often with sagebrush and up to moderate elevations

WESTERN WILD GINGER
Asarum caudatum

BIRTHWORT FAMILY
Aristolochiaceae
Perennial

OTHER NAMES: Indian Ginger
COLOUR: Brownish-purple
HEIGHT: 2–3 cm (¾–1¼″)
FLOWERS: Curiously shaped flowers arise on short stems from leaf-axils
EACH FLOWER: 2–2.5 cm (¾–1″) across, virtually no petals; calyx brownish-purple inside, deep cup-shaped with 3 triangular outcurved lobes tapering abruptly into long thin tails, sometimes curled, up to 7.5 cm (3″) long; inside of cup has 6 large yellow spots, outside, paler pinkish-brown, covered with long, downy hairs, in centre are 6 stamens, tightly bunched around a squat pistil
LEAVES: Opposite pairs of long, hairy-stalked leaves with large heart-shaped, almost leathery, short-haired blades, 4–10 cm (1½–4″) long, up to 15 cm (6″) broad; margins and veins are longer haired
STEMS: Flower-stems, 1.3–3 cm (½–1¼″) long with long soft hairs; main stem mostly trailing, softly long haired
BLOOMING PERIOD: April–July
HABITAT: Damp, shady woods, especially under cedar

GREAT BURDOCK
Arctium lappa

ASTER FAMILY
Asteraceae (Compositae)
Biennial

COLOUR: Purple to rose-purple
HEIGHT: Up to 2.4 m (8')
FLOWERS: In loose clusters at ends of flower-stems from leaf-axils
EACH FLOWER: Up to 4 cm (1½") across with tuft of purplish, tubular flowers surmounting almost globular involucre covered with green, hooked bracts, later forming brown burr
LEAVES: Large, leathery; long stalks ribbed, grooved on upper side, covered with short, stiff hairs; lower blades pointed, heart-shaped up to 50 cm (20") long, 30 cm (12") broad; upper blades smaller, oval-pointed
STEMS: Stout, tough, ribbed, rough, with branches from leaf-axils
BLOOMING PERIOD: August–October
HABITAT: Waste places and roadsides
NOTE: May cause dermatitis

SHOWY ASTER
Aster conspicuus

ASTER FAMILY
Asteraceae (Compositae)
Perennial

OTHER NAMES: Large Purple Aster
COLOUR: Bluish-purple
HEIGHT: 30–100 cm (12–40″)
FLOWERS: In open cluster at end of single stem
EACH FLOWER: Up to 3 cm (1¼″) across with from 12–35 narrow ray-petals and yellow disk up to 9 mm (⅜″) across; involucre up to 1.3 cm (½″) long with several rows of green bracts with pointed outcurved tips
LEAVES: Alternate, lower ones smaller, soon becoming dried and brown; upper leaves stemless, oval-pointed with saw-toothed margins, rough on both sides, up to 18 cm (7″) long, up to 7.5 cm (3″) broad
STEMS: Single, almost woody, sometimes hairy
BLOOMING PERIOD: July–September
HABITAT: Open wooded areas from lower to moderate elevations

GREAT NORTHERN ASTER
Aster modestus

ASTER FAMILY
Asteraceae (Compositae)
Perennial

Colour: Purple to violet
Height: 30–100 cm (12–39¼")
Flowers: 1 to a few at ends of stem-branches
Each Flower: About 2.5 cm (1") across with 20–45 ray-petals; bracts on involucre are narrow, smooth, outer ones often purple-tipped
Leaves: Alternate, smooth, lance-shaped, stalkless; blades almost clasping stem
Stems: Slender, almost smooth, often reddish with branches from leaf-axis
Blooming Period: July–August
Habitat: Moist, open woodlands, often near streams and sloughs

WESTERN ASTER
Aster occidentalis

ASTER FAMILY
Asteraceae (Compositae)
Perennial

COLOUR: Purple to violet-blue
HEIGHT: 20–100 cm (8–39¼")
FLOWERS: One to many in long clusters at ends of branches
EACH FLOWER: From 20–50 ray-petals from 7 mm–1.5 cm (¼–⅝") long; involucre 5–7 mm (³⁄₁₆–¼") high with narrow bracts, tips may be slightly purplish
LEAVES: Mainly lance-shaped; smooth, stemless from 2.7–15 cm (1⅛–6") long, from 2.7–10 cm (1⅛–4") broad; lower leaves larger, tapering to short stalks
STEMS: In clumps of single more or less smooth stems branching into flower-stems above
BLOOMING PERIOD: July–September
HABITAT: Mountainous elevations

DIFFUSE KNAPWEED
Centaurea diffusa

ASTER FAMILY
Asteraceae (Compositae)
Biennial

OTHER NAMES: Star-thistle
COLOUR: Pale purple to white
HEIGHT: 10–60 cm (4–24″)
FLOWERS: Small knapweed flowers at ends of many branched stems
EACH FLOWER: About 1.3 cm (½″) across with all disk or tubular flowers; narrow involucre 3–5 mm (⅛–³⁄₁₆″) long, green bracts which bear biscuit-coloured spines; top spine may be over 3 mm (⅛″) long, several pairs of shorter spines at sides
LEAVES: Many small, rough leaves, lower ones deeply lobed into long, narrow leaflets, upper ones become smaller; less lobed, uppermost may be unlobed, narrow
STEMS: Woody, rough, angled, many-branched, forming low bush
BLOOMING PERIOD: July–September
HABITAT: Dry waste places and roadsides
NOTE: Rapidly becoming a pest in drier areas

BROWN KNAPWEED
Centaurea jacea

ASTER FAMILY
Asteraceae (Compositeae)
Perennial

COLOUR: Red-purple
HEIGHT: 30 cm–1.2 m (1–4′)
FLOWERS: 1 flowerhead to each stem branch; plants many-branched, often grow in masses
EACH FLOWER: 2.5–4 cm (1–1½″) across with outer circle of ragged-looking disk flowers, inner disk flowers tightly packed; involucre almost round, several rows of rounded, brownish, papery bracts with somewhat coarsely dissected margins
LEAVES: Almost alternate throughout length of stems; lower ones may be lobed; stem leaves stalkless; blades narrow lance-shaped, covered with short, stiff hairs
STEMS: Woody, square, with short, stiff hairs, many branched
BLOOMING PERIOD: July–October
HABITAT: Waste ground, fields, and roadsides

COMMON CHICORY
Cichorium intybus

ASTER FAMILY
Asteraceae (Compositae)
Perennial

OTHER NAMES: Blue Sailors, Wild Succory
COLOUR: Bright blue
HEIGHT: 30 cm–1.2 m (1–4′)
FLOWERS: Many flat circular flowers in tight stemless clusters up many branched stems
EACH FLOWER: 2.5–4 cm (1–1½″) across with 12–16 strap-shaped ray-flowers, 5-toothed at tips; involucre has 2 rows of bracts, inner row about twice as many as, and longer than, outer ones; usually only one flower of each cluster opens at a time, closes at noon
LEAVES: Basal leaves have stalk, dandelion-like, 7.5–25 cm (3–10″) long, 1.3–6.5 cm (½–2½″) broad; stem leaves smaller, more lance-shaped, unlobed, clasping stem as it branches
STEMS: Hairy, ridged, many-branched
BLOOMING PERIOD: July–October
HABITAT: Waste ground, fields, and roadsides
NOTE: Poisonous. Flower closes when cloudy

CANADA THISTLE
Cirsium arvense

ASTER FAMILY
Asteraceae (Compositae)
Perennial

OTHER NAMES: Cursed Thistle, Soft Field Thistle, Creeping Thistle
COLOUR: Pinkish-purple
HEIGHT: 30 cm–1.8 m (1–6′)
FLOWERS: Numerous at ends of long stem branches. Male and female flowers on different plants
EACH FLOWER: 1.3–2 cm (½–¾″) across; male flowers longer than female flowers; male involucre rounded, female involucre more oblong; bracts on involucre stiff but not sharply spiny
LEAVES: Basal leaves long, with pointed, spine-tipped lobes; stem leaves short, lobes spine-tipped, stalkless; blades whitish beneath, often wavy
STEMS: Rigid, erect, more or less smooth, ridged
BLOOMING PERIOD: July–August
HABITAT: Pasture, waste ground, and roadsides

EDIBLE THISTLE
Cirsium edule

ASTER FAMILY
Asteraceae (Compositae)
Biennial

COLOUR: Deep red-purple
HEIGHT: 60 cm–1.8 m (2–6′)
FLOWERS: Usually in tight clusters at ends of stems
EACH FLOWER: 2.5–4 cm (1–1½″) across, with bristly-looking, deep red-purple ray-flowers; bracts on involucre slender, standing out, resembling sea-urchin; often downy
LEAVES: More regular-shaped than other thistles, perhaps less deeply-lobed and toothed with less and shorter spines; blades more delicate, but with prominent mid-rib; upper ones stalkless
STEM: Stout, succulent, hollow, slightly-hairy, tapering towards top where it may branch into flower-stems
BLOOMING PERIOD: July–September
HABITAT: Moister, open woods, wet meadows at more mountainous elevations

SPEAR THISTLE
Cirsium vulgare

ASTER FAMILY
Asteraceae (Compositae)
Biennial

OTHER NAMES: Common Thistle, Bur Thistle, Bull Thistle
COLOUR: Rose-purple
HEIGHT: 60 cm–1.5 m (2–5′)
FLOWERS: 1 to a few at tips of stems
EACH FLOWER: Up to 4 cm (1½″) across, consisting of dense, spreading tuft of very narrow ray-flowers; large-based almost conical involucre may be over 2.5 cm (1″) long with many green, spiny bracts
LEAVES: May be up to 20 cm (8″) long, dissected into pointed lobes with sharp, yellowish spines at tips; upper surfaces have short prickles; bases of leaves narrow, forming spiny wings down either side of stem; basal leaves in rosette
STEMS: Tough, rigid, and downy
BLOOMING PERIOD: July–September
HABITAT: Roadsides, waste places, and fields

SUBALPINE FLEABANE
Erigeron perigrinus

ASTER FAMILY
Asteraceae (Compositae)
Perennial

OTHER NAMES: Tall Purple Fleabane, Mountain Daisy
COLOUR: Pale purple
HEIGHT: Up to 60 cm (2′)
FLOWERS: Usually one daisy flower to a stem; several stems to a plant
EACH FLOWER: 30–80 ray-petals, 9 mm–2.5 cm (⅜–1″) long, surrounding large yellow disk; bracts on involucre loosely arranged, sometimes almost recurved, reddish
LEAVES: Basal and stem-leaves; mostly lance-shaped; basal leaves stalked, stem-leaves stalkless; all leaves central-veined
STEMS: Usually unbranched, slightly downy
BLOOMING PERIOD: July–August
HABITAT: Moist mountain meadows, streambanks to high elevations above timberline

SHAGGY FLEABANE
Erigeron pumilus

ASTER FAMILY
Asteraceae (Compositae)
Perennial

COLOUR: Pale purple to white
HEIGHT: 15–60 cm (6"–2')
FLOWERS: In loose groups at ends of long stems; grows in clumps
EACH FLOWER: Up to 2.5 cm (1") across with many, narrow ray-petals 9 mm (3/8") long, surrounding greenish-yellow disk; involucre has fine, green, hairy bracts about 5 mm (3/16") long
LEAVES: Many, long, narrow, strap-like leaves up to 7.5 cm (3") long, often twisted, covered with soft hairs, becoming smaller towards top of stem
STEMS: Green, rigid, hairy, branching into flower-stems above
BLOOMING PERIOD: May–July
HABITAT: Dry sagebrush flats and open plains

SHOWY FLEABANE
Erigeron speciosus

ASTER FAMILY
Asteraceae (Compositae)
Perennial

OTHER NAMES: Showy Daisy, Oregon Fleabane
COLOUR: Purplish-blue
HEIGHT: 20–80 cm (8–32″)
FLOWERS: Several single flowers at ends of long flower-stalks at upper ends of stems; may be several stems to a plant
EACH FLOWER: 2.5–4 cm (1–1½″) across with 65–150 narrow ray-flowers; disk-flowers in middle are yellow, many narrow, hairy bracts on involucre outcurved at their tips
LEAVES: Many narrow, lance-shaped leaves up stem; lowest ones may be short-stemmed, upper ones stemless, progressively smaller; blades have hairy margins, especially lower ones
STEMS: Rigid, hairy, almost square in section
BLOOMING PERIOD: June–August
HABITAT: Open wooded areas and banks from low to moderate elevations

BLUE-FLOWERED LETTUCE
Lactuca tatarica subsp. pulchella (Lactuca pulchella)

ASTER FAMILY
Asteraceae (Compositae)
Perennial

OTHER NAMES: Chicory Lettuce, Blue Lettuce
COLOUR: Blue to purple
HEIGHT: 20–100 cm (8–39¼")
FLOWERS: In loose clusters at ends of branches from upper leaf-axils
EACH FLOWER: Up to nearly 2.5 cm (1") across with about 15 ray-petals; many stamens; involucre up to 2 cm (¾") long with inner row of long, narrow, pointed bracts, middle row of shorter ones, outermost row of short, broad-based bracts; often all are pinkish-tinged
LEAVES: Lower ones dandelion-like with deep indentations, tapering into flat stalks; many narrow, lance-shaped leaves up stem, 5–16.5 cm (2–6½") long, 7 mm–3.5 cm (¼–1⅜") broad
STEMS: Unbranched below, rigid, round, smooth, exude a milky juice when broken
BLOOMING PERIOD: June–September
HABITAT: Dry to moist shrubby areas and meadows

COMMON SALSIFY
Tragopogon porrifolius

ASTER FAMILY
Asteraceae (Compositae)
Biennial

OTHER NAMES: Vegetable Oyster, Purple Salsify
COLOUR: Purple
HEIGHT: 30–90 cm (1–3′)
FLOWERS: Single flower-heads at ends of branched or single stems; closed in bright sunlight; similar to *Tragopogon dubius* except for colour
EACH FLOWER: 3.8–6.5 cm (1½–2½″) across with several rows of ray-petals, becoming progressively shorter towards middle, usually with toothed tips; involucre with long, pointed, green bracts, longer than ray-petals with keeled central ribs
LEAVES: Many smooth, long, narrow, tapering leaves clasp stems
STEMS: Flower-stems swell just below flower-head; several stems to a plant, branching at leaf-axils
BLOOMING PERIOD: April–August
HABITAT: Occasionally in moist, grassy areas, roadsides, and waste ground

ALKANET
Anchusa officinalis

BORAGE FAMILY
Boraginaceae
Perennial

COLOUR: Dark blue
HEIGHT: 30–80 cm (12–32″)
FLOWERS: In clusters at ends of stems and flower-stems from leaf-axils
EACH FLOWER: 7 mm (¼″) across, tubular, about 7 mm (¼″) long, opening into 5 rounded petals; 5 stamens within tube, hairy calyx has 5 pointed lobes, about as long as the tube
LEAVES: Lower leaves inverted lance-shaped, blades hairy both sides
STEMS: Rigid, hairy; may be several to each plant
BLOOMING PERIOD: May–July
HABITAT: Along drier roadsides

COMMON HOUND'S-TONGUE
Cynoglossum officinale

BORAGE FAMILY
Boraginaceae
Biennial

OTHER NAMES: Gypsy Flower, Dogbur, Woolmat
COLOUR: Reddish-purple
HEIGHT: 30–90 cm (1–3′)
FLOWERS: In almost one-sided, often drooping, loose, spike-like clusters at ends of stems
EACH FLOWER: 7 mm–1.5 cm (¼–⅝″) across, cup-shaped, with 5, rounded petals, uniting to form tube; 5 stamens; greenish-grey, stubby sepals, usually downy; seeds have stiff, barbed hairs which stick like a burr
LEAVES: Basal leaves downy, long lance-shaped, up to 20 cm (8″) long, tapering below into flattened stalk; many stem leaves, smaller and stalkless
STEMS: Slightly ridged, downy-haired
BLOOMING PERIOD: May–July
HABITAT: Dry waste places and roadsides
NOTE: May cause dermatitis

VIPER'S-BUGLOSS
Echium vulgare

BORAGE FAMILY
Boraginaceae
Biennial

OTHER NAMES: Blue-weed, Blue-devil
COLOUR: Bright blue, may be pink-tinged
HEIGHT: 30–60 cm (1–2′)
FLOWERS: In rigid spike
EACH FLOWER: Broad funnel-shaped, up to 1.3 cm (½″) long, opening into 5 lobes, upper 2 longer than lower 3; 5 reddish stamens, 4 of which protrude beyond lobes; hairy style longer than stamens; calyx 5-toothed, covered with bristly hairs; many pinkish buds; bristle-pointed bract at base of each flower
LEAVES: Few narrow, inverted lance-shaped basal leaves up to 23 cm (9″) long including stalks; stem leaves become progressively smaller up stem, upper ones stalkless; all stiffly hairy
STEMS: Unbranched, stout, green, covered with dark, bristly hairs
BLOOMING PERIOD: June–August
HABITAT: Poor soil on banks, roadsides, and fields
NOTE: May cause dermatitis

LONG-FLOWERED MERTENSIA
Mertensia longiflora

BORAGE FAMILY
Boraginaceae
Biennial

OTHER NAMES: Languid Ladies, Mountain Bluebell
COLOUR: Bright blue
HEIGHT: 10–25 cm (4–10″)
FLOWERS: In terminal drooping tassel
EACH FLOWER: 2–2.5 cm (¾–1″) long, tubular, expanding into 5 shallow lobes, expanded portion being ⅓–½ as long as tube; calyx cleft to below midway into 5 pointed teeth; 5 stamens attached to base of expanded portion of tube; long, thin style protrudes just beyond tube
LEAVES: Stalkless leaves arranged alternately up stem, fleshy, inverted lance-shaped to oblong, with rounded tips, often with pinkish mid-ribs beneath
STEMS: Sturdy, round, smooth, often pinkish-tinged
BLOOMING PERIOD: April–June
HABITAT: Open or slightly wooded sagebrush country with Ponderosa pine up to middle elevations

MOUNTAIN FORGET-ME-NOT
Myosotis asiatica
(Myosotis sylvatica var. alpestris)

BORAGE FAMILY
Boraginaceae
Perennial

COLOUR: Sky-blue
HEIGHT: 5–40 cm (2–16″)
FLOWERS: Small clusters from upper leaf-axils
EACH FLOWER: 9 mm (⅜″) across; 5 rounded petals form tube below; centre of flower has yellow "eye"; 5 stamens within tube; calyx has 5 green, hairy, pointed lobes about as long as tube
LEAVES: Basal leaves short-stemmed with inverted lance-shaped or long, pointed-oval blades and up to 15 cm (6″) long and 3 cm (1¼″) broad; stem-leaves alternate, stemless, and much narrower
STEMS: One to several from base, angled, softly hairy
BLOOMING PERIOD: June–August
HABITAT: Moist, open meadows and slopes from middle to high mountainous elevations

SMALL-LEAVED FORGET-ME-NOT
Myosotis laxa

BORAGE FAMILY
Boraginaceae
Annual

COLOUR: Pale blue
HEIGHT: 10–40 cm (4–16″)
FLOWERS: Several along ends of long thin stems
EACH FLOWER: Up to 7 mm (¼″) across with 5 petals which form short tube below; centre of flower yellow; 5 stamens, 5-toothed, hairy calyx about as long as tube
LEAVES: Alternate, 1.5–7.5 cm (⅝–3″) long and 3 mm–1.3 cm (⅛–½″) broad; lower leaves inverted lance-shaped; upper ones more lance-shaped
STEMS: Long and slender, often lying close to ground
BLOOMING PERIOD: June–September
HABITAT: Moist or wet places, often in water at low to moderate elevations

DRUMMOND'S ROCK CRESS
Arabis drummondii

MUSTARD FAMILY
Brassicaceae (Cruciferae)
Perennial

COLOUR: Pale purple to white
HEIGHT: 30–80 cm (12–32")
FLOWERS: Small flowers in loose cluster at top of unbranched stem; may be several stems to a plant
EACH FLOWER: 7 mm (¼") long, tubular opening into 4 tiny petals, 6 stamens, 2 of which are short; 4 pale yellowish-pink sepals
LEAVES: Several long elliptic leaves at base; stem leaves numerous, almost overlaping, stemless; blades narrow, lance-shaped and eared where they join stem
STEMS: Unbranched, slender, smooth
BLOOMING PERIOD: May–July
HABITAT: Dry to moist, open wooded areas from lower to sub-alpine elevations

LYALL'S ROCK CRESS
Arabis Lyallii

MUSTARD FAMILY
Brassicaceae (Cruciferae)
Perennial

COLOUR: Pale purple
HEIGHT: 10–24 cm (4–10″)
FLOWERS: Several at top of stem; several stems to a root-stock
EACH FLOWER: 4 rounded petals each 7 mm–1 cm (¼–⅖″) long; 4 smooth sepals, 3–4 mm (⅛–⅙″) long; may be purple-tinged; usually 6 stamens
LEAVES: Pointed-oblong, 1.5–3 cm (⅝–1¼″) long and 1.5–5 mm (1/16–3/16″) broad; smooth, bright-green, almost fleshy, arranged in rosette at base. A few smaller lobed leaves clasp the stem
STEMS: Several stems from root-stock, may be smooth or hairy
BLOOMING PERIOD: June–August
HABITAT: Dry, rocky areas in sub-alpine and alpine regions

COMMON HAREBELL
Campanula rotundifolia

BLUEBELL FAMILY
Campanulaceae
Perennial

OTHER NAMES: Scotch Bluebell, Bluebells of Scotland
COLOUR: Pale blue
HEIGHT: 15–46 cm (6–18″)
FLOWERS: Several almost nodding flowers at tops of long, thin stems; grow in clumps
EACH FLOWER: Bell-shaped, 2 cm (¾″) long and 2 cm (¾″) across, flaring into 5 pointed lobes; 5 curled stamens inside base of bell; 3-branched style almost as long as petals; calyx dark green, narrowly 5-lobed
LEAVES: Basal leaves long stalked, roundly heart-shaped blades; usually withered by time flowers appear; stem leaves grass-like up to 5 cm (2″) long, becoming progressively smaller up stem
STEMS: Dark green, slender, smooth, slight-ridged, sometimes twisted
BLOOMING PERIOD: June–August
HABITAT: Grassy roadsides and open woods at most elevations below sub-alpine

KALM'S LOBELIA
Lobelia kalmii

HAREBELL FAMILY
Campanulaceae
Perennial

OTHER NAMES: Brook Lobelia
COLOUR: Pale blue and white
HEIGHT: 10–40 cm (4–16″)
FLOWERS: 1 to several at top of long, slender stem
EACH FLOWER: 1.3 cm (½″) long, tubular, opening into 5 lobes, lower 3 larger and forming lip, with 2 white blotches towards base, upper 2 narrower, shorter, erect; distinct darker vein down middle of each lobe; calyx has 5 small, pointed lobes; flower-stems thin, 7 mm (¼″) long, arranged alternately with tiny bract at base
LEAVES: Few basal leaves, spatula-shaped, 9 mm–2.5 cm (⅜–1″) long; several alternate, narrow, pointed stem-leaves, reducing in size towards top of stem
STEMS: Unbranched, slender smooth
BLOOMING PERIOD: July–August
HABITAT: Sphagnum bogs, lakeshores, and wet meadows at low elevations

RUSSIAN THISTLE
Salsola kali
subsp. ruthenica
(Salsola kali var. tenuifolia)

GOOSEFOOT FAMILY
Chenopodiaceae
Annual

OTHER NAMES: Tumbleweed, Wind Witch
COLOUR: Purple through pink
HEIGHT: 20 cm–1.2 m (8″–4′)
FLOWERS: In long spikes of tiny flowers in axils of spiny bracts; plants have faintly sweet scent
EACH FLOWER: Stemless, 7–9 mm (¼–⅜″) across with purplish to whitish papery sepals
LEAVES: Lower leaves may be up to 5 cm (2″) long, very narrow, thick, rubbery string-like, spine-tipped, becoming much smaller and more triangular bract-like towards ends of stems, making whole plant prickly
STEMS: Many curving upwards from one root-stock forming large, rounded bush, becoming tumbleweed later in year; stems are round, pale green with purple stripes
BLOOMING PERIOD: June–September
HABITAT: Massed on gravelly waste ground and dry roadsides

TIMBER MILK-VETCH
Astragalus miser

PEA FAMILY
Fabaceae (Leguminosae)
Perennial

COLOUR: Pale blue-purple
HEIGHT: 10–50 cm (4–20″)
FLOWERS: In long, loose spikes on long, thin stems
EACH FLOWER: 9 mm–1.3 cm (⅜–½″) long, tubular, opening into a standard, backward-curved at sides, 2 wings slightly longer than keel and enclosing it from sides; 5-toothed slightly hairy calyx; flower-stems up to 3 mm (⅛″) long
LEAVES: Long, thin stalks from base with 4–8 pairs of opposite 7 mm–2.5 cm (¼–1″) long, narrow leaflets and 1 terminal leaflet; stalks have stipules at base
STEMS: Flower-stems long, thin, wiry
BLOOMING PERIOD: May–July
HABITAT: Open, grassy areas from foothills to high altitudes

ARCTIC LUPINE
Lupinus arcticus
subsp. canadensis
(Lupinus latifolius)

PEA FAMILY
Fabaceae (Leguminosae)
Perennial

COLOUR: Pale blue to pinkish-blue
HEIGHT: 30 cm–1.2 m (1–4′)
FLOWERS: Many in long spike on long flower-stem
EACH FLOWER: 1.3–2 cm (½–¾″) long; standard curves backwards, edges almost meeting behind; wings almost completely enclose upcurved keel which encloses pistil and stamens; frequently front part of standard is white; calyx has 2 softly hairy, pointed cup-shaped lobes; each little flower-stem 7 mm (¼″) long
LEAVES: Alternate at intervals up stem; stalks 5–7.5 cm (2–3″) long, terminating in 7–9 pointed, elliptic, 5 cm (2″) leaflets, flatly haired above and more so below, arranged like spokes of wheel; 2 pointed stipules where leaf-stalks join main stem
STEMS: Woody, hollow, softly hairy, unbranched below
BLOOMING PERIOD: June–August
HABITAT: Moist alpine meadows and open wooded mountain slopes

DWARF MOUNTAIN LUPINE
Lupinus lyallii

PEA FAMILY
Fabaceae (Leguminosae)
Perennial

OTHER NAMES: Low Mountain Lupine
COLOUR: Blue
HEIGHT: 5–20 cm (2–8″)
FLOWERS: In squat close cluster about 2.5 cm (1″) across, at top of short stem
EACH FLOWER: 1.3 cm (½″) long; standard curled backwards at sides which touch behind, front often white; wings completely enclose keel; calyx silky-haired with 1 long, pointed tooth below and 2 smaller ones above; about 10 flowers to a cluster
LEAVES: Mostly basal with grey-green appearance due to flat, silky hairs, which are thicker below showing as paler margin on slightly rolled up edges of leaflets; downy stalks, 1.3–3 cm (½–1¼″) long with 5–7 narrow pointed leaflets, 3 mm–1.3 cm (⅛–½″) long, radiating like spokes of wheel
STEMS: Flower-stems downy and reddish; plants tend to be mat-forming
BLOOMING PERIOD: July–August
HABITAT: Sandy or gravelly slopes and ridges to above timberline, sparsely scattered

SILKY LUPINE
Lupinus sericeus

PEA FAMILY
Fabaceae (Leguminosae)
Perennial

COLOUR: Pale blue to pinkish-blue
HEIGHT: 30–60 cm (1–2')
FLOWERS: Many flowers in long spikes
EACH FLOWER: 1.3 cm (½") long, standard curled backwards; wings touch at tips and enclose keel which contains stamens and pistil. 2 silky-haired sepals of unequal length, lower one much longer and standing away from keel, upper one hugs outer surface of standard; each flower-stem, 3–5 mm (⅛–³⁄₁₆") long
LEAVES: Stalks up to 7.5 cm (3") long, terminating in 7–9 narrow, pointed leaflets, 2.5–5 cm (1–2") long, radiating like spokes of wheel; leaflets silky-haired on both surfaces, perhaps more so beneath, giving greyish appearance beneath and green above
STEMS: Woody, round, hollow, green, finely hairy; several stems to a plant
BLOOMING PERIOD: May–August
HABITAT: Dry, sagebrush country

PRAIRIE GENTIAN
Gentiana affinis

GENTIAN FAMILY
Gentianaceae
Perennial

OTHER NAMES: Large Gentian, Oblong-leaved Gentian
COLOUR: Bright deep blue and green
HEIGHT: 15–45 cm (6–18″)
FLOWERS: Several terminal flowers and single flowers from upper leaf-axils
EACH FLOWER: 2.5–4 cm (1–1½″) long, up to 1.5 cm (⅝″) across, tubular with 5 pointed lobes mottled or streaked with pastel green; pleats between lobes may have 2 to 5 tooth-like segments; calyx 5-toothed, short, tubular, green, tinged with blue or purple; 5 stamens, shorter than corolla-tube, anthers pale-yellow; short style with cleft stigma at maturity
LEAVES: Several opposite pairs of stalkless leaves up stem with pointed-oblong toothless blades, 2–5 cm (¾–2″) long, 5 mm–2 cm (³⁄₁₆–¾″) broad; some smaller leaves with stalks at base
STEMS: 1 to several from root-stock, prostrate at first and becoming erect; generally purplish-tinged
BLOOMING PERIOD: July–October
HABITAT: Damp meadows from valleys and foothills to mountains. Uncommon, found in Summerland area

GLAUCOUS GENTIAN
Gentiana glauca

GENTIAN FAMILY
Gentianaceae
Perennial

OTHER NAMES: Pale Gentian
COLOUR: Green-blue
HEIGHT: 4–15 cm (1½–6″)
FLOWERS: Several flowers at top of single stem
EACH FLOWER: 1–2 cm (⅜–¾″) long, tubular and 5-lobed; 5 stamens, filaments being joined to inside of corolla at lower ends; style is green, fairly thick, and terminates in 2-lobed white stigma; calyx parts joined and 5-lobed and unequal in length, roughly about ⅓ length of corolla and with bluish tinge
LEAVES: Basal leaves almost egg-shaped, 5–20 mm (³⁄₁₆–¾″) long, arranged in rosette; may be 2–4 pairs of opposite stalkless leaves up stem
STEMS: From creeping root-stocks, unbranched, smooth, green, and square-section
BLOOMING PERIOD: July–September
HABITAT: Alpine meadows above timberline

NORTHERN GENTIAN
Gentianella amarella

GENTIAN FAMILY
Gentainaceae
Annual

OTHER NAMES: Feltwort
COLOUR: Blue to lilac, pinkish
HEIGHT: 5–50 cm (2–20″)
FLOWERS: In small groups up stem
EACH FLOWER: 1.3–2 cm (½–¾″) long, apparently tubular opening into usually 5 lobes which are fringed inside; calyx about ⅓ as long as tube with 5 narrow lobes
LEAVES: In several opposite pairs up stem, stalkless, up to 5.5 cm (2⅜″) long, may be over 2.5 cm (1″) broad; several larger basal leaves
STEMS: May be single or branched, smooth, almost square
BLOOMING PERIOD: June–September
HABITAT: In moist, open, or wooded areas up to moderate elevations

BALLHEAD WATERLEAF
Hydrophyllum capitatum

WATERLEAF FAMILY
Hydrophyllaceae
Perennial

COLOUR: Lavender-blue
HEIGHT: 10–40 cm (4–16")
FLOWERS: Many fuzzy-looking flowers in globular head on short stem, sometimes partly obscured by leaves
EACH FLOWER: Up to 9 mm (⅜") long, cup-shaped with 5 spreading lobes, 5 stamens and forked style, protrude beyond petals to give fuzzy appearance; 5 narrow, hairy sepals; flower-heads appear to arise from long leaf-stalks and overshadowed by blades
LEAVES: All basal with long succulent, reddish-tinged stalks, sheathing below ground; softly hairy blades up to 10 cm (4") broad and 15 cm (6") long, deeply cleft into 5–7 lobes which are again dissected into 3 lobes with pointed arch-shaped tips
STEMS: As long as leaf-stalks, terminating in a leaf with flower-head situated below
BLOOMING PERIOD: March–July
HABITAT: In moist open woods and slopes from moderate to high elevations

THREAD-LEAVED PHACELIA
Phacelia linearis

WATERLEAF FAMILY
Hydrophyllaceae
Annual

COLOUR: Pale lavender-blue to pinkish
HEIGHT: 10–50 cm (4–20″)
FLOWERS: Loose clusters
EACH FLOWER: Saucer-shaped, up to 2 cm (¾″) across, 5 rounded petals with darker veins; 5 stamens with dark anthers; 5 narrow, hairy sepals
LEAVES: Alternate, stalkless, long and narrow, may be up to 10 cm (4″) long with central rib; lower ones may be segmented
STEMS: May be single and branched above into flowering stems or branched below; often reddish
BLOOMING PERIOD: April–June
HABITAT: Dry, open areas often with sagebrush
NOTE: May cause dermatitis

SILKY PHACELIA
Phacelia sericea
subsp. sericea

WATERLEAF FAMILY
Hydrophyllaceae
Perennial

OTHER NAMES: Scorpionweed, Mountain Phacelia, Purple Fringe
COLOUR: Pale to dark bluish-purple
HEIGHT: 10–46 cm (4–18″)
FLOWERS: Many small flowers in dense, fluffy, cylindrical spikes on single stems; may be several stems to a plant
EACH FLOWER: Bell-shaped with 5 lobes about 7 mm (¼″) across with 5 purplish stamens protruding with long, forked style, well beyond petals, giving fluffy appearance; narrow sepals are silky-haired
LEAVES: Basal leaves stalked, blades deeply dissected into opposite, elongated, cleft segments; alternate stem leaves smaller and shorter-stalked or stalkless; stalks and blades silky-haired giving silver-grey appearance
STEMS: Erect, softly silky-haired, especially towards top; may be pinkish-tinged
BLOOMING PERIOD: June–August
HABITAT: Open rocky and wooded areas from below to above timberline
NOTE: May cause dermatitis

WESTERN BLUE IRIS
Iris missouriensis

IRIS FAMILY
Iridaceae
Perennial

OTHER NAMES: Fleur-de-lis, Rocky Mountain Iris, Snake Lily
COLOUR: Violet-blue
HEIGHT: 30–60 cm (1–2′)
FLOWERS: 1 to 3 at upper ends of stems
EACH FLOWER: Up to 7.5 cm (3″) across with 3 narrow, deep violet-blue upcurved petals; shorter than the 3 broad, downcurved petal-like sepals, which are paler in colour and yellow-blotched at their bases, boldly purple-lined; style has 3 petal-like branches; 3 stamens are opposite sepals and under style branches; flower-stems up to 6.5 cm (2½″) long with sheath-like bracts from which flowers emerge
LEAVES: Alternate up stem, stiff, sword-like, up to 40 cm (16″) long and up to 2 cm (¾″) broad, finely-ribbed, sheathing the stem
STEMS: Stout, rigid, round, branched above
BLOOMING PERIOD: May to early June
HABITAT: Wet meadows, streambanks
NOTE: Poisonous. May cause dermatitis

IDAHO BLUE-EYED GRASS
Sisyrinchium idahoense
(Sisyrinchium angustifolium)

Iris Family
Iridaceae
Perennial

Colour: Deep blue to purplish-blue
Height: 10–30 cm (4–12")
Flowers: 1 to few flowers on thin stems at summit of single stems
Each Flower: 2 cm (¾") across, shallow saucer-shaped with 6 oblong petal-like segments with fine points, finely lined with dark veins; centre of flower often yellow; stamens have yellow anthers, ovary below flower, round and green; thin flower-stem, reddish, about 2.5 cm (1") long; where it joins main stem there are 2 sheathing bracts which do not reach flower; from same node is long single spathe up to 5 cm (2") long, narrow, pointed
Leaves: Several basal leaves, almost grass-like, 5–15 cm (2–6") long
Stems: Unbranched, flattened, ridged
Blooming Period: April–July
Habitat: Moist areas, marshes, and damp meadows near lake edges from low to middle elevations

FIELD MINT
Mentha arvensis

MINT FAMILY
Lamiaceae (Labiatae)
Perennial

OTHER NAMES: Canada Mint
COLOUR: Purple-blue to pink or white
HEIGHT: 20–80 cm (8–32")
FLOWERS: Small flowers clustered in leaf-axils forming several whorls
EACH FLOWER: Tubular, opening into 2 lips, upper lip shallowly 2-lobed, lower lip deeply 3-lobed; 4 stamens and long style with 2 stigmas; 5-toothed calyx often purplish-tinged
LEAVES: Opposite with short stalks; blades pointed-elliptical, toothed, softly hairy; strongly mint-scented when crushed
STEMS: Square and rigid below, becoming greener and less rigid above
BLOOMING PERIOD: July–September
HABITAT: Moist ground near streams and lakes

COMMON CATNIP
Nepeta cataria

MINT FAMILY
Lamiaceae (Labiatae)
Perennial

OTHER NAMES: Catmint
COLOUR: White to pale mauve or lilac-spotted
HEIGHT: 30 cm–1.5 m (1–5′)
FLOWERS: Many small flowers in dense, round-topped spikes at ends of long stems from opposite leaf-axils
EACH FLOWER: Small, tubular, opening into 2 lips; upper lip slightly-hooded with black stamens hugging the inside; lower lip 3-lobed, spreading; calyx green, hairy, 5-toothed
LEAVES: Opposite, short stalks off main stem; blades heart-shaped, 2.5 cm–6.5 cm (1–2½″) long, 2–5 cm (¾–2″) wide, sharply toothed, covered with soft hairs; aromatic when crushed
STEMS: Stout, square, downy, branching at leaf-axils
BLOOMING PERIOD: June–September
HABITAT: Moist roadsides, waste places, and ditches

COMMON SELF-HEAL
Prunella vulgaris

MINT FAMILY
Lamiaceae (Labiateae)
Perennial

OTHER NAMES: Heal-all, Carpenter Weed
COLOUR: Purple, bluish-purple to pink
HEIGHT: 7.5–40 cm (3–16")
FLOWERS: Small closely-packed flowers in short fat spike
EACH FLOWER: 1.3–2.5 cm (½–1") long, tubular, with 2 lips; upper lip forms hood enclosing 4 stamens, lower lip has broad, fringed central lobe with small lobe either side; often purplish-tinged; 2-lobed calyx, upper lobe sharply, shallowly 3-toothed, narrower lower lobe, deeply 2-toothed
LEAVES: Opposite, with stalks; blades lance-shaped or pointed-oval, 2–9 cm (¾–3½") long, 7 mm–4 cm (¼–1½") broad
STEMS: Erect or lying on ground, square, slightly hairy
BLOOMING PERIOD: May–September
HABITAT: From lower to middle elevations in damp meadows, lakesides, and streambanks

MARSH SKULLCAP
Scutellaria galericulata

MINT FAMILY
Lamiaceae (Labiatae)
Perennial

OTHER NAMES: Hooded Skullcap
COLOUR: Pale blue and white
HEIGHT: 20–60 cm (8″–2′)
FLOWERS: Single flowers in upper, opposite leaf-axils, appearing to be in pairs
EACH FLOWER: Up to 2 cm (¾″) long, tubular, opening into 2 lips; upper lip hood-like; lower lip has 2 side lobes and broader, protruding central lip-like lobe; upward-curved tube, whitish; 4 stamens; calyx short, stubby
LEAVES: Opposite, narrow lance-shaped, slightly toothed, very short stalked or stalkless
STEMS: Slender, mostly unbranched, square, slightly hairy
BLOOMING PERIOD: June–August
HABITAT: Marshes, bogs, and wet meadows to moderate elevations

SWAMP HEDGE-NETTLE
Stachys palustris
subsp. pilosa

MINT FAMILY
Lamiaceae (Labiateae)
Perennial

COLOUR: Pale purple
HEIGHT: 20–70 cm (8–28″)
FLOWERS: About 6 small flowers in whorls at upper leaf-axils
EACH FLOWER: 9 mm (⅜″) long, tubular, opening into 2 lips; lower lip 3-lobed; middle lobe broad, purple-spotted; 4 stamens under upper lip; calyx has 5 sharply pointed, hairy teeth
LEAVES: Opposite; lower ones with short stalks; upper ones stalkless; blades pointed-oblong, toothed, softly hairy, 3–9 cm (1¼–3½″) long, 9 mm–4 cm (⅜–1½″) broad
STEMS: May be single or branched, green, square, covered with stiff hairs
BLOOMING PERIOD: June–August
HABITAT: Moist places along streambanks, lakeshores, and moist meadows at lower elevations

COMMON BUTTERWORT
Pinguicula vulgaris

BLADDERWORT FAMILY
Lentibulariaceae
Perennial

COLOUR: Violet-blue
HEIGHT: 5–15 cm (2–6″)
FLOWERS: Single flower to a stem
EACH FLOWER: 1.5–2.5 cm (⅝–1″) long including spur 1.3 cm (½″) across, wide funnel-shaped, opening into 2 lips, upper lip roundly 2-lobed, lower, roundly 3-lobed and longer, middle lobe greyish and hairy; funnel tapers backwards into 7 mm (¼″) round-ended spur; green, short-haired, 5-lobed calyx grasps tube at back of upper lip
LEAVES: In flattish, basal rosette; broad-elliptic, pale green with rolled-up edges; upper surface sticky, insectivorous
STEMS: Flower-stems unbranched, green, covered with short hairs
BLOOMING PERIOD: July–August
HABITAT: Bogs, damp river banks, from foothills to mountainous elevations
NOTE: Insectivorous

SAGEBRUSH MARIPOSA LILY
Calochortus macrocarpus

LILY FAMILY
Liliaceae
Perennial

OTHER NAMES: Green-banded Mariposa Lily, Star Tulip
COLOUR: Pale purple
HEIGHT: 20–56 cm (8–22″)
FLOWERS: 1–3 at top of slender stem
EACH FLOWER: Tulip-shaped, up to 5 cm (2″) across, 5 cm (2″) long, with 3 broad, rounded wedge-shaped petals, with central green band; inside base of each petal, creamy-white with yellow hairs, bounded above by purplish blotch; 6 stamens reaching to purple blotches, surround pistil with 3-lobed outcurved stigma; alternating with petals are 3 longer, narrow, pointed sepals, greenish with lavender margins
LEAVES: Lower leaf long, thin, grass-like; stem-leaves small, arranged alternately up stem
STEMS: Sturdy, smooth, slender, unbranched
BLOOMING PERIOD: May–July
HABITAT: Dry, open, grassy meadows and banks in sagebrush country

LARGE-FLOWERED TRITELEIA
Triteleia grandiflora
(Brodiaea douglasii)

LILY FAMILY
Liliaceae
Perennial

OTHER NAMES: Wild Hyacinth, Cluster Lily
COLOUR: Blue
HEIGHT: 30–90 cm (1–3′)
FLOWERS: Several flowers in loose cluster on unequal length umbrella-stems
EACH FLOWER: 2–2.5 cm (¾–1″) long, bell-shaped, 1.5 cm (⅝″) across; tube opens into 6 pointed petal-like segments, 3 inner petals, 3 larger outer sepals; petals and sepals have darker blue central vein; 6 stamens with bluish anthers, 3 higher ones seemingly attached to petals, appear to have darker anthers; lower ones seemingly attached to sepals; pointed, papery bracts below flower cluster
LEAVES: 1 to 4 basal leaves, almost grass-like, keeled, up to 40 cm (16″) long, often purplish at base
STEMS: Round, smooth, and leafless
BLOOMING PERIOD: April–July
HABITAT: Open grassy banks and sagebrush flats

WESTERN BLUE FLAX
Linum lewisii
subsp. lewisii
(Linum perenne var. lewisii)

FLAX FAMILY
Linaceae
Perennial

OTHER NAMES: Prairie Flax, Lewis Flax
COLOUR: Sky-blue
HEIGHT: 10–60 cm (4–24″)
FLOWERS: Several in loose elongated clusters swaying at ends of stems
EACH FLOWER: Shallow, saucer-shaped up to 3 cm (1¼″) across with 5 broad petals, pencilled with darker lines; 5 yellow stamens; 5 stigmas protruding beyond stamens; 5 green sepals about 3 mm (⅛″) long
LEAVES: Alternate, stalkless, narrow; pointed, up to 2.5 cm (1″) long, 3 mm (⅛″) broad, crowded on main stem, further apart on stem branches
STEMS: Smooth, slender, branching above into flower-stems
BLOOMING PERIOD: May–July
HABITAT: Dry areas at most elevations

PURPLE LOOSESTRIFE
Lythrum salicaria

LOOSESTRIFE FAMILY
Lythraceae
Perennial

COLOUR: Reddish-purple
HEIGHT: 60 cm −2.1 m (2−7′)
FLOWERS: Many small flowers in long spike
EACH FLOWER: Up to 9 mm (⅜″) long with 5 petals, lower parts form tube; 8 to 10 stamens of varying lengths, some protrude beyond petals as flowers mature; style also protrudes; hairy calyx forms tube with 5−7 pointed lobes, greenish with purple veins; several flowers from each leaf-axil
LEAVES: Usually opposite, almost clasping, lance-shaped blades softly hair, 2.5−10 cm (1−4″) long
STEMS: Rigid, square, branching into flower-stems above
BLOOMING PERIOD: August−September
HABITAT: Marshes and lake edges
NOTE: Becoming a pest in ponds and waterways

SPOTTED CORALROOT
Corallorhiza maculata
subsp. maculata

ORCHID FAMILY
Orchidaceae
Perennial

OTHER NAMES: Large Coral-root, Mottled Coralroot
COLOUR: Pinkish-purple
HEIGHT: 20–46 cm (8–18″)
FLOWERS: Loose spike-like arrangement on single stem
EACH FLOWER: 1.3 cm (½″) long; broad, white purple-spotted lip up to 9 mm (⅜″) long, 3-lobed at tip; sepals and petals all alike, purplish, may be purple-spotted; petals may be shorter than sepals
LEAVES: None
STEMS: Reddish to pinkish-purple, with several sheathing bracts
BLOOMING PERIOD: May–August
HABITAT: Dry to moist forests, sometimes on dry, open ground
NOTE: Saprophyte

WESTERN CORALROOT
Corallorhiza maculata subsp. mertensiana
(*Corallorhiza mertensiana*)

ORCHID FAMILY
Orchidaceae
Perennial

OTHER NAMES: Merten's Coralroot
COLOUR: Reddish to pinkish-purple
HEIGHT: 15–46 cm (6–18″)
FLOWERS: In loose spike-like arrangement on upper half of single stems
EACH FLOWER: Sepals and petals more or less same colour; hanging, often paler lip, broad, up to 9 mm (3/8″) long with short, rounded tooth on either side where it narrows, 2 narrow, oblong, reddish slightly outcurved sepals either side of base; above sepals are 2 similar shaped petals; at top is third more incurved sepal
LEAVES: None
STEMS: Reddish-purple, naked except for 2 or 3 sheathing bracts
BLOOMING PERIOD: June–August
HABITAT: Mostly in damp humus under coniferous trees, occasionally in more open areas
NOTE: Saprophyte

STRIPED CORALROOT
Corallorhiza striata

ORCHID FAMILY
Orchidaceae
Perennial

OTHER NAMES: Bigelow's Coralroot, Madder-stripes
COLOUR: Brownish-purple
HEIGHT: 15–50 cm (6–20″)
FLOWERS: Almost nodding in loose, spike-like arrangement
EACH FLOWER: Has broad oval, biscuit to purple lip with darker purple stripes; upper sepal and 2 lateral petals rounded-oblong, biscuit-coloured with fine purple stripes, arching forward, almost forming shallow hood; 2 lateral incurved sepals, similar in shape and colour
LEAVES: None
STEMS: May be dark and reddish-purple or pinkish with a few similar-coloured bracts
BLOOMING PERIOD: April–August
HABITAT: Moist, shady coniferous forests
NOTE: Saprophyte

ONE-FLOWERED BROOMRAPE
Orobanche uniflora

BROOMRAPE FAMILY
Orobanchaceae
Perennial

OTHER NAMES: Naked Broomrape
COLOUR: Purple
HEIGHT: 1.3–13 cm (½–5″)
FLOWERS: Single flower to stem
EACH FLOWER: Curved horn-shaped, 1.5–2 cm (⅝–¾″) long opening into 2 lips; upper lip 2-lobed; lower lip 3-lobed with darker purple veins inside; 2 bright orange folds between lobes; whole flower finely hairy; 4 stamens usually hairy; style white; 5 lobes of calyx pointed, pale biscuit to yellowish
LEAVES: None
STEMS: Unbranched, naked, finely hairy with 1 or 2 brown scales near base
BLOOMING PERIOD: April–August
HABITAT: Moist, grassy banks and open woodlands in valleys to middle elevations
NOTE: This specimen parasitic upon *Sedum*

TUFTED PHLOX
Phlox caespitosa

PHLOX FAMILY
Polemoniaceae
Perennial shrub

COLOUR: Blue to purplish
HEIGHT: 7.5–15 cm (3–6″)
FLOWERS: Many single flowers on many-branched stems; grows in mat-like clumps
EACH FLOWER: 1.3 cm (½″) across with 5, broad petals, narrowing to form tube 9 mm (⅜″) long; yellow stamens conspicuous in the middle, 3 long and 2 short; style with 2-branched stigma; calyx with 5, narrow, pointed sepals, half as long as tube, joined at their lower half
LEAVES: In many close whorls up stem, with 3 mm (⅛″) long, narrow almost needle-pointed blades
STEMS: Many-branched, tough
HABITAT: Dryish, grassy banks and open Ponderosa pine stands

JACOB'S-LADDER
Polemonium pulcherrimum

PHLOX FAMILY
Polemoniaceae
Perennial

OTHER NAMES: Blue Skunkleaf, Showy Polemonium
COLOUR: Blue
HEIGHT: 5–30 cm (2–12″)
FLOWERS: Small loose clusters at the tops of single stems; several stems to plant
EACH FLOWER: 2 cm (¾″) across, shallow bell-shaped with 5 rounded, finely darker-veined petals, orange as they narrow, forming orange centre to flower; 5 stamens with white anthers and pistil with forked stigma protrude beyond petals. Tiny bract where flower-stems branch
LEAVES: Mostly basal, up to 20 cm (8″) long, with many opposite pairs of small, pointed egg-shaped leaflets and terminal leaflet; stem leaves much smaller
STEMS: Herbaceous, smooth below, slightly sticky-haired above; may be reddish-tinged
BLOOMING PERIOD: May–August
HABITAT: Mostly at higher elevations in moist open or wooded, shady areas

COLUMBIAN MONKSHOOD
Aconitum columbianum

BUTTERCUP FAMILY
Ranunculaceae
Perennial

OTHER NAMES: Wolfbane
COLOUR: Blue
HEIGHT: 50 cm—1.8 m (20″—6′)
FLOWERS: In long loose spike on single stem
EACH FLOWER: May be over 2.5 cm (1″) long; sepals and petals same blue colour with many darker veins; upper sepal forms helmet-like hood, resembling a monk's hood; 2 broad lateral sepals, 2 narrow, pointed lower sepals; 2 petals enclosed within hood and concealed
LEAVES: Lower leaves stalked, terminating in blade 2—15 cm (2—6″) broad; cleft into usually 5 lobes, dissected into toothed segments; upper leaf-stalks quite short, blades reduced in size
STEMS: Sturdy, hollow, woody, may be slightly hairy especially at upper end
BLOOMING PERIOD: June—August
HABITAT: Damp, shady woods and along streambanks
NOTE: Poisonous

WESTERN BLUE CLEMATIS
Clematis occidentalis
subsp. grosseserrata
(Clematis columbiana)

BUTTERCUP FAMILY
Ranunculaceae
Perennial liana

OTHER NAMES: Virgin's Bower, Bell-rue
COLOUR: Lavender-blue to purplish
HEIGHT: Climbing or trailing up to 3.5 m (12')
FLOWERS: 1 nodding flower to a long stem, from opposite leaf-axils
EACH FLOWER: 4 thin, long, narrow, down-pointed petal-like sepals up to 5 cm (2") long; numerous stamens tightly packed in middle
LEAVES: Opposite or whorled at intervals along stems; stalks wiry about 5 cm (2") long, dividing into 3 shorter stalks with oval lance-shaped lobes up to 6.5 cm (2½") long 6.5 cm (2½") broad
STEMS: Woody, wiry; climbing with tendrils at leaf-nodes
BLOOMING PERIOD: May–July
HABITAT: Damp, open, often mixed deciduous and coniferous woods
NOTE: Poisonous. May cause dermatitis

UPLAND DELPHINIUM
Delphinium nuttallianum

BUTTERCUP FAMILY
Ranunculaceae
Perennial

OTHER NAMES: Larkspur
COLOUR: Deep purplish-blue to greyish-blue
HEIGHT: 15–40 cm (6–16″)
FLOWERS: 3–15 in loose spike-like arrangement
EACH FLOWER: About 2.5 cm (1″) across with 5 petal-like sepals; 1 at top, 2 at sides; 2 at bottom; spur extends backwards and is from as long, to twice as long as blade of upper sepal; smaller petals vary in colour from purplish-blue to whitish, arranged in upper and lower pairs, upper pair short, curved upwards, lower pair deeply 2-lobed, curved downwards, almost furry and covering numerous stamens
LEAVES: Lower leaves stalked, stem leaves stalkless; blades 2–8 cm (¾–3¼″) broad, dissected into several segments, which are in turn dissected into 2 or 3 long, narrow segments
STEMS: Usually unbranched, solid, sturdy; slightly downy, especially towards top
BLOOMING PERIOD: March–July
HABITAT: Dry sagebrush country to middle, more moist elevations
NOTE: Poisonous

PRAIRIE CROCUS
Pulsatilla patens
subsp. multifida
(Anemone patens)

BUTTERCUP FAMILY
Ranunculaceae
Perennial

OTHER NAMES: Pasqueflower, Windflower
COLOUR: Lavender-blue
HEIGHT: 5–25 cm (2–10″)
FLOWERS: Single showy flower to a stem; often grows in clumps
EACH FLOWER: Deeply cup-shaped 4–5 cm (1½–2″) across with 5–7 lavender-blue sepals, no petals; many bright yellow stamens; involucre has several narrowly-dissected leaves covered with long, greyish downy hairs
LEAVES: Several leaves from base, long, downy stalks dissected into many long, narrow downy segments
STEMS: Flower stem upright, covered with long, greyish, downy hairs
BLOOMING PERIOD: April–August
HABITAT: Open, dryish, wooded areas or prairies and up to mountain slopes
NOTE: Poisonous. May cause dermatitis

WESTERN MEADOW-RUE
Thalictrum occidentale

BUTTERCUP FAMILY
Ranunculaceae
Perennial

COLOUR: Greenish-white to greenish-purple
HEIGHT: 30–90 cm (1–3')
FLOWERS: Small clusters at ends of thin stems
EACH FLOWER: Petals none, sepals numerous and small, up to 5 mm (¼") long; male and female flowers on separate plants; male flowers–numerous (15–30) stamens with purplish filaments and yellowish-green anthers that hang like a tassel; female flowers–numerous (8–15) greenish-white free, unfused pistils with feathery stigmas usually purplish
LEAVES: Mostly opposite; stem leaves with long stalks which branch into 3 smaller branches which branch again into opposite pairs bearing 3-lobed leaflets cleft into small, round-ended lobes
STEMS: Slender, rigid, more or less smooth
BLOOMING PERIOD: June–July
HABITAT: Moist, shady woods at middle elevations

VIOLET SAXIFRAGE
Suksdorfia violacea

SAXIFRAGE FAMILY
Saxifragaceae
Perennial

COLOUR: Pinkish to violet
HEIGHT: 10–20 cm (4–8″)
FLOWERS: Several in loose cluster on single stem
EACH FLOWER: Up to 1.3 cm (½″) across with 5 pointed petals with 5 short stamens; 5-pointed calyx with short hairs
LEAVES: Several leaves from base with thin stalks, almost circular blades up to 2 cm (¾″) broad with scalloped margins; stem leaves become smaller up stem, more irregularly shaped
STEMS: Slightly hairy; unbranched except for flower stems from upper leaf-axils
BLOOMING PERIOD: March–June
HABITAT: Usually in wet mossy banks, and rock crevices at middle elevations

SMALL-FLOWERED BLUE-EYED MARY
Collinsia parviflora

FIGWORT FAMILY
Scrophulariaceae
Annual

OTHER NAMES: Blue-lips, Innocence, Blue-eyes
COLOUR: Blue and white
HEIGHT: 5–30 cm (2–12")
FLOWERS: Small flowers in small clusters from upper leaf-axils
EACH FLOWER: 7 mm (¼") long and 3 mm (⅛") across, tubular, opening into 2 lips; upper lip 2-lobed, whitish, erect, lower lip 3-lobed, blue; 2 side lobes much larger than middle one which is very small, pouch-like, enclosing 4 stamens and pistil; calyx unequally 5-toothed
LEAVES: Lower leaves short spatula-shaped with stalks; upper leaves opposite, more oblong, narrower, less than 5 cm (2") long
STEMS: Slender, with very short hairs branching from leaf-axils
BLOOMING PERIOD: March–July
HABITAT: Moist or dry, open or sparsely wooded areas from low to high elevations

COMMON FOXGLOVE
Digitalis purpurea

Figwort Family
Scrophulariaceae
Biennial

Colour: Pinkish-purple
Height: 60 cm −1.5 m (2−5′)
Flowers: In loose, 1-sided spike of drooping flowers
Each Flower: 4−5 cm (1½−2″) long, shaped like a finger-stall with 5 slight lobes, lower one longer almost lip-like, hairy, paler, purple-spotted inside; 4 stamens curve up from base meeting just at top of pistil; 5 broad, pointed sepals; flower-stems 1.3 cm (½″) long with leaf-like bracts as they join main stem
Leaves: Alternate up stem, pear-shaped, up to 15 cm (6″) long and 6.5 cm (2½″) broad, slightly-toothed, downy both sides; basal leaves have short, winged stalks
Stems: Rigid, green, and downy
Blooming Period: June−July
Habitat: Mainly roadsides from low to middle elevations
Note: Poisonous

SHRUBBY BEARDTONGUE
Penstemon fruticosus
var. scouleri

FIGWORT FAMILY
Scrophulariaceae
Perennial shrub

COLOUR: Lavender-blue to purple-pink
HEIGHT: 2.5–5 cm (1–2")
FLOWERS: Loose, short clusters of opposite pairs at ends of stems; grows in large clumps
EACH FLOWER: Up to 4 cm (1½") long, tubular, opening into 2 lips, upper one 2-lobed, lower one 3-lobed, hairy inside; 4 stamens with woolly anthers, 1 sterile stamen; calyx has 5 narrow-pointed teeth; flower-stems short
LEAVES: Many, mostly in opposite pairs up length of stems, narrow, pointed, may be untoothed or slightly toothed, up to 5 cm (2") long and 7 mm (¼") broad, dark green, smooth above, dull beneath
STEMS: Woody, brittle, lower parts rough and reddish
BLOOMING PERIOD: May–August
HABITAT: Dry, rocky, open places from lower foothills to moderate mountain elevations

SLENDER BLUE PENSTEMON
Penstemon procerus

FIGWORT FAMILY
Scrophulariaceae
Perennial

OTHER NAMES: Tall Penstemon, Small Purple Beardtongue
COLOUR: Pale to deep blue-purple
HEIGHT: 7.5–25 cm (3–10")
FLOWERS: Many, small flowers often drooping in tufty clusters at tops of single stems
EACH FLOWER: 9 mm (⅜") long, tubular, opening into 2 lips, upper 2-lobed, lower 3-lobed, longer; calyx 5-toothed; 2 opposite bracts below each cluster
LEAVES: In several opposite pairs up stem; lower ones short stalked, upper stalkless; blades pointed-oblong, up to 10 cm (4") long and 1.5 cm (⅝") broad, smooth
STEMS: Many flower-stems from mat-forming plant, unbranched, slender, smooth
BLOOMING PERIOD: June–August
HABITAT: Dry, open meadows and open wooded slopes from moderate elevations to above timberline

CHELAN PENSTEMON
Penstemon pruinosus

FIGWORT FAMILY
Scrophulariaceae
Perennial

COLOUR: Deep blue to purplish
HEIGHT: 10–40 cm (4–16″)
FLOWERS: Clusters at ends of short stalks from opposite leaf-axils
EACH FLOWER: Tubular, 1.3 cm (½″) long up to 1.3 cm (½″) across; tube opens into 2 lips, upper lip 2-lobed, lower lip 3-lobed; 4 stamens; calyx with 5 narrow, pointed, hairy lobes
LEAVES: Basal leaves with stalks often longer than blade, up to 10 cm (4″) long and 5 cm (2″) broad, shallowly but sharply toothed; stem leaves opposite, stalkless, narrow lance-shaped shallowly toothed, reducing in size up stem
STEMS: Several smooth, woody stems from one root stock
BLOOMING PERIOD: May to beginning of July
HABITAT: Open, dry, and often rocky terrain up to middle elevations
LOCATION: More southerly part of the Dry Interior

AMERICAN SPEEDWELL
Veronica americana

FIGWORT FAMILY
Scrophulariaceae
Perennial

OTHER NAMES: American Brooklime
COLOUR: Blue
HEIGHT: 15–80 cm (6–30")
FLOWERS: In loose open clusters at ends of long stems from upper leaf-axils
EACH FLOWER: 3–7 mm (⅛–¼") across, saucer-shaped with 4 rounded petals often whitish at base; lower petal usually narrower; 2 stamens with light purplish anthers protrude from middle of flower; 4 pointed, green sepals; each small stem 7 mm (¼") long
LEAVES: Opposite, 4 cm (1½") long, 2 cm (⅞") broad with slightly toothed, lance-shaped blades, short, thickish stalks
STEMS: Round, stout, smooth with opposite trailing branches; upper part may be reddish-tinged
BLOOMING PERIOD: May–July
HABITAT: Wet places and slow-running streams, from low to middle elevations

CUSICK'S SPEEDWELL
Veronica cusickii

FIGWORT FAMILY
Scrophulariaceae
Perennial

OTHER NAMES: Mountain Veronica
COLOUR: Pale blue
HEIGHT: Up to 20 cm (8")
FLOWERS: Several in cluster at top of single stem
EACH FLOWER: 9 mm −1.3 cm (⅜–½") across with 4 slightly darker-veined petals; lower one narrower than others; 2 stamens with pale anthers just longer than petals; style up to 9 mm (⅜") long protrudes beyond petals; sepals of unequal length
LEAVES: In several opposite pairs up stem, pointed egg-shaped, up to 2.5 cm (1") long, stalkless
STEMS: Erect, thin, unbranched, slightly downy, especially above where they are also reddish
BLOOMING PERIOD: July–August
HABITAT: Open alpine meadows and high, rocky, mountain slopes

BLUE VERVAIN
Verbena hastata

VERVAIN FAMILY
Verbenaceae
Perennial

OTHER NAMES: False Vervain
COLOUR: Deep blue-purple
HEIGHT: 46 cm–1.5 m (18"–5')
FLOWERS: In several, long, narrow spikes at ends of flowering stem branches
EACH FLOWER: 9 mm (⅜") long, tubular opening into 5 lobes; calyx 5-toothed; a pair of small bracts on upper part of flowering stems where they branch
LEAVES: Opposite, long spear-shaped, finely toothed, hairy on both surfaces and either short-stalked or stalkless; blades 4 cm (1½") to over 10 cm (4") long and 2–5 cm (¾–2") broad
STEMS: Rigid, hollow, four-sided, often reddish-tinged and branching into flowering stems at upper leaf-axils
BLOOMING PERIOD: July–September
HABITAT: In moist places, roadside ditches, moist waste ground

EARLY BLUE VIOLET
Viola adunca

VIOLET FAMILY
Violaceae
Perennial

COLOUR: Pale to deep violet-blue
HEIGHT: Up to 20 cm (8")
FLOWERS: Single flower to long stem; several stems to a plant
EACH FLOWER: 7 mm–1.3 cm (¼–½") long with 5 broad-ended petals, upper 2 smaller than lower 3 which are often whitish at base and finely lined with darker veins, 2 side petals are hairy inside; lower petal extends backwards into a spur, usually over half its length and slightly hooked; style is hairy
LEAVES: Mostly up the stem with narrow, pointed, toothed stipules at base of stalks; blades are heart to kidney-shaped, 1.3–4 cm (½–1¼") broad with slightly round-toothed margins
STEMS: Grow longer through flowering season and branch into flower-stems at the leaf-axils; 2 tiny bracts halfway up flower-stems
BLOOMING PERIOD: April–August
HABITAT: Moist to drier areas, banks and meadows
NOTE: In *Viola nephrophylla* the spur is short

NORTHERN BOG VIOLET
Viola nephrophylla

VIOLET FAMILY
Violaceae
Perennial

OTHER NAMES: Swamp Violet
COLOUR: Violet-blue
HEIGHT: Up to 25 cm (10")
FLOWERS: Solitary flower to a single long stem; may be several flowers stems to plant
EACH FLOWER: 9 mm–2 cm (⅜–¾") long with 5 broad-ended petals, upper 2 smaller than lower 3 which are often whitish at the base and hairy inside; spur is short; sepals pale green and pointed
LEAVES: All basal with long stalks, may be up to 25 cm (10") long; blades heart-shaped and may be up to 6.5 cm (2½") broad
STEMS: Flower-stems from the base and leafless except for single pair of tiny, pointed bracts halfway up
BLOOMING PERIOD: May–July
HABITAT: Wet sphagnum bogs and meadows

YELLOW *and* ORANGE FLOWERS

DESERT PARSLEY
Lomatium ambiguum

PARSLEY FAMILY
Apiaceae (Umbelliferae)
Perennial

OTHER NAMES: Wyeth Biscuitroot
COLOUR: Bright yellow
HEIGHT: 10–60 cm (4–24")
FLOWERS: Many tiny flowers in flat-topped clusters on umbrella-stems; each cluster at summit of longer umbrella-stem; the several longer stems of unequal length
EACH FLOWER: 2 mm (1/16") across 5 outcurved petals, 5 stamens with yellow anthers; no sepals, no circle of bracts below each cluster
LEAVES: Borne on stalks which are broadened, reddish, and sheath-like at base; as sheath narrows above, generally branches into 3 smooth, green, thin stems each bearing 3 pairs of narrow, elongated leaflets which may, or may not divide again
STEMS: May be single or branched, smooth and green
BLOOMING PERIOD: April–July
HABITAT: Drier, open, often rocky slopes and sagebrush flats to moderate elevations

NARROW-LEAVED PARSLEY
Lomatium triternatum

PARSLEY FAMILY
Apiaceae (Umbelliferae)
Perennial

OTHER NAMES: Nineleaf Biscuitroot
COLOUR: Yellow
HEIGHT: 20–80 cm (8–32")
FLOWERS: Small tight clusters at ends of unequal length umbrella-stems
EACH FLOWER: Minute, 5 tiny petals, 5 yellow stamens
LEAVES: Mostly basal stalks broaden at base and terminate in 3 divisions which again divide into 3 long, narrow leaf-segments which again divide into 3 elongated segments; may be one or two smaller leaves with short, sheathed stalks at flower-stem branches
STEMS: Rigid and may be slightly hairy
BLOOMING PERIOD: April–July
HABITAT: Dry, lower elevations

SIERRA SANICLE
Sanicula graveolens

PARSLEY FAMILY
Apiaceae (Umbelliferae)
Perennial

OTHER NAMES: Western Snakeroot
COLOUR: Yellow
HEIGHT: 5–50 cm (2–20″)
FLOWERS: Tiny male and female flowers in small tight clusters from umbrella-stems terminating long stems
LEAVES: Alternate, lower ones with stalks from base; blades 1.5 cm (⅝″) to over 4 cm (1½″) long, 2.1–4 cm (⅞–1½″) broad, divided into opposite leaflets which are again divided and lobed
STEMS: Single from base and irregularly branched above
BLOOMING PERIOD: May–July
HABITAT: From low to moderate elevations on open or sparsely wooded slopes

AMERICAN SKUNK-CABBAGE
Lysichiton americanum
(Lysichitum americanum)

ARUM FAMILY
Araceae
Perennial

OTHER NAMES: Yellow Arum, Swamp Lantern
COLOUR: Yellow
HEIGHT: Up to 90 cm (3′)
FLOWERS: Numerous tiny, tightly packed flowers on thick, pointed spadix (cluster); whole sheathed by large, pointed, yellow spathe (hood) up to 20 cm (8″) long
EACH FLOWER: Minute, greenish-yellow with 4 sepals and 4 stamens
LEAVES: Appear later; large, broad, and tapering to point; may be up to 90 cm (3′) long and 30 cm (1′) broad; all basal; skunk-like odour
STEMS: Fleshy and thick
BLOOMING PERIOD: April–July
HABITAT: Swampy, muddy areas often near cedar stands at lower elevations
NOTE: Poisonous

SHORT-BEAKED FALSE DANDELION
Agoseris glauca

ASTER FAMILY
Asteraceae (Compositae)
Perennial

COLOUR: Yellow
HEIGHT: 10–70 cm (4–28")
FLOWERS: Solitary terminal flower on unbranched stem; may be several stems in a small group
EACH FLOWER: Up to 5 cm (2") across with all ray-petals, which may be finely toothed; involucre has several rows of bracts
LEAVES: All from base, long, narrow, and lance-shaped with conspicuous midrib and may be toothed, lobed, or entire
STEMS: Unbranched and may be hairy
BLOOMING PERIOD: May–September
HABITAT: Open meadows at higher elevations

CHAMISSO'S ARNICA
Arnica chamissonis

ASTER FAMILY
Asteraceae (Compositae)
Perennial

COLOUR: Yellow
HEIGHT: 20 cm–1 m (8–39¼″)
FLOWERS: Several at upper end of single stem
EACH FLOWER: About 13 ray-petals from 1.3–2 cm (½–¾″) long; hairy bracts on involucre have longer, more crowded white hairs at or near tips
LEAVES: 5–10 pairs of stemless leaves spaced up stem; blades covered with short hairs, mostly lance-shaped, often with dented margins
STEMS: Single and covered with short hairs
BLOOMING PERIOD: June–August
HABITAT: Moist meadows and streambanks

HEART-LEAVED ARNICA
Arnica cordifolia

ASTER FAMILY
Asteraceae (Compositae)
Perennial

COLOUR: Yellow
HEIGHT: 20–60 cm (8–24″)
FLOWERS: 1–3 flowers to single stem
EACH FLOWER: Up to 5 cm (2″) across with 10–15 broad, pointed ray-petals; involucre 1.3–2 cm (½–¾″) deep and usually hairy
LEAVES: Basal leaves have long stalks and large, heart-shaped, often toothed blades 4–24 cm (1½–8¾″) long and 2.5–9 cm (1–3½″) broad; 2–4 opposite pairs of smaller stem-leaves; stalks and blades softly hairy
STEMS: Single, downy, and branching into flower-stems above
BLOOMING PERIOD: April–June
HABITAT: Moist woodlands from foothills to high elevations

BROWN-HAIRED ORANGE-FLOWERED ARNICA
Arnica fulgens

ASTER FAMILY
Asteraceae (Compositae)
Perennial

COLOUR: Yellow
HEIGHT: 20–60 cm (8–24″)
FLOWERS: Usually 1 flower to a stem, occasionally 3
EACH FLOWERHEAD: Up to 5 cm (2″) across with 10–23 ray-petals; yellow disk 9 mm (3/8″) across; narrow, downy bracts on involucre become narrower and pointed towards tips
LEAVES: Basal leaves have stalks which broaden into narrow, inverted lance-shaped blades, with longitudinal veins, softly hairy; 2 or 3 opposite pairs of smaller, pointed, stalkless leaves up stem
STEMS: Sturdy, downy, and usually unbranched
BLOOMING PERIOD: May–July
HABITAT: Grassy meadows and open woods from the foothills to moderate elevations

BROAD-LEAVED ARNICA
Arnica latifolia

ASTER FAMILY
Asteraceae (Compositae)
Perennial

COLOUR: Yellow
HEIGHT: 23–50 cm (9–20″)
FLOWERS: Single terminal bloom with 1 pair of opposite buds below
EACH FLOWER: Daisy-like, 4 cm (1½″) or more across; 8–10 broad ray-petals up to 2 cm (¾″) long, slightly concave disk up to 7 mm (¼″) across; involucre 1.5 cm (⅝″) deep with 8–10 smooth, green, ribbed bracts
LEAVES: 1 pair of opposite leaves 5–6.5 cm (2–2½″) below terminal flower; almost triangular blades, toothed, and stemless with flower-bud from each axil; 3–4 pairs of opposite stalkless leaves up rest of stem but more oval and roundly toothed; may be over 2.5 cm (1″) wide, 5 cm (2″) long and slightly hairy at the edges, 2 basal leaves smaller, rounded, and less toothed
STEM: Green and more or less smooth
BLOOMING PERIOD: July and August
HABITAT: Sub-alpine, alpine, and above timberline at elevations from 914 m–2,438 m (3,000–8,000′)

HAIRY ARNICA
Arnica mollis

ASTER FAMILY
Asteraceae (Compositae)
Perennial

COLOUR: Yellow
HEIGHT: 10–60 cm (4–24")
FLOWERS: Single flower at ends of simply-branched stems
EACH FLOWER: 2–5 cm (1½–1¾") across with 12–18 ray-petals surrounding disk which is up to 1.5 cm (⅝") across; bracts on involucre hairy especially at base
LEAVES: Opposite, lance-shaped, hairy, and stalkless; may be 5 pairs up stem
STEMS: Rigid, green, hairy, and mostly oppositely branched above
BLOOMING PERIOD: June–September
HABITAT: Moist, more open places from middle to high elevations

PRAIRIE SAGEBRUSH
Artemisia frigida

ASTER FAMILY
Asteraceae (Compositae)
Perennial shrub

OTHER NAMES: Fringed Sagebrush, Pasture Sage
COLOUR: Yellow
HEIGHT: 10–46 cm (4–18″)
FLOWERS: Loose, sometimes slightly drooping spikes of small flowerheads
EACH FLOWER: In tight globular bunch about 3 mm (⅛″) across with grey-green sepals
LEAVES: Many, finely-dissected, fringe-like leaves, mostly on upper part of stem; softly downy giving grey-green appearance; highly aromatic when crushed
STEMS: Many thin, wiry, unbranched stems; greyish and downy above and brownish below
BLOOMING PERIOD: July–September
HABITAT: Dry to arid, open areas at moderate elevations

WESTERN MUGWORT
Artemisia ludoviciana

Aster Family
Asteraceae (Compositae)
Perennial

Colour: Greenish-yellow
Height: 30 cm–1 m (12–39¼")
Flowers: Many small flowers crowded in spike-like clusters on long stems from upper leaf-axils
Each Flower: 3 mm (⅛") across with tiny male and female flowers; involucre up to 3 mm (⅛") high with downy, green bracts
Leaves: Alternate, highly aromatic, stalkless and lance-shaped, 3–11 cm (1¼–4¼") long and up to 9 mm (⅜") broad; covered with short, whitish downy hairs beneath and green above
Stems: Single, but one to several from one root-stock, almost woody and often reddish below
Blooming Period: June–October
Habitat: Dry, open areas and roadsides

BIG BASIN SAGEBRUSH
Artemisia tridentata

Aster Family
Asteraceae (Compositae)
Perennial shrub

Colour: Yellow to brownish-yellow
Height: 46 cm–1.5 m (18″–5′)
Flowers: Slender spikes composed of many smaller spikes each bearing many tiny flowers; at ends of branched stems
Each Flower: Tiny, up to 3 mm (⅛″) long with 5 stamens and a style
Leaves: Many small, narrow, untoothed leaves within flower-spikes; stem-leaves on side branches in groups; small blades grey-green, narrow, fan-shaped, and up to 2.5 cm (1″) long and 7 mm (¼″) broad, 3-toothed at tip and with 3 longitudinal veins
Stems: Woody, many branched, downy, greyish-green above and brown and rough below. Whole plant highly aromatic when crushed
Blooming Period: July–September, later than Rabbitbrush in southern British Columbia
Habitat: Dry, open, flat areas and hillsides

ARROW-LEAVED BALSAM-ROOT
Balsamorhiza sagittata

ASTER FAMILY
Asteraceae (Compositae)
Perennial

OTHER NAMES: Spring Sunflower
COLOUR: Yellow
HEIGHT: 20–80 cm (8–32″)
FLOWERS: Single large daisy-flower to a stem; grows in clumps
EACH FLOWER: Up to 10 cm (4″) across with up to 25 pointed ray-petals; pale orange disk becoming brownish with age; downy bracts on involucre in two layers, inner ones short and narrow, outer ones broader and longer standing out like frill
LEAVES: Mostly basal with long stalks and large arrowhead-shaped, silver-green blades, up to 30 cm (12″) long and 15 cm (6″) broad and untoothed
STEMS: Unbranched, usually with a few small leaves
BLOOMING PERIOD: April–July
HABITAT: Drier, open slopes and sagebrush flats from low to moderate elevations

NODDING BEGGARTICKS
Bidens cernua

ASTER FAMILY
Asteraceae (Compositae)
Annual

OTHER NAMES: Bur Marigold, Sticktight
COLOUR: Yellow
HEIGHT: 20 cm–1.5 m (8″–5′)
FLOWERS: Nodding, 1 terminal and 2 lower ones on opposite stems
EACH FLOWER: 4 cm (1½″) across with 6–10 broad, ray-petals surrounding brownish-yellow disk; sometimes ray-petals absent; bracts on involucre greenish-yellow. Below each flower 6–7 green, out-curved, leaf-like bracts often irregular in length
LEAVES: Opposite, long lance-shaped, and toothed; lower ones 13–15 cm (5–6″) long, upper ones becoming more pointed and narrower. All stalkless
STEMS: Round, smooth above and slightly hairy below, branching into three flower-stems, which may again be three-branched
BLOOMING PERIOD: July–September
HABITAT: Roadside ditches and boggy areas

PINEAPPLEWEED
Chamomilla suaveolens
(Matricaria matricarioides)

ASTER FAMILY
Asteraceae (Compositae)
Annual

COLOUR: Greenish-yellow
HEIGHT: 5–46 cm (2–18″)
FLOWERS: 1 to several at ends of branched stems and having a pineapple scent when crushed
EACH FLOWER: Round, cone-shaped, from 5–9 mm (3/16–3/8″) across consisting of many tiny, tightly packed disk-flowers; bracts on involucre generally in 2 rows and about 5 mm (3/16″) long with darker green central rib; flower-stems from 1.3 mm–2.5 cm (½–1″) long with usually fringed leaflet below flowerheads
LEAVES: On stem where it branches and up to 5 cm (2″) long with several pairs of opposite finely-dissected leaflets
STEMS: Tough, green, ridged, and angling as it branches
BLOOMING PERIOD: May–September
HABITAT: Waste places and poor ground on roadsides

COMMON RABBITBRUSH
Chrysothamnus nauseosus

ASTER FAMILY
Asteraceae (Compositae)
Perennial shrub

OTHER NAMES: Goldenbush, False Goldenrod
COLOUR: Yellow
HEIGHT: 46–60 cm (1½–2′)
FLOWERS: Compact mass at ends of many branches, up to 20 flowers in each head
EACH FLOWER: Tubular receptacle bearing 5 tiny, tubular flowers, each with 4 pointed petals forming star; protruding beyond petals, a long 2-branched style, giving general fluffy appearance
LEAVES: Many on branches, very narrow and pointed and up to 2.5 cm (1″) long; pale grey-green due to very short velvet hairs
STEMS: Bare and woody with many thin branches above; same colour and texture as leaves. Both stems and leaves have acrid smell when crushed
BLOOMING PERIOD: August and September—before sagebrush
HABITAT: Arid parts alongside sagebrush
NOTE: Poisonous

GOLDEN FLEABANE
Erigeron aureus

ASTER FAMILY
Asteraceae (Compositae)
Perennial

COLOUR: Yellow
HEIGHT: 5–15 cm (2–6")
FLOWERS: Solitary, terminal daisy flower; often growing in clumps
EACH FLOWER: Up to 2 cm (¾") across with from 25–60 ray-petals; bracts on involucre downy
LEAVES: Basal except for perhaps tiny one half-way up stem; blades are dull green, and oval, spatula-shaped with stalks
BLOOMING PERIOD: July–August
HABITAT: Open, rocky places in the mountains at high elevations to above timberline

FINE-LEAVED FLEABANE
Erigeron linearis

ASTER FAMILY
Asteraceae (Compositae)
Perennial

COLOUR: Golden yellow
HEIGHT: 5–30 cm (2–12″)
FLOWERS: Single daisy flowers at tops of usually single stems; grows in clumps
EACH FLOWER: May be up to 2.5 cm (1″) across with 15–45 ray-petals surrounding disk from 9 mm–1.3 cm (⅜–½″) across; involucre from 3–7 mm (⅛–¼″) long with bracts covered with short, fine, greyish hairs
LEAVES: Long and very narrow, may be up to 9 cm (3½″) long, the basal ones having straw-coloured stalks
STEMS: Sturdy, finely hairy, straw-coloured below and greenish above
BLOOMING PERIOD: May–July
HABITAT: Dry, rocky open areas from lower sagebrush flats to middle elevations

WESTERN GOLDENROD
Euthamia occidentalis
(Solidago occidentalis)

ASTER FAMILY
Asteraceae (Compositae)
Perennial

COLOUR: Yellow
HEIGHT: 60 cm–2.1 m (2–7′)
FLOWERS: Small fuzzy clusters at ends of branches at upper part of stems
EACH FLOWER: 7–9 mm (¼–⅜″) across with 15–30 ray-petals and fewer disk-flowers; bracts of involucre narrow and pointed
LEAVES: Many long, narrow, almost strap-like leaves without stalks, 10–13 cm (4–5″) long and up to 9 mm (⅜″) broad; become progressively smaller up stem
STEMS: Rigid, smooth, and branching into flower-stems at leaf-axils above
BLOOMING PERIOD: July–October
HABITAT: Moist, lush open areas near ditches and on roadsides at lower elevations

BROWN-EYED SUSAN
Gaillardia aristata

ASTER FAMILY
Asteraceae (Compositae)
Perennial

OTHER NAMES: Blanket Flower
COLOUR: Yellow
HEIGHT: 25–60 cm (10–24″)
FLOWERS: In clumps with 1 flower to each stem
EACH FLOWER: Up to 5 cm (2″) across with reddish-brown disk about 2 cm (¾″) across and surrounded by 8–20 ray-petals usually deeply 2- or 3-notched; in some plants lower ⅓ of petals are reddish and veined. As flower matures, disk becomes larger. Involucre has several rows of green, pointed bracts
LEAVES: Narrow and pointed, alternate and hairy on both sides; lower leaves taper into stalk and are about 10 cm (4″) long; upper leaves about 6.5 cm (2½″) long and almost clasping stem; some may be irregularly notched
STEMS: Rigid, round, hairy, and may be reddish above; may be 1 or 2 branches from leaf-axils; smells like chrysanthemum when crushed
BLOOMING PERIOD: June–August
HABITAT: Open, dry ground, grassy roadsides and fields in dry areas

CURLYCUP GUMWEED
Grindelia squarrosa

ASTER FAMILY
Asteraceae (Compositae)
Biennial

OTHER NAMES: Tarweed, Resinweed
COLOUR: Yellow
HEIGHT: 20–90 cm (8–36″)
FLOWERS: Yellow daisy-like flowers at ends of branched stems
EACH FLOWER: 2.5–3 cm (1–1¼″) across when fully open; yellow disk surrounded by many distinct ray-petals; involucre has several rows of out-curved, sticky, shiny green bracts
LEAVES: Lower leaves up to 5 cm (2″) long and roundly spear-shaped, dull green, and tough; many stem-leaves serrated, almost clasping, and becoming progressively smaller up stem
STEMS: Several woody stems from one root-stock and becoming many-branched above
BLOOMING PERIOD: July–September
HABITAT: Very dry open areas, gravelly roadsides and waste places
NOTE: Poisonous

HAIRY GOLDEN ASTER
Heterotheca villosa
(Chrysopsis villosa)

ASTER FAMILY
Asteraceae (Compositae)
Perennial

COLOUR: Yellow
HEIGHT: 10–50 cm (4–20")
FLOWERS: One to several in loose clusters at ends of stems
EACH FLOWER: Up to 2.5 cm (1") across with 10–25 ray-flowers; involucre 6–9 mm (3/10–3/8") high with overlapping, hairy, tapered bracts of varying lengths
LEAVES: Alternate up to 5 cm (2") long and 2 cm (3/4") broad, covered with short stiffish hairs; lower leaves usually fall early
STEMS: Several often spreading, hairy stems from one rootstock, lower parts frequently reddish
BLOOMING PERIOD: June–September
HABITAT: Open, sunny, gravelly, or sandy banks

ORANGE HAWKWEED
Hieracium aurantiacum

ASTER FAMILY
Asteraceae (Compositae)
Perennial

OTHER NAMES: Devil's Paintbrush
COLOUR: Orange
HEIGHT: 15–50 cm (6–20")
FLOWERS: Loose, short cluster at top of single stem
EACH FLOWER: 1.3–2.5 cm (½–1") across composed of star-shaped, 5-toothed, ray-flowers only; involucre 5 mm–1.3 cm (⅓–½") long with 2 or 3 rows of narrow, lance-shaped bracts covered with black-tipped hairs
LEAVES: Cluster of lance-shaped, basal leaves 7.5–20 cm (3–8") long and 7 mm–2.5 cm (¼–1") broad and very bristly; may be 1 or 2 small stem-leaves
STEMS: Unbranched, rigid, and strongly hairy
BLOOMING PERIOD: June–September
HABITAT: Fields and roadsides

PRICKLY LETTUCE
Lactuca serriola

ASTER FAMILY
Asteraceae (Compositae)
Annual

OTHER NAMES: Compass Plant, Weed Milk Thistle
COLOUR: Pale yellow
HEIGHT: 30 cm–1.8 m (1–6′)
FLOWERS: Terminal clusters
EACH FLOWER: Up to 1.3 cm (½″) across with ray-flowers only; involucre about 9 mm (⅜″) long
LEAVES: 5–30 cm (2–12″) long and 1.3–10 cm (½–4″) broad, smooth, almost fleshy, stalkless and eared where they clasp stem; margins finely serrated and prickly as are backs of the midribs, reducing in size up stem
STEMS: Stout and covered with prickly hairs
BLOOMING PERIOD: July–September
HABITAT: Waste places and roadsides

FALSE AGOSERIS
Nothocalais troximoides
(Microseris troximoides)

ASTER FAMILY
Asteraceae (Compositae)
Perennial

COLOUR: Pale yellow
HEIGHT: 5–30 cm (2–12")
FLOWERS: Solitary, terminal flower
EACH FLOWER: Composed of unequal length ray-petals; involucre 1.5–2.5 cm (⅝–1") deep with long, narrow bracts with midribs
LEAVES: All basal, long, narrow, and tapered with slightly wavy edges and may be up to 30 cm (12") long and 1.3 cm (½") broad, often folded up at edges especially near base
STEMS: Often reddish and smooth
BLOOMING PERIOD: April–June
HABITAT: Dry, open slopes at lower elevations, ponderosa pine-bunchgrass
NOTE: Uncommon

ONE-STEMMED RAGWORT
Senecio integerrimus var. exaltatus

ASTER FAMILY
Asteraceae (Compositae)
Perennial

COLOUR: Bright yellow
HEIGHT: 20–70 cm (8–28″)
FLOWERS: Several in loose flat-topped cluster at top of single stem
EACH FLOWER: Up to 2.5 cm (1″) across with about 8 broad ray-petals; involucre up to 9 mm (⅜″) long with smooth, black-tipped bracts
LEAVES: Leaves from base have stalks about 7.5 cm (3″) long and 4 cm (1½″) broad with indented margins; alternate stem-leaves become narrow, lance-shaped, downy, toothed, and almost clasping stem
STEMS: Ridged and downy
BLOOMING PERIOD: May–August
HABITAT: Moist to dry, open meadows from middle elevations to near timberline

ARROW-LEAVED RAGWORT
Senecio triangularis

ASTER FAMILY
Asteraceae (Compositae)
Perennial

OTHER NAMES: Giant Ragwort
COLOUR: Yellow
HEIGHT: 30 cm–1.5 m (1–5′)
FLOWERS: Almost flat-topped loose cluster from upper stem-branches
EACH FLOWER: Daisy-like with 7–10 ray-petals 9 mm–1.3 cm (⅜–½″) long surrounding yellowish-brown disk with protruding 2-lobed stigmas; involucre 7–9 mm (¼–⅜″) long with green, brownish-tipped bracts
LEAVES: Triangular, lance-shaped, and sharply pointed with irregularly toothed margins; blades from 4–15 cm (1½–6″) long and 2–5 cm (¾–2″) broad at base; lower leaves have stalks while upper ones may be stalkless and arranged alternately
STEMS: Green, ribbed, and hollow
BLOOMING PERIOD: June–September
HABITAT: Moist, open woodlands and streambanks from middle to high elevations

CANADA GOLDENROD
Solidago canadensis

ASTER FAMILY
Asteraceae (Compositae)
Perennial

COLOUR: Yellow
HEIGHT: 60 cm–1.8 m (2–6′)
FLOWERS: Many small flowers on one side of many flower-stems at upper part of stem, forming large, pyramidal cluster, 20–30 cm (8–12″) across
EACH FLOWER: About 13 tiny ray-petals; involucre has thin, narrow bracts
LEAVES: Many, dark green, leathery, narrow, lance-shaped leaves up length of stem; may be slighty serrated; blades with longitudinal veins narrow as they join main stem
STEMS: Woody below and may be slightly hairy
BLOOMING PERIOD: July–October
HABITAT: Lush, grassy meadows and roadsides

NORTHERN GOLDENROD
Solidago multiradiata

ASTER FAMILY
Asteraceae (Compositae)
Perennial

COLOUR: Golden yellow
HEIGHT: 5–50 cm (2–20")
FLOWERS: Short compact clusters at ends of plant stems
EACH FLOWER: Larger flowers with longer ray-petals than most goldenrods; about 13 ray-petals 5 mm (3/16") long surround larger number of disk-flowers, involucre 3–5 mm (1/8–3/16") long with thin, narrow, pointed bracts
LEAVES: Basal leaves and lower stem-leaves spatula-shaped, 2–10 cm (3/4–4") long, 9 mm–1.5 cm (3/8–5/8") broad with long-haired stalks; smooth blades
STEMS: Slightly hairy and more so above
BLOOMING PERIOD: July–August
HABITAT: In gravelly or rocky places at high mountain elevations to above timberline

SPIKE-LIKE GOLDENROD
Solidago spathulata

ASTER FAMILY
Asteraceae (Compositae)
Perennial

COLOUR: Yellow
HEIGHT: 7.5–60 cm (3–24")
FLOWERS: Dense, often tufted, cylindrical spike
EACH FLOWER: 5–7 mm (3/16–1/4") long; 5–10 ray-petals surrounding about 13 disk-flowers; involucre has 2 rows of narrow, round-ended bracts, outer row shorter than inner row
LEAVES: Many, long, spatula-shaped, basal leaves; blade tapers down into short stalk, whole being up to 15 cm (6") long and over 2.5 cm (1") wide, mostly shallowly toothed and smooth; few stem-leaves are narrower and become progressively smaller
STEMS: Usually unbranched, rigid, slightly hairy, and often reddish
BLOOMING PERIOD: June–September
HABITAT: Variable habitats in open areas from lower to mountain elevations

ROUGH PERENNIAL SOW-THISLTE
Sonchus arvensis

ASTER FAMILY
Asteraceae (Compositae)
Perennial

COLOUR: Yellow
HEIGHT: 46 cm–1.8 m (18″–6′)
FLOWERS: Loose clusters at upper ends of stems; closed in bright sunlight
EACH FLOWER: 4 cm (1½″) across with many ragged ray-petals and 2-branched stigmas; lower part of each ray-petal surrounded by fluffy plume; involucre has many, pointed, green hairy bracts; inner row longer than outer row and may be 2 cm (¾″) long
LEAVES: Lowest leaves large and deeply, oppositely lobed similar to dandelion leaf with soft spines on margins and on backs of midribs; stem-leaves smaller, clasping and unlobed above, becoming coarsely toothed lower down stem
STEMS: Hollow, becoming thick and ribbed below
BLOOMING PERIOD: July–October
HABITAT: Roadsides and waste places

COMMON TANSY
Tanacetum vulgare

ASTER FAMILY
Asteraceae (Compositae)
Perennial

COLOUR: Bright yellow
HEIGHT: 60 cm–1.2 m (2–4′)
FLOWERS: Flat compact cluster 13–15 cm (5–6″) across with smaller, shorter-stemmed clusters from upper leaf-axils and having spicey-sweet scent
EACH FLOWER: Flat-topped velvety disc from 7–9 mm (¼–⅜″) across, consisting of both ray and disc-flowers which are hardly distinguishable
LEAVES: Dark green, large, carrot-like, and deeply lobed; arranged alternately up stem; when crushed they have pungent aroma
STEM: Smooth, ribbed, and slightly angled at leaf axils
BLOOMING PERIOD: July–September
HABITAT: Scattered throughout, on moist, grassy roadsides and fields
NOTE: Poisonous. May cause dermatitis

YELLOW SALSIFY
Tragopogon dubius

ASTER FAMILY
Asteraceae (Compositae)
Biennial

OTHER NAMES: Oyster Plant, Goat's-beard
COLOUR: Pale lemon-yellow
HEIGHT: 30–90 cm (1–3')
FLOWERS: Single dandelion-like flowers at ends of stems
EACH FLOWER: 4–6.5 cm (1½–2½") across with several rows of ray-flowers, becoming progressively shorter towards middle; usually with toothed tips; involucre usually has 13 long, pointed bracts with keeled central ribs arranged in 2 rows; stem swollen below flower-head. Seed-head resembles that of large dandelion
LEAVES: Many broadly-clasping, smooth leaves which taper to long point
STEMS: Several stems branching at leaf-axils; hollow, green with darker green, narrow stripes and appearing jointed at leaf-axils
BLOOMING PERIOD: May–July
HABITAT: Drier roadsides and waste ground
NOTE: Flower closes when cloudy

SPOTTED TOUCH-ME-NOT
Impatiens capensis

BALSAM FAMILY
Balsaminaceae
Annual

OTHER NAMES: Jewelweed
COLOUR: Orange and brown
HEIGHT: 30–60 cm (12–24")
FLOWERS: Several on hair-like stems from upper leaf-axils of branched stems
EACH FLOWER: Up to 2.5 cm (1") long and horn-shaped; large lip-like sepal reddish-blotched and extends backwards into long recurved spur, resembling shepherd's crook; flower suspended on thin stem attached to upper part of horn
LEAVES: Alternate, with 2.5 cm (1") long stalks terminating in small, slightly serrated, pointed, almost egg-shaped blades
STEMS: Hollow, almost translucent, greenish-yellow, and branched; appear jointed at branches
BLOOMING PERIOD: July–September
HABITAT: Moist, open woods and ditches

COLUMBIA GROMWELL
Lithospermum ruderale

FORGET-ME-NOT FAMILY
Boraginaceae
Perennial

OTHER NAMES: Puccoon, Lemonweed
COLOUR: Lemon-yellow
HEIGHT: 20–60 cm (8–24″)
FLOWERS: Many small inconspicuous flowers crowded in upper leaf-axils, in clumps
EACH FLOWER: 7 mm (¼″) across, with 7 mm (¼″) long tube opening into 5 rounded petals; 5 stamens each attached to petal; 5 pointed sepals covered with stiff hairs
LEAVES: Many, narrow, pointed leaves up full length of stems; stalkless, 6.5–7.5 cm (2½–3″) long and 5 mm (⅜″) broad with strong midrib down the back and covered with short, stiff hairs; become progressively smaller up stem
STEMS: Stout, woody and green, covered with longish hairs and slightly ribbed
BLOOMING PERIOD: April–June
HABITAT: Dry, open meadows and hillsides up to middle elevations

CLASPING-LEAVED PEPPER-GRASS
Lepidium perfoliatum

MUSTARD FAMILY
Brassicaceae (Cruciferae)
Annual

COLOUR: Pale yellow
HEIGHT: 10–60 cm (4–24″)
FLOWERS: Many small flowers in rounded cluster at ends of single or branched stems
EACH FLOWER: About 1.5 mm (¹⁄₁₆″) long with 4 petals with usually 6 stamens
LEAVES: Basal and lower stem-leaves up to 6.5 cm (2½″) long with opposite, finely-dissected leaflets; upper leaves teardrop-shaped with rounded end encircling stem and point outermost
STEMS: May be single or branched, smooth, and deep reddish-purple
BLOOMING PERIOD: March–June
HABITAT: Open, dry slopes and waste land

BRITTLE PRICKLY-PEAR CACTUS
Opuntia fragilis

CACTUS FAMILY
Cactaceae
Perennial

OTHER NAMES: Pigmy-tuna, Fragile Opuntia
COLOUR: Pale yellow
HEIGHT: Up to 20 cm (8″)
FLOWERS: Several flowers to a matted clump
EACH FLOWER: 2.5–5 cm (1–2″) across with many, very thin, spreading petals and numerous stamens surrounding sturdy pistil
LEAVES: Scale-like and fall early
STEMS: Jointed, thick, fleshy, almost circular in cross-section; each segment may be up to 5 cm (2″) long and armed with sharp spines up to 2.5 cm (1″) long; top segment easily broken off
BLOOMING PERIOD: May–June
HABITAT: Dry to arid hillsides and sagebrush slopes

COMMON ST. JOHN'S-WORT
Hypericum perforatum

St. John's Wort Family
Clusiaceae (Hypericaceae)
Perennial

Colour: Yellow
Height: 30–90 cm (1–3′)
Flowers: Loose cluster at ends of opposite flower-stems from upper leaf-axils
Each Flower: 2–2.5 cm (¾–1″) across with 5 narrow, pointed petals, black-dotted along margins; petals open flat to show tight cluster of many stamens; pointed, lance-shaped sepals are half the length of petals
Leaves: Many opposite pairs of small, stalkless, narrow, oval leaves on stem-branches; fewer larger, opposite leaves on main stem; leaves appear to be perforated by transparent pinholes when held up to light
Stems: Woody, grey-green, and smooth and branched into flower-stems at upper portion
Blooming Period: June–July
Habitat: In large or small masses on roadsides and waste places
Note: May cause dermatitis

LANCE-LEAVED STONECROP
Sedum lanceolatum

STONECROP FAMILY
Crassulaceae
Perennial

COLOUR: Yellow
HEIGHT: 5–20 cm (2–8″)
FLOWERS: Star-like flowers in tight clusters at stem summits; grows in clumps
EACH FLOWER: 7 mm–1.3 cm (¼–½″) across with usually 5 pointed petals and 5 shorter, lance-shaped sepals; usually twice as many stamens as petals
LEAVES: Thick, short, fleshy leaves, fatter than *Sedum stenopetalum,* in tight rosettes at base; stem-leaves are alternate, slightly incurved and almost overlapping
STEMS: Single except for short flower-stems above
BLOOMING PERIOD: June–August
HABITAT: Open, rocky, or gravelly places from low to subalpine elevations

NARROW-PETALED STONECROP
Sedum stenopetalum

Stonecrop Family
Crassulaceae
Perennial

Colour: Yellow
Height: 5–20 cm (2–8″)
Flowers: Star-like flowers in almost flat-topped clusters at tops of single stems; several stems to a plant
Each Flower: 7 mm–1.3 cm (¼–½″) across with 4 or 5 pointed petals and 4 or 5 short, lance-shaped sepals; usually twice as many stamens as petals
Leaves: Bunched, thick, short, pointed, fleshy leaves at base, often reddish; stem-leaves are alternate, 7 mm–1.3 cm (¼–½″) long
Stems: Single, smooth, and branching into short flower-stems above
Blooming Period: May–July
Habitat: Dry grassland, sagebrush flats, and open ponderosa pine forests

SULPHUR HEDYSARUM
Hedysarum sulphurescens

PEA FAMILY
Fabaceae (Leguminosae)
Perennial

OTHER NAMES: Yellow Loments
COLOUR: Pale yellow
HEIGHT: 30–60 cm (12–24″)
FLOWERS: Close, one-sided drooping spikes at upper ends of stems; several stems to a plant
EACH FLOWER: 1.3 cm −1.5 cm (½–⅝″) long with prominent keel which is longer than the wings; calyx is 5-toothed, upper 2 teeth broader and shorter than lower 3
LEAVES: Divided into 1.3 cm (½″) opposite leaflets
STEMS: Several stems from base, slightly hairy and branching into long flower-stems from leaf-axils
BLOOMING PERIOD: June–August
HABITAT: Open, wooded areas

YELLOW SWEET-CLOVER
Melilotus officinalis

PEA FAMILY
Fabaceae (Leguminosae)
Biennial

COLOUR: Yellow
HEIGHT: Up to 1.5 m (5′)
FLOWERS: Numerous sweet-smelling spikes of tiny flowers, on long stems from leaf-axils
EACH FLOWER: 3 mm (⅛″) long; standard deeply cleft; narrow wings point forward and enclose keel; green calyx is 5-pointed
LEAVES: 1.3 cm (½″) long stalks terminating in 3 leaflets, 1.3–2.8 cm (½–1⅛″) long, rounded at tip, finely toothed, and smooth
STEMS: Several rigid stems from one root-stock; upper part square and ribbed, lower part rounded and ribbed; branches into flower-stems at leaf-axils
BLOOMING PERIOD: May to July and often into September
HABITAT: Waste places and roadsides

FIELD LOCOWEED
Oxytropis campestris

PEA FAMILY
Fabaceae (Leguminosae)
Perennial

COLOUR: Pale yellow to white
FLOWERS: Compact short spikes at upper end of single stems; several stems to a plant
EACH FLOWER: 9 mm–2 cm (⅜–¾") long; standard slightly outcurved at sides; keel may be purplish and is enclosed by wings; calyx about half as long as petals; 5-pointed and softly hairy with tiny, green, hairy bract below
LEAVES: Many basal leaves 10–15 cm (4–6") long; stalks half-round, 2.5–5 cm (1–2") long, terminating in 5–41 almost opposite, flat-haired leaflets which have a greyish appearance
STEMS: Flower-stems are leafless, thin, and hairy
BLOOMING PERIOD: May–July
HABITAT: Drier ground from lower elevations to low mountainous areas

YELLOW CLOVER
Trifolium aureum
(Trifolium agrarium)

Pea Family
Fabaceae (Leguminosae)
Biennial

Colour: Yellow
Height: 20–50 cm (8–20″)
Flowers: 30–100 tiny flowers in almost globular clusters, 9 mm–1.5 cm (⅜–⅝″) across; on thin stems from leaf-axils
Each Flower: 5–7 mm (³⁄₁₆–¼″) long with flared standard
Leaves: Lower leaves have long stalks and upper ones very short stalks; all stalks have stipules where they join main stem; each stalk terminates in 3 elliptical leaflets, serrated around upper ⅔, more so in lower leaves
Stems: Several thin, rigid stems from one root-stock
Blooming Period: June–September
Habitat: Roadsides and waste ground

GOLDEN CORYDALIS
Corydalis aurea

FUMITORY FAMILY
Fumariaceae
Biennial

COLOUR: Yellow
HEIGHT: 10–40 cm (4–16″)
FLOWERS: Short, loose, spike-like clusters on spreading stems
EACH FLOWER: 1.3 cm–2 cm (½–¾″) long with 4 petals; upper one roundly spurred at base; inner lateral petals joined at tips; 6 stamens often united into 2 groups; 2 small sepals
LEAVES: Alternate with long stalks which divide and bear up to 4 pairs of opposite, deeply-dissected segments, giving almost carrot-leaf appearance
STEMS: Several, smooth, spreading, freely branched stems from one root-stock
BLOOMING PERIOD: May–July
HABITAT: Rocky places and dry to moister open places

YELLOW IRIS
Iris pseudacorus

IRIS FAMILY
Iridaceae
Perennial

OTHER NAMES: Water Flag
COLOUR: Yellow
HEIGHT: 90 cm–1.2 m (3–4′)
FLOWERS: 1 to a few showy flowers at upper ends of stems; grows in large clumps
EACH FLOWER: 3 narrow, upcurved petals shorter than 3 broad downcurved petal-like sepals and purple pencil-lined on inside; up to 5 cm (2″) long, lower parts of both petals and sepals form tube about 1.3 cm (½″) long; style has 3 petal-like branches and 3 stamens opposite sepals under style branches; flower-stems 5–7.5 cm (2–3″) long with usually 2 sheath-like bracts from which flowers emerge
LEAVES: Alternate up stem, stiff and sword-like, and up to 90 cm (3′) long and 2 cm (¾″) broad, finely-ribbed, and sheathing stem
STEMS: Stout, rigid, round, and jointed at shorter stem-leaves
BLOOMING PERIOD: June–July
HABITAT: Marshes, sloughs, lakes, and streambanks
NOTE: Poisonous. May cause dermatitis

GREATER BLADDERWORT
Utricularia vulgaris

BLADDERWORT FAMILY
Lentibulariaceae
Perennial

COLOUR: Yellow
HEIGHT: 5–20 cm (2–8″)
FLOWERS: 1 to several in loose cluster at upper end of single stem
EACH FLOWER: 2 cm (¾″) long with 2 lips; upper lip short and flared upwards, lower lip much larger and forms palate with edges flared outwards; below lower lip is forward pointing spur; 2 sepals
LEAVES: Basal and usually under water, having feathery segments bearing tiny bladders
STEMS: Floating, with flower-stems smooth and upright
BLOOMING PERIOD: April–June
HABITAT: Very wet areas, sloughs, and slow-moving streams

YELLOW GLACIER LILY
Erythronium grandiflorum

LILY FAMILY
Liliaceae
Perennial

OTHER NAMES: Fawn Lily, Dog-tooth Violet, Snow Lily
COLOUR: Yellow
HEIGHT: 15–25 cm (6–10″)
FLOWERS: Nodding, 1–3 per plant
EACH FLOWER: 5 pointed, outcurved petals up to 4 cm (1½″) long; 5 pendulous stamens with yellow or deep purple-red anthers; style terminates in 3-lobed outcurved stigma
LEAVES: 2 basal spear-shaped, green, shiny leaves, one usually larger, 13–20 cm (5–8″) long
STEMS: Leafless, green above and becoming pinkish below; may branch into 1 or 2 flower-stems
BLOOMING PERIOD: March to August, according to elevation, as snow melts
HABITAT: Open alpine and sub-alpine meadows, also at lower elevations on most mountains

YELLOWBELL FRITILLARY
Fritillaria pudica

LILY FAMILY
Liliaceae
Perennial

OTHER NAMES: Yellow Snowdrop
COLOUR: Yellow
HEIGHT: 7.5–23 cm (3–9")
FLOWERS: 1 or 2 nodding on long stems
EACH FLOWER: 2 cm (¾") long and deep bell-shaped with 6 oblong, lance-shaped tepals which are often reddish near base; 6 stamens are almost as long as tepals
LEAVES: Usually 2 almost opposite long, narrow leaves about halfway up stem
STEMS: Smooth, round, and often reddish below
BLOOMING PERIOD: March–June
HABITAT: Dry, grassy slopes, sagebrush flats, and open ponderosa pine areas

COLUMBIA LILY
Lilium columbianum

LILY FAMILY
Liliaceae
Perennial

OTHER NAMES: Tiger Lily, Oregon Lily
COLOUR: Orange
HEIGHT: 60–90 cm (2–3′)
FLOWERS: 1 to several, nodding on long stem-branches at upper part of plant
EACH FLOWER: 4 cm (1½″) across with 6 long, pointed, shiny tepals completely recurved backwards to show many maroon spots on broader parts; 6 long stamens with yellow to brownish anthers surround robust style almost as long as stamens which hang about 2 cm (¾″) below tepals
LEAVES: 1 or 2, pointed, leaf-like bracts at flower-stem branches; may be pair of narrow, pointed leaves further down stem; rest of stem has whorls of 5–9 pointed leaves with midribs; up to 7.5 cm (3″) long and 1.5 cm (⅝″) broad
STEMS: Rigid, round, smooth, and unbranched except for flower-stems
BLOOMING PERIOD: June–July
HABITAT: Moist open woods from low to middle elevations throughout the area

WHITE-STEMMED BLAZING-STAR
Mentzelia albicaulis

BLAZING-STAR FAMILY
Loasaceae
Annual

COLOUR: Yellow
HEIGHT: 10–40 cm (4–16″)
FLOWERS: Loose terminal cluster
EACH FLOWER: 7–9 mm (¼–⅜″) across with 5 yellow petals becoming brownish at bases; 15–35 stamens shorter than petals; 5-pointed calyx joined below
LEAVES: Stemless or short-stemmed up to 10 cm (4″) long; upper ones sometimes unnotched, lower leaves deeply notched, giving a ladder-like appearance; basal ones become pinkish with age; all leaves covered with very short, stiff hairs which tend to cling
STEMS: Thin, wiry, white or pinkish, and shining
BLOOMING PERIOD: May–June; opens in sunshine
HABITAT: Sandy soil in the Dry Interior

BLAZING-STAR
Mentzelia laevicaulis

BLAZING STAR FAMILY
Loasaceae
Biennial

OTHER NAMES: Stick-leaf
COLOUR: Yellow
HEIGHT: 46–60 cm (18–24″)
FLOWERS: 9–10 cm (3½–4″) across with 5 pointed petals; many yellow stamens about same length as petals; outer 5 stamens flattened to look like very narrow, greenish-yellow lobes
LEAVES: Lower leaves with stalks may be over 18 cm (7″) long, narrow, and deeply notched; upper stalkless leaves become progressively smaller and less deeply notched up stem; covered with very short, stiff, pale hairs which give a greyish appearance and a burr-like feel
STEMS: Woody and pale grey becoming swollen beneath flower; thickly covered with short, stiff, pale grey hairs; may be several single stems to a plant, freely branching above
BLOOMING PERIOD: June–September
HABITAT: Arid, desert areas in valleys and foothills

PINEDROPS
Pterospora
andromedea

INDIAN PIPE FAMILY
Monotropaceae
(Heath Family) (Ericaceae)
Perennial

OTHER NAMES: Albany Beechdrop
COLOUR: Yellow
HEIGHT: 30–90 cm (1–3′)
FLOWERS: Many urn-shaped, nodding flowers in long spike
EACH FLOWER: Up to 9 mm (⅜″) long, urn-shaped with 5 lobes outcurved at tips; 10 short stamens; narrow, lance-shaped sepals half as long as flower; small, pointed bract at base of each flower
LEAVES: Scale-like and narrow, lance-shaped and more crowded towards base of stem and brownish as plant does not need chlorophyll
STEMS: Unbranched, fleshy, rigid, and reddish-brown, with very short, sticky hairs
BLOOMING PERIOD: June–August
HABITAT: Mostly in shady coniferous woods with deep humus, especially under yellow pine but also under fir, from lower to high elevations
NOTE: Saprophyte

YELLOW POND-LILY
Nuphar lutea
subsp. polysepala
(Nuphar polysepala)

WATER LILY FAMILY
Nymphaeaceae
Perennial

OTHER NAMES: Spatterdock, Wokas, Cowlily
COLOUR: Yellow
HEIGHT: Floating on water or erect above surface
FLOWERS: Single, large flower terminating thick stem
EACH FLOWER: Large globular or goblet-shaped flower, 7.5–13 cm (3–5″) across with 5 or more broad, thick, waxy, petal-like sepals; outer ones smaller and usually greener than inner ones which may be reddish-tinged inside; on looking into flower, top of stigma appears round and flat with radiating ribs and slightly scalloped edges surrounded by 10–20 tiny petals and numerous stamens
LEAVES: Usually floating; several long, thick, round-stalked leaves; stalks mostly under water; large, broad, round heart-shaped and leathery blades are 23–25 cm (9–10″) broad, usually floating but sometimes upstanding
STEMS: Leafless, thick, fleshy, smooth, round, and green
BLOOMING PERIOD: May–August
HABITAT: Sloughs, slow-running streams, and lakes at most elevations

YELLOW EVENING PRIMROSE
Oenothera depressa
subsp. strigosa (Oenothera biennis)

EVENING PRIMROSE FAMILY
Onograceae
Biennial

COLOUR: Yellow
HEIGHT: 30–90 cm (1–3′)
FLOWERS: Several in short, loose spike on single or branched stems
EACH FLOWER: 2.5–4 cm (1–1½″) across and saucer-shaped, with 4 large, almost wedge-shaped petals, slightly dented; 8 stamens; stigma is 4-lobed; 4 long, pointed sepals sharply recurved downwards; long, green ovary below flower rising from leaf-axils
LEAVES: Alternate, lance-shaped, and up to 9 cm (3½″) long and 4 cm (1½″) broad, softly hairy beneath and slightly serrated; lower stalked leaves wither and leave shorter-stalked stem-leaves which reduce in size up stem
STEMS: Woody, pale biscuit-coloured, and slightly hairy
BLOOMING PERIOD: June–September
HABITAT: Moist meadows, streambanks, and roadsides at lower elevations

YELLOW CORALROOT
Corallorhiza trifida

ORCHID FAMILY
Orchidaceae
Perennial

OTHER NAMES: Northern Coralroot, Pale Coralroot, Early Coralroot
COLOUR: Greenish-yellow
HEIGHT: 10–35 cm (4–14")
FLOWERS: Loose spike-like arrangement on upper part of slender stem. May be single plants or in clusters
EACH FLOWER: 1 cm long; greenish-yellow sepals and petals atop long greenish-yellow ovary; white lip may be purple-spotted and bordered on either side by a sepal; hood formed by 2 petals and third sepal which are all similar
LEAVES: None
STEM: Pale green to yellowish, erect and smooth with a few sheath-like bracts
BLOOMING PERIOD: May–July
HABITAT: Moist, mossy ground in humus beneath coniferous trees, bogs and swampy areas
NOTE: Saprophyte

SMALL YELLOW LADY'S-SLIPPER
Cypripedium calceolus subsp. parviflorum

ORCHID FAMILY
Orchidaceae
Perennial

OTHER NAMES: Yellow Moccasin-flower, Golden Slipper, Yellow Indian-shoe
COLOUR: Yellow
HEIGHT: 15–60 cm (6–24″)
FLOWERS: 1–3 on long stems
EACH FLOWER: Large moccasin-shaped lip, 2–5 cm (¾–2″) long with small, roundish opening revealing purple-veined inside; petals and sepals greenish-yellow to purple-bronze; 2 lateral petals twisted; up to 4.5 cm (1¾″) long and 1.3 cm (½″) broad; upper sepal broader and a little shorter; 2 lateral sepals joined together and below lip; ovary elongated and ribbed; pointed leaf-like bract below flower
LEAVES: May be several broad, pointed, lance-shaped, ribbed, softly hairy leaves, clasping stem, arranged alternately 10–15 cm (4–6″) long
STEMS: Rigid, slightly hairy, and may branch into flower-stems above
BLOOMING PERIOD: May–June
HABITAT: Bogs, swamps, and damp, mossy woods
NOTE: May cause dermatitis

SULPHUR FLOWERED UMBRELLAPLANT
Eriogonum umbellatum

BUCKWHEAT FAMILY
Polygonaceae
Perennial

COLOUR: Pale to deep yellow
HEIGHT: 10–30 cm (4–12″)
FLOWERS: Arranged on umbrella-stems forming dense cluster of tiny flowers at top of single stem
EACH FLOWER: 3 mm (⅛″) across with usually 6 petal-like almost papery sepals; vary from cream to yellow or pinkish tinged; 9 stamens; each tiny flower has 5–8-toothed involucre; below converging point of short umbrella-stems is whorl of bracts forming frilly collar
LEAVES: Basal, pointed, paddle-shaped on spreading stems, forming mats; blades have short stalks, 3 cm (1¼″) long and 1.3 cm (½″) wide, green above and greyish beneath; edges often curled under
STEMS: Flower-stems round, rigid, and slightly woolly, the creeping stems woody
BLOOMING PERIOD: June–August
HABITAT: Quite varied habitats from lower altitudes in sagebrush deserts, to foothills and up to alpine elevations

FRINGED LOOSESTRIFE
Lysimachia ciliata
(Steironema ciliata)

PRIMROSE FAMILY
Primulaceae
Perennial

COLOUR: Yellow
HEIGHT: 30 cm–1.2 m (1–4′)
FLOWERS: Single flowers on opposite long stems from leaf-axils
EACH FLOWER: 5 rounded petals up to 9 mm (⅜″) long, 5 stamens; 5 pointed, greenish sepals
LEAVES: Opposite, broad, lance-shaped with short, softly hairy stalks; blades are 5–13 cm (2–5″) long and 2.5–3 cm (1–1¼″) broad
STEMS: Thin and almost smooth
BLOOMING PERIOD: June–August
HABITAT: Damp meadows and streambanks

TUFTED LOOSESTRIFE
Lysimachia thyrsiflora

PRIMROSE FAMILY
Primulaceae
Perennial

COLOUR: Yellow
HEIGHT: 20–46 cm (8–18")
FLOWERS: Several opposite, long, thin-stemmed almost globular clusters from upper-middle leaf-axils; clusters about 1.3 cm (½") across
EACH FLOWER: About 3 mm (⅛") long with 5–7 narrow petals; usually as many stamens as petals which, with style, are longer than petals, producing a fuzzy appearance; calyx has tiny green sepals; flower-stems wiry, about 2.5 cm (1") long
LEAVES: Several pairs of stalkless, narrow, pointed, lance-shaped leaves up stem, 5–13 cm (2–5") long, up to 2.5 cm (1") broad, with central vein
STEMS: Woody, hollow, and pale brownish-green; unbranched
BLOOMING PERIOD: May–July
HABITAT: Bogs, swamps, ditches, and lake edges

YELLOW COLUMBINE
Aquilegia flavescens

BUTTERCUP FAMILY
Ranunculaceae
Perennial

OTHER NAMES: Granny's Nightcap, Rock Bells
COLOUR: Pale yellow
HEIGHT: 20–60 cm (8″–2′)
FLOWERS: 1 or 2 nodding at ends of thin stems
EACH FLOWER: 2.5–5 cm (1–2″) across with 5 pale yellow horn-shaped petals, each tapered end forming spur about as long as width of mouth of horn; each petal joined to its neighbour as it narrows; all 5 spurs point upwards; on looking into flower, petals appear as 5 cups; 5 greenish-yellow, pointed sepals close to spurs and alternate with petals; numerous stamens protrude as brush from each flower
LEAVES: Lower ones have long stalks which branch into 3 smaller stalks each having 3-lobed blade; each lobe broadens, is again 3-lobed and notched; where stem branches into flower-stems, there is whorl of narrower, pointed leaves; on flower-stems 1 or 2 pointed leaves
STEMS: Smooth, thin, and rigid
BLOOMING PERIOD: July and August
HABITAT: Mountain slopes in open, wooded, damp areas at 914 m–1524 m (3,000–5,000′) scattered throughout area

SITKA COLUMBINE *Aquilegia formosa*

BUTTERCUP FAMILY
Ranunculaceae
Perennial

OTHER NAMES: Western Columbine
COLOUR: Orange and yellow
HEIGHT: 20 cm–1 m (8″–3′6″)
FLOWERS: Several nodding flowers at ends of thin stems
EACH FLOWER: 2.5–4 cm (1–1½″) across with 5 horn-shaped petals, each tapered forming an orange-red spur 2–2.5 cm (¾–1″) long; flared mouth of horn is yellow; each petal joined to neighbour with spurs pointing upwards; broad, pointed sepals 2.5–3 cm (1–1¼″) long, 1.3–1.5 cm (½–⅝″) wide, orange-red, often green-tipped; numerous stamens protrude as brush from each flower
LEAVES: Basal leaves have long stalks which branch into smaller stalks, each having 3-lobed blade; each lobe broadens, is again 3-lobed, notched; whorl of stalkless, narrower, pointed leaves at stem branches; 1 or 2 leaves on flower stems
STEMS: Smooth, thin, and rigid
BLOOMING PERIOD: May–August
HABITAT: Middle to high elevations in moist meadows, open wooded areas

SHORE BUTTERCUP
Ranunculus cymbalaria
var. saximontanus

BUTTERCUP FAMILY
Ranunculaceae
Perennial

COLOUR: Yellow
HEIGHT: 20–30 cm (8–12″)
FLOWERS: Single flowers at ends of branched or unbranched stems; may be several stems to plant
EACH FLOWER: 5 petals, 3–9 mm (⅛–⅜″) long, and numerous stamens surrounding green cone; 5 greenish-yellow sepals
LEAVES: All basal; stalks may be 1–5 times as long as blades which are roundly heart-shaped, fleshy, with scalloped margins
STEMS: Smooth, green, and leafless but may have flower-stem branches towards top
BLOOMING PERIOD: May–August
HABITAT: Marshes and wet muddy meadows, alkaline places
NOTE: May cause dermatitis

SUB-ALPINE BUTTERCUP
Ranunculus eschscholtzii

BUTTERCUP FAMILY
Ranunculaceae
Perennial

COLOUR: Yellow
HEIGHT: 10–25 cm (4–10″)
FLOWERS: Single flower to stem; may be several stems to plant
EACH FLOWER: 5 broad petals, 7–15 mm (¼–⅝″) long, forming shallow cup; 5 sepals are softly hairy; many stamens
LEAVES: Basal leaves have long stalks with blade deeply lobed; each lobe 2- or 3-toothed; may be a few bracts below each flower
STEMS: Smooth and green
BLOOMING PERIOD: June–August
HABITAT: Wet slopes in the mountains
NOTE: May cause dermatitis

YELLOW WATER BUTTERCUP
Ranunculus flabellaris

BUTTERCUP FAMILY
Ranunculaceae
Perennial

COLOUR: Yellow
HEIGHT: 10–20 cm (4–8″)
FLOWERS: Single small flowers at ends of branched stems; grows in masses
EACH FLOWER: Saucer-shaped, up to 1.3 cm (½″) across, 5 rounded petals and many stamens surrounding green, rounded, cone-shaped receptacle; 5 yellowish sepals tend to recurve
LEAVES: Round in outline from 2–15 cm (¾–6″) across, deeply cleft into 3 lobes, each lobe deeply notched and finely dissected; mostly from base and with short stalks
STEMS: Smooth, creeping, and branching into flower-stems
BLOOMING PERIOD: May–August
HABITAT: Mud flats, slough edges, streambanks, and marshes
NOTE: May cause dermatitis

CELERY-LEAVED BUTTERCUP
Ranunculus sceleratus subsp. multifidus

BUTTERCUP FAMILY
Ranunculaceae
Annual

COLOUR: Yellow
HEIGHT: 20–50 cm (8–20″)
FLOWERS: Several at ends of branched stems
EACH FLOWER: Saucer-shaped, up to 1.3 cm (½″) across; 5 petals and 5 greenish-yellow sepals
LEAVES: Lower leaves have long, fleshy stalks and celery leaf-shaped blades which are deeply 3-cleft, each segment 3-lobed and each lobe 3-lobed
STEMS: Fleshy and hollow; may be several to 1 root-stock
BLOOMING PERIOD: May–September
HABITAT: Moist meadows, marshes, and shallow streams
NOTE: May cause dermatitis

YELLOW MOUNTAIN AVENS
Dryas drummondii
var. drummondii

ROSE FAMILY
Rosaceae
Perennial

OTHER NAMES: Yellow Dryas
COLOUR: Yellow
HEIGHT: 15–25 cm (6–10″)
FLOWERS: Single flower often nodding at summit of unbranched stem; often grows in masses
EACH FLOWER: 2.5 cm (1″) across with 7–10 petals and numerous stamens; egg-shaped sepals covered with short dark hairs
LEAVES: Many, close to ground, oblong, 1.5–5 cm (⅝–2″) long and up to 2 cm (¾″) broad; leathery blades creased in herring-bone fashion and roundly toothed; upper surface dark green, underside silvery with white, matted hairs
STEMS: Upright and softly hairy
BLOOMING PERIOD: May–July
HABITAT: Rocky or gravelly ridges and slopes from higher elevations to above timberline

COMMON SILVERWEED
Potentilla anserina

ROSE FAMILY
Rosaceae
Perennial

COLOUR: Yellow
HEIGHT: 2.5–10 cm (1–4″)
FLOWERS: 1 to a thin stem
EACH FLOWER: 2 cm (¾″) across with 5 rounded petals and many stamens; 5 pointed, hairy sepals; 5 sepal-like bracts
LEAVES: Up to 15 cm (6″) long with many oblong, opposite leaflets, coarsely serrated; very silky and silvery beneath, green above; all basal
STEMS: Creeping, thin, and reddish; flower-stems arise from main creeping stem where it roots
BLOOMING PERIOD: May–August
HABITAT: Slough edges, streambanks, and moist meadows

DRUMMOND'S CINQUEFOIL
Potentilla drummondii
subsp. drummondii

ROSE FAMILY
Rosaceae
Perennial

COLOUR: Golden yellow
HEIGHT: 25–30 cm (10–12″)
FLOWERS: Several in loose cluster; grows in clumps
EACH FLOWER: Shallow saucer-shaped; 5 broad petals, slightly dented at outer margins, 7–9 mm (¼–⅜″) long; about 20 stamens and numerous pistils; 5 sepals are hairy and about half as long as petals; below sepals are tiny bracts
LEAVES: Basal leaves have long stalks and opposite pairs of deeply toothed leaflets; 2 or 3 small, short-stalked leaves with stipules up stem
STEMS: Branching above into flower-stems
BLOOMING PERIOD: June–August
HABITAT: Wet slopes and meadows from sub-alpine to alpine elevations

GRACEFUL CINQUEFOIL
Potentilla gracilis

Rose Family
Rosaceae
Perennial

OTHER NAMES: Five Finger Cinquefoil
COLOUR: Pale yellow
HEIGHT: 30–90 cm (1–3′)
FLOWERS: Open clusters at summits of stems; grows in masses
EACH FLOWER: Up to 2.5 cm (1″) across with 5 heart-shaped, dull, pale yellow petals and numerous stamens; 5 green, hairy, pointed sepals; 5 similar-looking small bracts
LEAVES: Alternate, lower ones with long stalks; blades fan-shaped with from 5 to 7 deeply toothed finger-like leaflets; both stalks and blades covered with coarse hairs; upper leaves become progressively smaller and stalkless
STEMS: Rigid, coarsely hairy, branched at summit into flower-stems
BLOOMING PERIOD: June–August
HABITAT: Dry to moist grasslands including sagebrush areas and up to sub-alpine elevations

ANTELOPEBUSH
Purshia tridentata

ROSE FAMILY
Rosaceae
Perennial shrub

OTHER NAMES: Greasewood, Bitter Brush
COLOUR: Yellow
HEIGHT: 90 cm–2.8 m (3–9′)
FLOWERS: Many small flowers along stem
EACH FLOWER: 7 mm (¼″) across with 5 rounded petals and usually 25 stamens; calyx covered with hairs
LEAVES: Narrow fan-shaped with 3 teeth at tip; covered with greyish hairs beneath; 9 mm–2 cm (⅜–¾″) long
STEMS: Woody, greyish, becoming gnarled below
BLOOMING PERIOD: April–June
HABITAT: Open dry sagebrush and ponderosa pine areas

CREEPING SIBBALDIA
Sibbaldia procumbens

ROSE FAMILY
Rosaceae
Perennial

OTHER NAMES: Barren Strawberry
COLOUR: Yellow
HEIGHT: 5–9 cm (2–3½")
FLOWERS: Several on stems from leaf-axils of mat-forming plants
EACH FLOWER: 5 narrow, pointed petals alternating with 5 short stamens; green, pointed sepals twice as long as petals with which they alternate
LEAVES: Mostly arise from creeping stems; blades have 3 almost fan-shaped leaflets, each with 3 teeth across top, 1–2 cm (⅜–1½") long
STEMS: Creeping
BLOOMING PERIOD: June–August
HABITAT: Open alpine and sub-alpine meadows

BREWER'S MITREWORT
Mitella breweri

SAXIFRAGE FAMILY
Saxifragaceae
Perennial

OTHER NAMES: Bishop's Cap
COLOUR: Yellow to greenish-yellow
HEIGHT: 15–30 cm (6–12″)
FLOWERS: Long cylindrical spike
EACH FLOWER: Lacy appearance due to 5 petals modified by being finely dissected into several oppositely paired thread-like segments; alternating with petals are lobes of saucer-shaped calyx; 5 stamens opposite calyx lobes
LEAVES: Several basal leaves with reddish, downy stalks; blades kidney-shaped and very shallowly several lobed; lobes shallowly toothed, 4–7.5 cm (1½–3″) broad
STEMS: Thin, leafless, slightly hairy, and reddish below
BLOOMING PERIOD: May–August
HABITAT: Moist mountain meadows and slopes up to timberline

FIVE-STAMENED MITREWORT
Mitella pentandra

SAXIFRAGE FAMILY
Saxifragaceae
Perennial

COLOUR: Pale greenish-yellow
HEIGHT: 10–30 cm (4–12″)
FLOWERS: Single flowers at intervals up upper portion of slender stem
EACH FLOWER: 5 modified petals similar to *Mitella breweri*; dissected into several oppositely paired, thread-like segments which alternate with pale yellow lobes of saucer-shaped calyx; 5 stamens opposite thread-like petals
LEAVES: Basal leaves have stalks 2.5–3 cm (1–1¼″) long; blades long, heart shaped, 2–5 cm (¾–2″) broad, mostly longer than broad; slightly several-lobed, toothed, and hairy on both sides
STEMS: Slender and hairy
BLOOMING PERIOD: June–August
HABITAT: Moist woods and meadows in the mountains

DALMATION TOADFLAX
Linaria dalmatica

FIGWORT FAMILY
Scrophulariaceae
Perennial

COLOUR: Yellow and orange
HEIGHT: 46 cm–1 m (18–39¼")
FLOWERS: Spikes at upper ends of several stems from 1 root-stock
EACH FLOWER: 4.2–5 cm (1¾–2") long including spur; distinctly 2-lipped, upper lip longer than lower lip and 2-lobed and creased down middle; lower lip has 3 lobes, outer 2, folded downwards; lobes join to form pouch (palate-like swelling) which is furry and orange; lower lip extends downwards into long, thin spur
LEAVES: Many, pointed, almost triangular, almost fleshy, clasping leaves up full length of stem; margins often curled upwards; 5–6.5 cm (2–2½") long and 2.5–3.2 cm (1–1¼") broad, becoming progressively smaller up stems
STEMS: Woody, round, smooth, and green. May branch above
BLOOMING PERIOD: June–September
HABITAT: Roadsides and waste places

COMMON TOADFLAX
Linaria vulgaris

FIGWORT FAMILY
Scrophulariaceae
Perennial

OTHER NAMES: Snapdragon, Butter-and-Eggs
COLOUR: Yellow and orange
FLOWERS: Several in loose spike; may be many stems to plant
EACH FLOWER: 2.5–3 cm (1–1¼″) long, including spur; 2 distinct lips, upper lip cleft into 2 lobes; lower lip 3 lobes which join to form pouch (palate) which is orange and furry; lower lip then extends downwards into thin, straight spur about 9 mm (⅜″) long; flower-stems 7 mm (¼″) long with small, pointed bract where they join main stem; 5 green sepals
LEAVES: Many strap-like leaves up full length of stem, 4–6.5 cm (1½–2½″) long
STEMS: Rigid and branching into slender, flowering stems at upper leaf-axils
BLOOMING PERIOD: June–September
HABITAT: Meadows, roadsides, and waste ground

PURPLE-STEMMED MONKEYFLOWER
Mimulus floribundus

FIGWORT FAMILY
Scrophulariaceae
Annual

COLOUR: Yellow and reddish brown
HEIGHT: 5–25 cm (2–10″)
FLOWERS: Usually in pairs, one from each opposite leaf-axil; grows in masses
EACH FLOWER: 7 mm–1.3 cm (¼–½″) long, tubular, opening into 2 rather indistinct lips, upper lip 2-lobed, lower lip 3-lobed; pale green calyx is 5-pointed
LEAVES: Opposite with short stalks; blades broad at base and tapering to rounded point
STEMS: Smooth and often reddish
BLOOMING PERIOD: May–October
HABITAT: Moist open places up to middle elevations

COMMON MONKEY FLOWER
Mimulus guttatus

FIGWORT FAMILY
Scrophulariaceae
Perennial

COLOUR: Yellow and reddish-brown
HEIGHT: A few to 90 cm (3′)
FLOWERS: Few in loose cluster at upper part of oppositely-branched stems at leaf-axils
EACH FLOWER: 1.3–3 cm (½–1¼″) long, tubular, opening into 2 lips, upper lip is 2-lobed, lower lip much larger and roundly 3-lobed; throat hairy and often red-spotted; 5-pointed calyx up to 2 cm (¾″) long, ridged and hairy; flower-stems up to 9 mm (⅜″) long
LEAVES: Opposite, up to 5.7 cm (2¼″) long, broadly oval with irregularly dented margins; lower ones taper into short stalk, upper ones smaller and stalkless
STEMS: Light green, stout, hollow, and ridged
BLOOMING PERIOD: March–September
HABITAT: Moist to wet, open places from sea level to moderate mountain elevations

BRACTED LOUSEWORT
Pedicularis bracteosa

FIGWORT FAMILY
Scrophulariaceae
Perennial

OTHER NAMES: Fern Leaf, Wood Betony
COLOUR: Yellowish or reddish-green
HEIGHT: 30–50 cm (12–20″)
FLOWERS: Dense, pointed spike
EACH FLOWER: 1.3 cm (½″) long, consisting of flattened, yellowish hood, curved over at top and reddish below; enclosing 3 stamens and long style with reddish, curved end; lower lip green, 3-lobed, veined, and reddish below; calyx has 3 parts: 2 large lobes and 1 small one at back
LEAVES: At base of flower-spike is long, green, pointed bract; 2 or 3 leaves lower down on stem, 7.5–10 cm (3–4″) long with 8–10 pairs of opposite, deeply toothed leaflets and 1 terminal leaflet, giving fern-like appearance
STEM: Woody, hollow, smooth, reddish, and stout below with 3 or 4 brown scale-like leaves at base
BLOOMING PERIOD: July and August
HABITAT: Mountains from 914–2743 m (3,000–9,000′), in moist meadows and open woodlands throughout the area

YELLOW PENSTEMON
Penstemon confertus

FIGWORT FAMILY
Scrophulariaceae
Perennial

COLOUR: Pale yellow
HEIGHT: 20–50 cm (8–20″)
FLOWERS: Many small flowers in tight whorls on upper part of single stems; may be several stems to plant
EACH FLOWER: 9 mm (⅜″) long and tubular opening into 2 lips, upper lip 2-lobed, lower lip 3-lobed; 5 green, shiny, pointed sepals; opposite pair of bracts below each whorl
LEAVES: At base there may be few long, narrow leaves with stalks and 2 or 3 opposite pairs of narrow, pointed leaves not extending further than half-way up stem, up to 6.5 cm (2½″) long and 1.5 cm (⅝″) wide and stalkless; all leaves are dull green and toothless
STEMS: Unbranched, rigid, green, and may be hairy above
BLOOMING PERIOD: May–August
HABITAT: Dry to moist open woods, streambanks from lower to middle mountain elevations

YELLOW RATTLE　　　　　　　**FIGWORT FAMILY**
Rhinanthus minor　　　　　　　Scrophulariaceae
(Rhinanthus crista galli)　　　　　　Annual

COLOUR: Pale yellow
HEIGHT: 15–80 cm (6–30″)
FLOWERS: In pairs in loose, leafy spike
EACH FLOWER: 5–13 mm (⅓–½″) long with 2 lips, upper lip hooded and enclosing 4 stamens, tip violet-spotted; lower lip 3-lobed and has 2 black spots; calyx 4-toothed, inflated but constricted round petals, pale green with dark longitudinal veins
LEAVES: Opposite, stalkless, lance-shaped, and toothed
STEMS: May be single or slightly branched and 4-sided
BLOOMING PERIOD: June–August
HABITAT: Moist fields and meadows at varying elevations

GREAT MULLEIN
Verbascum thapsus

FIGWORT FAMILY
Scrophulariaceae
Biennial

OTHER NAMES: Common Mullein, Beggar's Blanket, Flannel-plant
COLOUR: Pale yellow
HEIGHT: 30 cm–1.8 m (2–6′)
FLOWERS: Tall, tight spike
EACH FLOWER: Up to 4 cm (1½″) across with 5 rounded petals almost fringed at margins; 5 stamens, upper 3 short, curled and covered with downy hairs, lower 2 almost as long as lower petal; calyx pale green and 5-pointed
LEAVES: Flannelly and whitish-green due to fine woolly hairs; basal leaves in a rosette, large lance-shaped, broad end outermost and tapering into stalk, blade up to 30 cm (12″) long and 13 cm (5″) wide; stem-leaves stalkless, becoming progressively smaller up stem and clasping
STEM: Unbranched, thick, and woody, becoming very downy above
BLOOMING PERIOD: June–August
HABITAT: Roadsides and waste ground

YELLOW WOOD VIOLET
Viola glabella

VIOLET FAMILY
Violaceae
Perennial

OTHER NAMES: Smooth Violet
COLOUR: Yellow
HEIGHT: 10–30 cm (4–12″)
FLOWERS: Single on long stems
EACH FLOWER: 9 mm–1.3 cm (⅜–½″) long with short spur and 5 petals, lower 3 purplish-pencilled; 2 side ones softly hairy
LEAVES: Some basal with long succulent stalks and pointed kidney- or heart-shaped blades; 1 or 2 smaller, similar shaped leaves on upper part of flower-stem
STEMS: Flower-stem branches above and has 1 pair of stipules
BLOOMING PERIOD: March–July
HABITAT: Moist woods and shady streambanks, from low to higher elevations

NUTTALL'S PRAIRIE YELLOW VIOLET
Viola nuttallii

VIOLET FAMILY
Violaceae
Perennial

COLOUR: Yellow
HEIGHT: 2.5–15 cm (1–6")
FLOWERS: 1 to several on long stems
EACH FLOWER: 7 mm–1.5 cm (¼–⅝") long with short spur and 5 rounded petals; lower middle one usually broader and together with its neighbours on either side, pencilled with brownish-purple; side ones are also softly hairy; 2 upper petals usually brownish on back
LEAVES: Large, thick, and elongated egg-shaped, tapering down into often winged stalks
STEMS: Flower-stems unbranched with stipules part way up
BLOOMING PERIOD: April–July
HABITAT: Dry, open areas and sagebrush flats

EVERGREEN YELLOW VIOLET
Viola orbiculata

VIOLET FAMILY
Violaceae
Perennial

COLOUR: Yellow
HEIGHT: Up to 5 cm (2")
FLOWERS: One to each long flower-stem; several flowers to a plant
EACH FLOWER: 7 mm–1.5 cm (¼–⅝") long with short spur; 5 petals, side ones hairy, lower 3 have pencilled, purple lines; spur is short; 5 pointed sepals
LEAVES: Mostly from base with stalks 2–15 cm (¾–6") long; blades almost round or broad kidney-shaped and slightly serrated, 2–3 cm (¾–1¼") broad, thin, smooth, and green; often remain green through winter
STEMS: Smooth, up to 5 cm (2") long; 1 or 2 small leaves with stipule where stalk joins main stem
BLOOMING PERIOD: May–August
HABITAT: Alpine and sub-alpine slopes

WHITE GREEN *and* BROWN FLOWERS

POISON-IVY
Toxicodendron rydbergii
(Rhus radicans)

SUMAC FAMILY
Anacardiaceae
Perennial shrub

COLOUR: Greenish-white
HEIGHT: 46 cm–1.3 m (18–50")
FLOWERS: Many small flowers in tight clusters in leaf-axils
EACH FLOWER: Up to 3 mm (⅛") long with mostly 5 petals, 5 sepals, and 5 stamens. Berries are whitish
LEAVES: 3 shiny, pointed, egg-shaped, often wavy-edged leaflets 5–15 cm (2–6") long
STEMS: Woody, usually with short hairs and branched above
BLOOMING PERIOD: April–July
HABITAT: Drier gravelly areas
NOTE: All parts of this shrub contain a poisonous oil which on contact with the skin causes severe irritation

COMMON POISON-HEMLOCK
Conium maculatum

PARSLEY FAMILY
Apiaceae (Umbelliferae)
Biennial

COLOUR: White
HEIGHT: 60 cm–3 m (2–10′)
FLOWERS: Many flat-topped, lacy-looking clusters from umbrella-like stems at ends of many branches
EACH FLOWER: 3 mm (⅛″) across, 5 tiny, heart-shaped petals; 5 white stamens a little longer than petals. Below each large flower-cluster several pointed bracts each with dark green central band
LEAVES: On thin stalks sheathing main stem, blades divide into several pairs of opposite lobes and a terminal one; lobes again divide into several opposite, tiny, toothed lobes giving fern-like effect, lower leaves opposite, upper ones alternate at stem-branches
STEMS: Stout, ribbed, green-purple, spotted, and hollow; freely branched
BLOOMING PERIOD: May–August
HABITAT: Damp roadsides, ditches and waste ground
NOTE: Poisonous

COMMON COW-PARSNIP
Heracleum sphondylium subsp. montanum
(Heracleum lanatum)

PARSLEY FAMILY
Apiaceae (Umbelliferae)
Perennial

COLOUR: White
HEIGHT: 1.2–3 m (4–10′)
FLOWERHEADS: Dense, flat, umbrella-clusters up to 25 cm (10″) across, composed of tiny flowers at top of single stem. May be several stems to plant, large cluster made up of many smaller clusters each at end of single stem. Stems radiate like ribs of umbrella
LEAVES: Large with thick stalks which come off main stem in form of large, pale green, ribbed sheath. Blades divided into 3 large leaflets, terminal ones may be up to 30 cm (12″) long. Leaflets cleft into 3 lobes, deeply-toothed. Leaves hairy beneath
STEMS: Stout, woody, hollow, and hairy
BLOOMING PERIOD: June–August
HABITAT: Moist meadows and streambanks from lowlands to middle elevations
NOTE: May cause dermatitis

GEYER'S LOMATIUM
Lomatium geyeri

PARSLEY FAMILY
Apiaceae (Umbelliferae)
Perennial

OTHER NAMES: Biscuit-root, Pepper and Salt
COLOUR: White
HEIGHT: 15–30 cm (6–12″)
FLOWERS: Many tiny flowers in several small clusters on unequal length umbrella stems, forming larger, almost flat-topped cluster
EACH FLOWER: 4 mm (1/10″) across with 5 out-rolled petals each with central band; 5 stamens with purple anthers, giving "pepper and salt" effect
LEAVES: Basal with purplish stalks 5–15 cm (2–6″) long, terminating in 3 branches each bearing 2 or 3 pairs of opposite leaflets which are dissected into elongated segments with rounded tips, dark green, and almost carrot-like
STEMS: Flower-stems unbranched, smooth, green, ridged, and becoming purplish below
BLOOMING PERIOD: March–April
HABITAT: Dry to very dry slopes and sagebrush flats up to moderate elevations

LARGE-FRUITED LOMATIUM
Lomatium macrocarpum

Parsley Family
Apiaceae (Umbelliferae)
Perennial

Colour: White to purplish-white
Height: Up to 20 cm (8")
Flowers: Very small flowers in tight fuzzy clusters on short umbrella-stems which radiate at ends of longer umbrella-stems
Each Flower: 1.2 mm (1¹⁄₁₆") across with tiny outcurved petals and 2 long, protruding white stamens. Circle of tiny, downy bracts below each tight cluster
Leaves: Mostly from base with long, downy stalks, sheathing below. The many opposite, downy leaflets finely dissected
Stems: Round, ridged, downy, and reddish, especially below
Blooming Period: End of March–May
Habitat: Open, dry, gravelly, or rocky areas at lower elevations

GAIRDNER'S YAMPAH
Perideridia gairdneri
subsp. borealis

PARSLEY FAMILY
Apiaceae (Umbelliferae)
Perennial

COLOUR: White
HEIGHT: 30 cm–1.5 m (1–5′)
FLOWERS: Many tiny flowers at end of umbrella-stems forming small flat-topped clusters which in turn are at ends of larger umbrella-stems, thus forming larger flat-topped clusters up to 6.5 cm (2½″) across
LEAVES: Spaced up stem with stalks; blades divided into 1 or 2 opposite pairs of very narrow, elongated segments and 1 terminal segment; leaves frequently dried up by the time flowers bloom
STEMS: Single and rigid
BLOOMING PERIOD: July–August
HABITAT: Open, dry to wet woodlands and meadows up to moderate elevations

HEMLOCK WATER-PARSNIP
Sium suave

PARSLEY FAMILY
Apiaceae (Umbelliferae)
Perennial

COLOUR: White
HEIGHT: 60 cm–1.8 m (2–6′)
FLOWERHEADS: Flattish head of clusters of tiny flowers from umbrella-stems which are divided into smaller groups of umbrella-stems which bear clusters
LEAVES: Lower leaves have long stalks sheathing stem; blades in opposite, lance-shaped leaflets which may or may not be finely toothed; each leaflet up to 20 cm (8″) long; upper stem-leaves very narrow and pointed and practically stalkless
STEMS: Stout, hollow, ribbed, and branching into flower-stems at upper leaf-axils
BLOOMING PERIOD: July–August
HABITAT: Ditches and marshy places at lower elevations

INDIAN-HEMP DOGBANE
Apocynum cannabinum

DOGBANE FAMILY
Apocynaceae
Perennial

COLOUR: White to greenish-white
HEIGHT: 30–100 cm (12–39¼″)
FLOWERS: Small flowers in clusters at ends of stems and upper stem branches
EACH FLOWER: Tubular, up to 3 mm (⅛″) long and opening into 5 pointed, erect petals; green calyx has 4 narrow, pointed lobes; 5 stamens enclosed in tube
LEAVES: Opposite; upper ones have short stalks, lower ones stalkless; blades smooth and pointed oblong from 5 cm (2″) to over 10 cm (4″) long and up to 4 cm (1½″) broad, having conspicuous whitish mid-rib
STEMS: Smooth, round, rigid, and usually reddish, especially above; reddish opposite stem branches from upper leaf-axils; stems and leaves exude milky juice when cut
BLOOMING PERIOD: June–September
HABITAT: Usually in damper areas, roadsides, and waste ground
NOTE: Poisonous

WILD SARSAPARILLA
Aralia nudicaulis

GINSENG FAMILY
Araliaceae
Perennial

COLOUR: White to greenish-white
HEIGHT: 20–46 cm (8–18")
FLOWERS: 1 to 5 almost globular clusters up to 5 cm (2") across from 1 to 5-branched flower-stem; branches radiate from central point, each branch terminates in smaller, umbrella formation with 28–35 stems radiating to form globular cluster
EACH FLOWER: Very small and conspicuous by 5 stamens which protrude beyond 5 tiny greenish-white, outcurved petals with green ovary beneath
LEAVES: Single, smooth, long leaf-stalk from root-stock divides into 2 to 5 branches, each 7.5–15 cm (3–6") long, each one again dividing into 3 short-stalked leaflets; spreading leaves obscure flowerheads
STEMS: Flower-stem leafless and shorter than leaf-stalk
BLOOMING PERIOD: May–June
HABITAT: Moist, shaded, woody areas

DEVIL'S-CLUB
Oplopanax horridus

GINSENG FAMILY
Araliaceae
Perennial shrub

COLOUR: Greenish-white. Red berries
HEIGHT: 1–3 m (3–10′)
FLOWERS: In long terminal, pyramidal spike of small clusters of tiny flowers borne on umbrella-stems. Replaced by pyramid of bright red berries
EACH FLOWER: Up to 7 mm (¼″) long and almost stemless with 5 petals and 5 stamens
LEAVES: Large, tough, like maple leaf, 30 cm (12″) broad and 20 cm (8″) long with coarsely-toothed lobes. Stalks up to 23 cm (9″) long and together with veins, sharply spiny
STEMS: Thick, armed with sharp spines
BLOOMING PERIOD: May–July. Berries from August onwards
HABITAT: Moist, shady woods from low to middle elevations
NOTE: Poisonous

LOW PUSSYTOES
Antennaria dimorpha

ASTER FAMILY
Asteraceae (Compositae)
Perennial

COLOUR: Greyish-white
HEIGHT: 1.3–4 cm (½–1½″)
FLOWERS: Solitary, at end of short leafy stem
EACH FLOWER: Male and female flowers on separate plants
MALE FLOWERS—involucre about 5–7 mm (³⁄₁₆–¼″) high, blackish-green or brownish except for margins and tips which are colourless; anthers have a tail-like terminal appendage; whorl of barbed bristles
FEMALE FLOWERS—involucre 10–15 mm (⅖–⅗″) high, narrow, slightly pointed tips, darkened petals form a slender tube; cleft style; whorl of long soft bristles
LEAVES: Numerous, mat-like and narrow lance-shaped but broader towards middle, up to 3 cm (1¼″) long and 5 mm (³⁄₁₆″) broad, covered with silky hairs
STEMS: Flower stems very short and leafy
BLOOMING PERIOD: April–May
HABITAT: Dry open slopes in sagebrush areas

WOOLLY PUSSYTOES
Antennaria lanata

ASTER FAMILY
Asteraceae (Compositae)
Perennial

COLOUR: Greyish-white
HEIGHT: 10–20 cm (4–8")
FLOWERS: Several tightly packed heads gives effect of the pads of a cat's-paw
EACH FLOWERHEAD: Composed of many, tiny flowers; male and female flowers are on separate plants
LEAVES: Many grey, woolly, basal leaves, long spatula-shaped and tapering towards base, 2.5–10 cm (1–4") long and 3–9 mm (⅛–⅜") broad, several small leaves up the stem
STEMS: Unbranched, grey, and woolly
BLOOMING PERIOD: July–August
HABITAT: Moist sub-alpine and alpine slopes

BIENNIAL WORMWOOD
Artemisia biennis

Aster Family
Asteraceae (Compositae)
Annual

Other Names: Biennial Sagewort
Colour: Pale yellowish-green
Height: 46 cm–1.8 m (18″–6′)
Flowers: Very small flowers, densely packed in spikes from upper leaf-axils
Each Flower: Minute yellowish-green flowers and pointed, green bracts; several tiny flowerheads form small spikes
Leaves: 5–13 cm (2–5″) long, deeply narrow lobed almost to midrib; lobes again dissected and toothed; many, reducing up the stem
Stems: Tough, stout, and often pinkish-tinged; several stems from 1 root-stock
Blooming Period: August–October
Habitat: Dry or moist waste places, open meadows, and roadsides
Note: Poisonous

TARRAGON
Artemisia dracunculus

ASTER FAMILY
Asteraceae (Compositae)
Perennial

OTHER NAMES: Dragon Sagewort
COLOUR: Olive-green to brownish-green
HEIGHT: 50 cm–1.5 m (20–60″)
FLOWERS: Many minute, rounded flowers in small spike-like arrangements from leaf-axils of branches of leaf-axils of main stem; whole plant has green feathery appearance from a distance
EACH FLOWER: Up to 2 mm (1/10″) across appearing like tiny green balls
LEAVES: Many long, narrow, alternate, dark green leaves from 2.5–10 cm (1–4″) long and 2–9 mm (1/10–3/8″) broad
STEMS: May be several stout, smooth stems from the base
BLOOMING PERIOD: July–October
HABITAT: Open, mostly dry, gravelly places and roadsides

**TUFTED WHITE
PRAIRIE ASTER**
Aster pansus

ASTER FAMILY
Asteraceae (Compositae)
Perennial

COLOUR: White
HEIGHT: 30 cm–1.2 m (1–4′)
FLOWERS: Many small daisy flowers forming loose, almost one-sided spikes on branched stems
EACH FLOWER: 7–9 mm (¼–⅜″) across with up to 25 narrow, white ray-petals; disc 3 mm (⅛″) across and surrounded by tiny hairs; involucre 3 mm (⅛″) deep with 3 rows of green bracts; flower-stems about 3 mm (⅛″) long
LEAVES: Many, narrow and strap-like 4–5 cm (1½–2″) long below, diminishing in size up the stem and branches
STEMS: Woody and brownish
BLOOMING PERIOD: July–September
HABITAT: Dry or damp, open areas and roadsides

HOARY FALSE YARROW
Chaenactis douglasii

Aster Family
Asteraceae (Compositae)
Biennial

Other Names: Hoary Chaenactis
Colour: White- to flesh-coloured
Height: 15–50 cm (6–20″)
Flowers: Loose candelabra-like cluster
Each Flower-head: 1.5 cm (⅝″) long and 1.3–1.5 cm (½–⅝″) across, composed of many, tiny tubular flowers flaring into 6 lobes, with style protruding and dividing into 2, curved parts, giving flower-head a fuzzy appearance; involucre looks green-ribbed with long bracts
Leaves: Arranged alternately up stem and 5–10 cm (2–4″) long with several crinkled looking leaflets arranged at right angles to midribs; slightly hairy
Stems: Green, slightly hairy, and branched above
Blooming Period: June–July
Habitat: Dry, open, rocky, or sandy areas

CANADIAN FLEABANE
Conyza canadensis

ASTER FAMILY
Asteraceae (Compositae)
Annual

OTHER NAMES: Horseweed
COLOUR: White to green or yellowish-white
HEIGHT: 20–100 cm (8–39¼″)
FLOWERS: Many small flowers in clusters at ends of branches from leaf-axils
EACH FLOWER: Up to 5 mm (³⁄₁₆″) long with tiny ray-petals surrounding disc-flowers; bracts on involucre, green and smooth and almost as long as ray-petals; base of involucre rounded
LEAVES: Many long, narrow, alternate leaves up to 10 cm (4″) long, with hairy edges
STEMS: Rigid, ridged, green, single below and branching at upper leaf-axils
BLOOMING PERIOD: July–September
HABITAT: Waste places and roadsides

OXEYE DAISY
Leucanthemum vulgare
(Chrysanthemum leucanthemum)

ASTER FAMILY
Asteraceae (Compositae)
Perennial

COLOUR: White
HEIGHT: Up to 50 cm (20″)
FLOWERS: 1 or 2 daisy flowers to single stem, often in clumps or masses
EACH FLOWER: Up to 5 cm (2″) across with 20–30 ray-petals 1.3 cm (½″) long; disc may be up to 2 cm (¾″) across; involucre has several rows of pointed, green bracts
LEAVES: Basal leaves up to 10 cm (4″) long, narrow and toothed, may be deeply-lobed with short stalks, becoming smaller and stalkless up main stem
STEMS: Green and ridged
BLOOMING PERIOD: May–July
HABITAT: Moist, grassy roadsides and fields
NOTE: May cause dermatitis

COMMON GROMWELL
Buglossoides arvensis
(Lithospermum arvense)

BORAGE FAMILY
Boraginaceae
Annual

COLOUR: White to bluish-white
HEIGHT: 10–70 cm (4–28")
FLOWERS: Small and practically stalkless in axils of upper leaves
EACH FLOWER: Tubular, up to 3 mm (⅛") across and 8 mm (5⁄16") long, tube opening into 5 lobes; 5 stamens attached to lower part of tube; calyx composed of 5 narrow, pointed, hairy sepals
LEAVES: Arranged alternately up stem, stalkless and becoming more crowded and lance-shaped towards top; lower leaves inverted, lance-shaped, 1.5–5.9 cm (⅝–2⅜") long and up to 7 mm (¼") broad; all leaves covered with short hairs and have prominent midrib
STEMS: Single or may be branched and may be in clumps; slightly ridged, stiffly haired, and often pinkish below
BLOOMING PERIOD: April–June
HABITAT: Wasteland, roadsides, and fields at lower elevations

HOLBOELL'S ROCK CRESS
Arabis holboellii

MUSTARD FAMILY
Brassicaceae (Cruciferae)
Biennial

COLOUR: White to purplish
HEIGHT: 15–90 cm (6–35")
FLOWERS: Many small flowers in long, thin almost one-sided spike
EACH FLOWER: 5 mm–1.5 cm (3/16–5/8") long, narrow below and opening into 4 lobes; calyx about half as long as petals and pale green; flower-stems thin, short, and downcurved
LEAVES: Narrow, inverted lance-shaped with wavy edges in loose rosette at base; many almost overlapping stem-leaves are long, narrow, and eared where they clasp stem
STEMS: Mostly single but occasionally branched
BLOOMING PERIOD: May–August
HABITAT: Sagebrush flats and slopes in dry desert areas

WHITLOW-GRASS
*Erophila verna
subsp. spathulata
(Draba verna)*

MUSTARD FAMILY
Brassicaceae (Cruciferae)
Annual

COLOUR: White
HEIGHT: 2–20 cm (¾–8″)
FLOWERS: Single to loose spike-like arrangement
EACH FLOWER: 4 petals up to 2 mm (¹⁄₁₀″) long and notched into 2 lobes; 6 stamens and 4 sepals
LEAVES: Flattish rosette at base, oblong to inverted lance-shaped, finely hairy, 1.3–2.5 cm (½–1″) long
STEMS: Leafless, slender, and slightly hairy below; may be several stems arising from rosette of leaves
BLOOMING PERIOD: Early spring
HABITAT: Open grassy areas often among sagebrush and in arid areas

COMMON WATER CRESS
Nasturtium officianale
(Rorippa nasturtium-aquaticum)

MUSTARD FAMILY
Brassicaceae (Cruciferae)
Perennial

COLOUR: White
HEIGHT: 10–50 cm (4–20″)
FLOWERS: Many small flowers in rounded clusters at ends of branched stems
EACH FLOWER: Up to 7 mm (¼″) across with 4 rounded petals and 6 stamens; pale green sepals in 2 pairs, with 1 opposite pair longer
LEAVES: 4 cm (1½″) to nearly 13 cm (5″) long with central main stalk bearing opposite pairs of oval leaflets
STEMS: Floating or erect, fleshy, and ridged
BLOOMING PERIOD: March–October
HABITAT: Usually in running fresh water, roadside ditches, and streams

THICK-LEAVED THELYPODY
Thelypodium laciniatum

MUSTARD FAMILY
Brassicaceae (Cruciferae)
Biennial

COLOUR: White
HEIGHT: 30 cm–2.5 m (1–8′)
FLOWERS: Numerous small flowers in long spike-like arrangement
EACH FLOWER: 1.3 cm (½″) long with 4 narrow, straggly petals, 6 stamens and long style; shorter greenish-white 5-pointed calyx
LEAVES: Alternate from 10–40 cm (4–16″) long, sharply and deeply lobed, similar to dandelion leaf, becoming progressively smaller up stem
STEMS: Woody, smooth, and green
BLOOMING PERIOD: April–July
HABITAT: Dry desert areas

BABY'S-BREATH
Gypsophila paniculata

PINK FAMILY
Caryophyllaceae
Perennial

COLOUR: White
HEIGHT: Up to 80 cm (32")
FLOWERS: Numerous tiny flowers on many, branched stems giving appearance of frozen breath; plants in large clumps
EACH FLOWER: 3–5 mm (⅛–³⁄₁₆") across with 5 slightly notched petals; 10 stamens, some longer than petals; each flower-stem almost hair-thin and 5 mm (³⁄₁₆") long with tiny bracts
LEAVES: Opposite and up to 7.5 cm (3") long, narrow and pointed and up to 1.3 cm (½") broad and greyish-green with prominent midrib; almost clasping at stem branches
STEMS: Rigid, smooth, greyish-green, and jointed at branches—simply branched at upper ⅔
BLOOMING PERIOD: June–July
HABITAT: Drier areas, roadsides, and waste places

WHITE CAMPION
Silene alba
subsp. alba
(Lychnis alba)

PINK FAMILY
Caryophyllaceae
Perennial

COLOUR: White
HEIGHT: 38–120 cm (15–48″)
FLOWERS: Loose, open clusters at ends of oppositely branched stems
EACH FLOWER: Up to 2.5 cm (1″) across with 5 deeply-notched petals which narrow abruptly and form 2.5 cm (1″) long tube at right-angles to blades. On looking into flower there appears to be a frill at top of tube; male and female flowers on separate plants; male flower has 10 stamens female flower has 5 styles; 5-pointed hairy calyx 2.5 cm (1″) long, veined, and inflated; that of female flower becomes much more inflated as it matures; veins on that of male flower are purplish and fewer
LEAVES: Opposite; lower ones lance shaped with stalks and blades up to 10 cm (4″) long and 4 cm (1½″) broad; several pairs of smaller stalkless leaves up stem
STEMS: Rigid, green, downy, and appearing jointed at opposite simple branches
BLOOMING PERIOD: June–August
HABITAT: Prolific in waste places, roadsides, and meadows

MENZIES' CAMPION
Silene menziesii

PINK FAMILY
Caryophyllaceae
Perennial

OTHER NAMES: Small-flowered Catchfly
COLOUR: White
HEIGHT: 5–30 cm (2–12")
FLOWERS: 4–6 flowers in loose clusters at ends of opposite branches from upper leaf-axils
EACH FLOWER: 7 cm (2¾") across with 5 rounded, deeply notched petals; 5 stamens; pale green, small, elongated, bladder-shaped 5-pointed calyx
LEAVES: Opposite, lance-shaped and dull green with midrib, up to 5 cm (2") long and 1.3 cm (½") broad; may be stalkless or very short stalked; may be several pairs up the stem
STEMS: Rigid, reddish, and slightly downy
BLOOMING PERIOD: May–August
HABITAT: Moist, open woodlands at low to moderate elevations

PARRY'S CAMPION
Silene parryi

PINK FAMILY
Caryophyllaceae
Perennial

COLOUR: White, purplish-tinged
HEIGHT: 20–40 cm (8–16")
FLOWERS: Usually on single stem which may be branched, with 1 terminal flower and 1 or 2 pairs of opposite buds; several stems to root-stock
EACH FLOWER: 5 petals up to 2 cm (¾") long and deeply notched into 2 almost square ended lobes; lower half of petals bend at right-angles from broader, notched blade and together with calyx form a tube; where bend occurs is a white frill; 10 stamens; calyx is 5-toothed, tubular, 1.3–1.5 cm (½–⅝") long, slightly inflated, pale green with 10 conspicuous purplish ribs
LEAVES: Many basal leaves, long, narrow, and spatula shaped, 2.5–7.5 cm (1–3") long and 3–9 mm (⅛–⅜") broad; stem-leaves are opposite and stalkless in 1 or 2 pairs up stem
STEMS: Thin, rigid, and slightly sticky haired; may branch at upper leaf-axils
BLOOMING PERIOD: July–August
HABITAT: Dry, open mountain slopes at high elevations

BLADDER CAMPION
Silene vulgaris
(Silene cucubalus)

PINK FAMILY
Caryophyllaceae
Perennial

OTHER NAMES: White Ben
COLOUR: White
HEIGHT: Up to 60 cm (2′)
FLOWERS: In clusters at ends of branched stems; often in clumps
EACH FLOWER: 2 cm (¾″) across with 5 deeply notched, rounded petals which taper to form loose tube surrounded by bladder-shaped 5-pointed calyx, greyish-green and appears mottled by network of light veins, up to 1.5 cm (⅝″) long, 3 styles; at flower-stem branches are opposite pairs of tiny leaves
LEAVES: Opposite, lance-shaped, and stalkless, lower ones up to 6.5 cm (2½″) long and pale, dull green with prominent midribs
STEMS: Pale green, round, rigid, and smooth with a hard, small swelling at leaf nodes
BLOOMING PERIOD: May–July
HABITAT: Waste ground, roadsides, and fields at lower elevations

LAMB'S-QUARTERS
Chenopodium album

GOOSEFOOT FAMILY
Chenopodiaceae
Annual

OTHER NAMES: Fat Hen, Goosefoot
COLOUR: Green to brownish-green
HEIGHT: 30 cm–1.2 m (1–4′)
FLOWERS: Small, green flowers in numerous spikes composed of tight clusters; terminal spike largest with small, lateral spikes from leaf-axils
EACH FLOWER: Very small and green with mealy, 5-lobed calyx and no petals
LEAVES: Alternate up full length of stem; roundly isosceles triangular, and irregularly toothed, with stems; blades are whitish beneath
STEMS: Many-branched, woody, pale green with darker green stripes, smooth and roundly ribbed
BLOOMING PERIOD: June–September
HABITAT: Roadsides and waste places

JERUSALEM-OAK GOOSEFOOT
Chenopodium botrys

GOOSEFOOT FAMILY
Chenopodiaceae
Annual

COLOUR: Yellowish-green
HEIGHT: 15–40 cm (6–16″)
FLOWERS: Many tiny, yellowish-green flowers in small clusters, forming long, thin spike and having very pungent odour
LEAVES: Lower leaves have reddish stalks 2–2.5 cm (¾–1″) long; blades are 2–4 cm (¾–1¼″) long; and deeply, oppositely-lobed, and 1 terminal lobe; lobes again shallowly round toothed; have appearance of a crinkly oak-leaf with reddish veins; smaller somewhat hairy leaves up stem
STEMS: Simple or branched, green above and reddish below
BLOOMING PERIOD: May–October
HABITAT: Gravelly roadsides and waste ground

GREEN EUROPEAN GLASSWORT
Salicornia europaea

GOOSEFOOT FAMILY
Chenopodiaceae
Annual

OTHER NAMES: Samphire, Saltwort
COLOUR: Green to red
HEIGHT: 5–30 cm (2–12″)
FLOWERS: Extremely small, in 3's and scarcely visible, sunken just above scales that serve as leaves
STEMS: Main stem brownish-green and branches into green, thin finger-like jointed stems with tiny scale-like leaves; finger-like stems up to nearly 3 mm (⅛″) thick; whole plant turns red when past maturity
BLOOMING PERIOD: June–September
HABITAT: Moist to dry alkaline soils round sloughs

FIELD BINDWEED
Convolvulus arvensis

MORNING GLORY FAMILY
Convolvulaceae
Perennial

OTHER NAMES: Morning Glory
COLOUR: White to pink
HEIGHT: Variable–trailing or climbing
FLOWERS: Single at intervals along trailing or climbing stems
EACH FLOWER: 2.5–5 cm (1–2") across when fully open; 5 joined, wedge-shaped petals with more or less straight edges; 5 stamens and long style with white 2-lobed stigma; calyx up to 7 mm (¼") deep and 2-lobed; flower-stems up to 5 cm (2") long
LEAVES: Alternately arranged along full length of trailing or climbing stems; blades small, arrow-head shaped, up to 4 cm (1½") long and 3.4 cm (1⅜") broad
STEMS: Several trailing or climbing to several feet long
BLOOMING PERIOD: May–September
HABITAT: Waste ground, fields, and gravelly roadsides

CANADIAN BUNCHBERRY
Cornus canadensis

Dogwood Family
Cornaceae
Perennial

Other Names: Dwarf Dogwood, Pigeon Berry
Colour: White to greenish or pale yellow
Height: 7.5–25 cm (3–10″)
Flowers: Single, terminal flower to a stem; often growing in masses
Each Flower: 2–2.5 cm (¾–1″) across with 4 broad, pointed, petal-like bracts; in centre is a tight cluster of greenish-white, ball-like flowers which later develop into red berries
Leaves: 2–2.5 cm (¾–1″) below the "flower" is whorl of broad, oval, pointed leaves, 2 of which are usually larger than rest; may be 1 or 2 smaller leaves down stem; all leaves appear ribbed with veins and are smooth
Stems: Smooth and reddish, often with opposite pair of brown, papery scales
Blooming Period: June–August
Habitat: Moist woods from low to sub-alpine elevations

GREAT SUNDEW
Drosera anglica

Sundew Family
Droseraceae
Perennial

Other Names: Long Leaved Sundew, Paddle-leaf Sundew
Colour: White
Height: 5–15 cm (2–6″)
Flowers: Loose, almost one-sided, drooping cluster at top of single stem
Each Flower: Very small with 4 or 5 oblong petals; calyx has similar shaped but shorter lobes; 4 or 5 stamens and equal number of styles
Leaves: From base with thin stalks which may be over 2.5 cm (1″) long and terminating in narrow, oblong or paddle-shaped leaf, which appears red with bristly red hairs terminating in tiny, sticky knobs
Stems: Long, thin, and unbranched
Blooming Period: June–August
Habitat: Sphagnum bogs and swamps
Note: Insectivorous

FOUR-ANGLED CASSIOPE
Cassiope tetragona

HEATH FAMILY
Ericaceae
Perennial shrub

OTHER NAMES: Moss Heather, Lapland Cassiope
COLOUR: White
HEIGHT: Up to 30 cm (12″)
FLOWERS: 1 to several with short stems at ends of stem-branches; often nodding
EACH FLOWER: Bell-shaped and up to nearly 1.3 cm (½″) long and flaring into 4 or 5 rounded lobes; 8–10 stamens and short style; calyx quite small and has 4 or 5 narrow, pointed, reddish lobes resembling a grasping claw
LEAVES: Many tightly packed opposite leaves up to 9 mm (⅜″) long, egg-shaped and in 4 rows
STEMS: Stout and leaf-covered
BLOOMING PERIOD: June–August
HABITAT: Rocky areas and meadows from alpine elevations to above timberline

CREAM MOUNTAIN-HEATHER
Phyllodoce glanduliflora

HEATH FAMILY
Ericaceae
Perennial shrub

COLOUR: Cream to greenish-white
HEIGHT: 10–15 cm (4–6″)
FLOWERS: Loose open clusters up stem which is mat-forming
EACH FLOWER: Urn-shaped with constricted mouth then flared, 7 mm (¼″) long with 6 narrow, pointed, pale greenish-yellow, hairy sepals; 6 stamens; several short, hairy flower-stems about 2 cm (¾″) long forming clusters at intervals
LEAVES: Many short, narrow, pointed, stalkless, evergreen leaves 7 mm (¼″) long, thickly distributed along stem-branches
STEMS: Woody and leafless, then spreading into many, leafed branches
BLOOMING PERIOD: July–August
HABITAT: Mountain slopes from just below to just above timberline

SULPHUR LUPINE
Lupinus sulphureus

PEA FAMILY
Fabaceae (Leguminosae)
Perennial

COLOUR: White to cream
HEIGHT: 30–60 cm (1–2′)
FLOWERS: Many spikes to plant
EACH FLOWERS: 1.3 cm (½″) long–the standard, wings and keel all white or cream; keel encloses stamens and long, wiry style; calyx has 2 sepals covered with long hairs
LEAVES: Hairy stalks up to 7.5 cm (3″) long, terminating in 7–10 long, narrow, radiating, hairy leaflets; arranged more or less alternately up the stem
STEMS: Sometimes branched, green, round, rigid, and brittle
BLOOMING PERIOD: May–August
HABITAT: Dry gravelly areas in Dry Interior

WHITE SWEET-CLOVER
Melilotus alba

PEA FAMILY
Fabaceae (Leguminosae)
Perennial

COLOUR: White
HEIGHT: Up to 3 m (10′)
FLOWERS: In numerous sweet-smelling spikes of tiny flowers, on long stems from leaf-axils
EACH FLOWER: 3 mm (⅛″) long, standard is deeply cleft; narrow wings point forwards and enclose keel, green calyx is 5-pointed
LEAVES: 1.3 cm (½″) long stalks terminating in 3 leaflets, 1.3–3 cm (½–1⅛″) long, rounded at tip, finely toothed and smooth
STEMS: Several rigid stems from one root-stock; upper part square and ribbed and lower part rounded and ribbed; stem branches into flower-stems at leaf-axils
BLOOMING PERIOD: May–July, and often into September
HABITAT: Waste places and roadsides

RICHARDSON'S CRANE'S-BILL
Geranium richardsonii

GERANIUM FAMILY
Geraniaceae
Perennial

COLOUR: White to pinkish
HEIGHT: 30–90 cm (12–36")
FLOWERS: One to several at ends of branched upper stem
EACH FLOWER: 1.3–2 cm (½–¾") across with 5 broad, rounded petals veined with purple and hairy on inside; sepals oblong and slightly hairy on edges and terminate in short, stiff bristle; 10 stamens
LEAVES: Mostly basal on long, slightly hairy stalks; blades 6.5–14 cm (2½–5½") broad and deeply cleft into from 5–7 irregularly shaped lobes which in turn are deeply toothed; hairy on veins beneath; small leaf where flower-stems branch off
STEMS: Leafless up to flower-stems and slightly hairy below; flower-stems smoother and purplish
BLOOMING PERIOD: June–August
HABITAT: Moist, light, shady places

SILVERLEAF PHACELIA
Phacelia hastata
subsp. hastata
(Phacelia hastata var. leucophylla)

WATERLEAF FAMILY
Hydrophyllaceae
Perennial

COLOUR: Dull white to pale lavender
HEIGHT: 30–60 cm (12–24")
FLOWERS: Very tight curled-over clusters at ends of stems; several straggly stems to each plant
EACH FLOWER: 5–7 mm (3/16–1/4") across with 5 rounded petals; 5 stamens protrude at least 7 mm (1/4") beyond petals, giving fuzzy appearance; 5 pointed, bristly sepals; flowers at base of cluster open first while ones towards tip unopened, giving the whole curl a neat, green appearance
LEAVES: Silvery green with short, downy hairs, especially beneath; lower leaves have long, hairy stalks; blades spear shaped with conspicuous veins; stem leaves become progressively smaller towards top
STEMS: Silvery and branched from base
BLOOMING PERIOD: May–August
HABITAT: Dry to arid, open, rocky, or sandy areas; often in sagebrush country
NOTE: May cause dermatitis

THREE-SPOT MARIPOSA LILY
Calochortus apiculatus

LILY FAMILY
Liliaceae
Perennial

COLOUR: White
HEIGHT: 10–25 cm (4–10″)
FLOWERS: 1 or 2 flowers to single thin stem
EACH FLOWER: Up to 4 cm (1½″) across and shallow saucer shaped with 3 broad, pointed petals with coarse yellow hairs on inside to about ¾ of the way up; dark, purplish spot on inside base of each petal; 6 stamens, stigma is 3 parted; 3 narrow sepals shorter than petals and green-veined
LEAVES: Single basal grass-like leaf up to 20 cm (9″) long and 1 cm (⅜″) broad and sheathing stem at base
STEMS: Thin, green, and round with pair of opposite bracts
BLOOMING PERIOD: May–June
HABITAT: Open coniferous woods and grassy slopes
LOCATION: Southeast British Columbia and adjacent parts of United States
NOTE: Seed pod hangs downward

BLUE-BEAD CLINTONIA
Clintonia uniflora

LILY FAMILY
Liliaceae
Perennial

OTHER NAMES: Alpine Beauty, Brides' Bonnet, Queen's Cup
COLOUR: White. Navy-blue berry
HEIGHT: 10–15 cm (4–6″)
FLOWERS: Usually single flower to single stem
EACH FLOWER: Up to 3 cm (1¼″) across with 6 tepals, softly hairy on outside; 6 stamens; small bract below flower
LEAVES: 2 or 3 basal, pointed, paddle-shaped up to 4 cm (1½″) broad with central rib, sheath-like at base and softly hairy especially at edges and underneath
STEMS: Hairy
BLOOMING PERIOD: June–August, according to altitude
HABITAT: From 360–2,500 m (1,200–5,000′) in shady, moist coniferous forests

HOOKER'S FAIRYBELLS
Disporum hookeri
var. oreganum

LILY FAMILY
Liliaceae
Perennial

OTHER NAMES: Smooth Fairybells, Small-flowered Fairybell
COLOUR: White to greenish-white
HEIGHT: 25.5–50 cm (10–20″)
FLOWERS: Hanging beneath leaves in 2's or 3's
EACH FLOWER: Up to 2 cm (¾″) long, bell-shaped with 6 ridged, pointed tepals and 6 stamens, which generally protrude beyond tepals
LEAVES: Arranged alternately in same plane as stems, pointed oval from 5–15 cm (2–6″) long with parallel veins and heart-shaped at junction with stem
STEMS: Branched at 45° angles, rigid and smooth
BLOOMING PERIOD: April–July
HABITAT: Moist, shady woods

CHOCOLATE LILY
Fritillaria lanceolata

LILY FAMILY
Liliaceae
Perennial

OTHER NAMES: Checker Lily, Mission Bells, Rice-root
COLOUR: Chocolate brown, mottled with greenish-yellow
HEIGHT: 20–50 cm (8–20″)
FLOWERS: 1–5 nodding at top of single stem
EACH FLOWER: 2.5 cm (1″) across; deep bell-shaped with 6 oblong, chocolate-coloured tepals mottled with greenish-yellow; 6 stamens with yellow anthers and shorter than tepals, hang clustered in middle together with longer style; behind nodding flower is a long, narrow pointed bract or spathe
LEAVES: Narrow lance shaped, 5–15 cm (2–6″) long and 3 mm–2 cm (⅛–¾″) broad and often in 1 or 2 whorls up stem or may be scattered
STEMS: Round, green, rigid, smooth and reddish below
BLOOMING PERIOD: April–June
HABITAT: Damp, open, grassy banks, and meadows

FALSE SOLOMON'S-SEAL
Smilacina racemosa

LILY FAMILY
Liliaceae
Perennial

OTHER NAMES: False Spikenard
COLOUR: White
HEIGHT: 30–90 cm (1–3′)
FLOWERS: Dense, terminal, fluffy plume on long stem
EACH FLOWER: Up to 6 mm (¼″) across with tiny, pointed tepals about 2 mm (¹⁄₁₆″) long; 6 stamens 2 to 3 times as long as tepals and having bell-shaped anthers; style is shorter
LEAVES: Alternate, large, broad, and oval-pointed without stalks; 15–20 cm (6–9″) long and 7.5–10 cm (3–4″) broad and ribbed; lower leaves almost clasp stemps; all leaves softly short-haired, especially beneath
STEMS: Stout, green, and slightly ribbed; softly hairy with brownish sheath at base
BLOOMING PERIOD: Late April–June
HABITAT: From low to medium elevations in moist woods and more open areas

STAR-FLOWERED SOLOMON'S-SEAL
Smilacina stellata

LILY FAMILY
Liliaceae
Perennial

OTHER NAMES: Wild Spikenard
COLOUR: White
HEIGHT: 20–50 cm (8–20″)
FLOWERS: Loose, short spray of star-shaped flowers
EACH FLOWER: 6 mm (¼″) across with 6 narrow, pointed, outcurved tepals and 6 yellow stamens; flower-stems 5 mm (³⁄₁₆″) long
LEAVES: 1 short, narrow, pointed, ribbed leaf 7 cm (2¾″) long and 13 mm (½″) broad, at base of each spray and several larger leaves up to 12 cm (4¾″) long, arranged alternately on upper part of stem as it angles, and almost clasping
STEMS: Round, smooth, green, rigid with scale-like bract below
BLOOMING PERIOD: May–June according to elevation 345 m (1,150′) and higher
HABITAT: Damp, mixed woods and open areas

WESTERN MOUNTAINBELLS
Stenanthium occidentale

LILY FAMILY
Liliaceae
Perennial

OTHER NAMES: Bronze Bells, Western Stenanthium
COLOUR: Brownish-purple, purplish-green, or greenish-yellow
HEIGHT: 25–40 cm (10–16")
FLOWERS: Several flowers nodding on thin stems in loose spike-like arrangement
EACH FLOWER: Up to 1.3 cm (½") long, narrow bell-shaped with 6 tepals recurved at tips; 6 stamens and 3 styles
LEAVES: Mostly basal where they sheathe stem, inverted lance-shaped, 15–30 cm (6–12") long and up to 2.5 cm (1") broad; may be 1 or 2 tiny bracts on stem
STEMS: Single, round, and green
BLOOMING PERIOD: June–August
HABITAT: Streambanks, damp slopes in mountain woods
NOTE: Poisonous

CUCUMBERROOT TWISTEDSTALK
Streptopus amplexifolius

LILY FAMILY
Liliaceae
Perennial

OTHER NAMES: White Mandarin, Liverberry, Large Twistedstalk
COLOUR: White to greenish or yellowish-white
HEIGHT: 50 cm–1 m (20–39¼″)
FLOWERS: Single, underneath leaves just beside axil
EACH FLOWER: Up to 13 mm (½″) across with 6 slender, pointed tepals, bell-like and hanging on a hair-like kinked stalk beneath the upper leaves; 6 short stamens surround a longer style
LEAVES: Clasp the stem and are pointed-oval and ribbed; 5–12 cm (2–4¾″) long and 2.5–5 cm (1–2″) broad; gray-green on underside
STEMS: Round, smooth, and branched
BLOOMING PERIOD: May–July
HABITAT: Moist, shady areas, streambanks and woodlands from low to high elevations

WESTERN WHITE TRILLIUM
Trillium ovatum

LILY FAMILY
Liliaceae
Perennial

OTHER NAMES: Wake Robin, Birthroot
COLOUR: White, aging to pinkish-purple
HEIGHT: 10–46 cm (4–18″)
FLOWERS: Solitary at top of stem
EACH FLOWER: 4–5 cm (1½–2″) across with 3 broad, lance-shaped petals; 6 stamens surrounding 3 stigmas; 3 sepals similar in shape to petals but narrower and almost as long; flower stem 2.5–6.5 cm (1–2½″) long
LEAVES: Often stalkless, broadly egg-shaped and abruptly pointed; may be 5–15 cm (2–6″) long and up to 15 cm (6″) broad; usually 3 arranged in whorl below flower-stem
STEMS: Stout, unbranched, and leafless below single whorl of leaves
BLOOMING PERIOD: March–May
HABITAT: Streambanks and moist woods from low elevations to mountainous areas
LOCATION: Sparsely scattered in the Okanagan and Kootenays

GREEN FALSE HELLEBORE
Veratrum viride
subsp. eschscholtzii

LILY FAMILY
Liliaceae
Perennial

OTHER NAMES: Indian Hellebore, Indian Poke, Corn Lily
COLOUR: Pale yellowish-green
HEIGHT: 90 cm–1.8 m (3–6′)
FLOWERS: Small flowers in dense, long, drooping, branching spikes from upper leaf-axils; terminal spike is usually erect
EACH FLOWER: 1.3 (½″) across with 6, pointed, yellowish-green tepals with darker green veins and slightly downy on outside; 6 stamens; tiny bract below each flower
LEAVES: Many leaves arranged spirally up stem as far as flowering branches; lower leaves broad, pointed-elliptic and may be up to 30 cm (12″) long and 6.5–15 cm (2½–6″) broad and softly hairy beneath; longitudinal parallel veins are so prominent that leaf looks almost pleated; they reduce in size up stem which they clasp
STEMS: Very stout, woody, hollow, smooth, and finely ribbed
BLOOMING PERIOD: June–September
HABITAT: Moist sub-alpine meadows and lower swamps
NOTE: Poisonous

BEAR-GRASS
Xerophyllum tenax

LILY FAMILY
Liliaceae
Perennial

OTHER NAMES: Basket Grass, Squaw Grass
COLOUR: White
HEIGHT: 60 cm–1.2 m (2–4′)
FLOWERS: Large white to cream, conical or club-shaped head of massed, small, sweet-smelling flowers at top of long stem
EACH FLOWER: 13 mm (½″) across with pointed petals and sepals all similar and totalling 6, with 6 stamens 13 mm (½″) long protruding beyond them; style terminates in 3-branched stigma; each white flower-stalk 13 mm (½″) long with thin grass-like bract about 2.5 cm (1″) long as it joins main stem; many bracts down stem become progressively longer and more leaf-like towards bottom
LEAVES: Many, basal in large tuft, grass-like with sharp edges and up to 45 cm (1½′) long
STEMS: Round and woody
BLOOMING PERIOD: June–September according to altitude
HABITAT: Open wooded areas on mountain slopes and alpine meadows
NOTE: Poisonous

ELEGANT DEATH-CAMAS
Zigadenus elegans
subsp. elegans

LILY FAMILY
Liliaceae
Perennial

OTHER NAMES: Green Lily, Wand Lily, Poison Sego
COLOUR: White
HEIGHT: 30–75 cm (1–2½′)
FLOWERS: Greenish-white, arranged in loose cluster at upper end of single stem
EACH FLOWER: About 13 mm (½″) across with 6 pointed tepals, similar to Bear-grass but each with a greenish spot at base; 6 stamens enclose shorter styles; stipule where each flower-branch joins main stem
LEAVES: Several long and narrow, thick, grass-like, mostly basal, and may be up to 30 cm (1′) long and 13 mm (½″) broad with ridged midrib down the back
STEMS: Pale green, rigid, thin, round, and smooth
BLOOMING PERIOD: July–August
HABITAT: Moist meadows and open wooded areas
NOTE: Poisonous

GRASS-LEAVED DEATH-CAMAS
Zigadenus venenosus

LILY FAMILY
Liliaceae
Perennial

COLOUR: White to cream
HEIGHT: 20–50 cm (8–20″)
FLOWERS: Short, cone-shaped cluster at top of single stem
EACH FLOWER: 7 mm (¼″) across with 6 pointed tepals; 6 stamens usually a little longer than tepals; at base of each flower-stalk is small bract
LEAVES: 3 or 4 basal grass-like leaves 5–18 cm (2–7″) long and folded longitudinally forming a keel; often a smaller leaf halfway up flower-stem
STEMS: Rigid, round, and green
BLOOMING PERIOD: March–July
HABITAT: Grassy slopes in drier sagebrush country, and in moist open areas at higher elevations
NOTE: Poisonous

BUCKBEAN
Menyanthes trifoliata

BUCKBEAN FAMILY
Menyanthaceae
Perennial

COLOUR: White to pink-tinged
HEIGHT: 15–49 cm (6–19")
FLOWERS: Clustered at top of single stem
EACH FLOWER: 2 cm (¾") across with 5–6 narrow, pointed petals covered with long, coarse, white hairs inside; 5 stamens and style often longer than these; 5–6 lobed green calyx
LEAVES: Basal, with 4.2 cm (1¾") long stalks, terminating in 3 separate, leathery, leaf segments each 6.5–7.5 cm (2½–3") long, egg-shaped with indented margins; each segment has short stalk
STEMS: Visible flower-stem round, smooth, and leafless
BLOOMING PERIOD: May–August
HABITAT: Lake edges and bogs
NOTE: Root and lower stem often submerged

MOUNTAIN LADY'S-SLIPPER
Cypripedium montanum

ORCHID FAMILY
Orchidaceae
Perennial

OTHER NAMES: Moccasin-flower, White Lady's-slipper
COLOUR: White
HEIGHT: 15–60 cm (6–24")
FLOWERS: 1 to 3 on long stems from leaf axils
EACH FLOWER: White, often pink-veined, moccasin-shaped, almost globular lip; behind are 2 lateral petals, long, twisted, and ribbon-like, greenish or bronze; upper sepal similar in colour and broader, 2 lower sepals smaller and united
LEAVES: Several broad, lance-shaped and almost sheathing stem; covered with short, soft hairs
STEMS: Green, rigid and softly hairy with 1 or 2 flower-stems from upper leaf-axils
BLOOMING PERIOD: May–July
HABITAT: Moist to dryish woods from lower to sub-alpine elevations

SPARROW'S-EGG LADY'S-SLIPPER
Cypripedium passerinum

ORCHID FAMILY
Orchidaceae
Perennial

OTHER NAMES: Franklin's Lady's-slipper, Small White Northern Lady's-slipper, Purple-spot White Slipper
COLOUR: White
HEIGHT: Up to 40 cm (16")
FLOWERS: Usually solitary, occasionally 2 on single stem
EACH FLOWER: Pouch or lip is 2–2.5 cm (¾–1") long, almost round moccasin-shaped, with small opening revealing purple spots on inside, petals white and up to 2 cm (¾") long and 5–7 mm (³⁄₁₆–¼") wide; sepals green and softly hairy, upper one broad and 2 lower ones smaller and often united and indistinct
LEAVES: Many stalkless, broad, lance-shaped leaves up stem 10–15 cm (4–6") long and ribbed, downy, especially beneath
STEMS: Very downy and unbranched
BLOOMING PERIOD: June–July
HABITAT: Sphagnum bogs, mossy woods, lake edges, and along streams
LOCATION: Mara Meadows, uncommon

LARGE-LEAVED RATTLESNAKE ORCHID
Goodyera oblongifolia

ORCHID FAMILY
Orchidaceae
Perennial

OTHER NAMES: Green-leaved Rattlesnake Orchid
COLOUR: White to greenish-white
HEIGHT: 20–50 cm (8–20″)
FLOWERS: Very slender spike arranged on 1 side or spirally
EACH FLOWER: Up to 7 mm (¼″) long; 2 lateral petals join with top petal-like sepal to form hood slightly upturned at tip; below hood is sac-like lip slightly downcurved at tip; lateral sepals almost envelop the lip but are outcurved
LEAVES: In basal rosette, long, oval, lance-shaped and up to 7.5 cm (3″) long; thick and rigid and dark green above, usually with white midrib and network of whitish veins
STEMS: Rigid and softly hairy with few pale, pointed, sheath-like bracts
BLOOMING PERIOD: June–September
HABITAT: Mossy, damp, or dryish areas in coniferous woods

LOESEL'S LIPARIS
Liparis loeselii

ORCHID FAMILY
Orchidaceae
Perennial

OTHER NAMES: Loesel's Twayblade, Fen Orchis
COLOUR: Yellowish-green
HEIGHT: 7.5–20 cm (3–8″)
FLOWERS: A few in loose spike-like arrangement
EACH FLOWER: 1.3 cm (½″) across; lip broadly rounded oblong, 5 mm (³⁄₁₆″) long and downcurved, 2 lateral petals about the same length, narrow, and almost cylindrical; sepals narrow, lance-shaped, and about 6 mm (⁵⁄₁₆″) long; a minute bract below each flower; all flower parts green
LEAVES: 2 basal leaves pointed oblong-oval, 5–15 cm (2–6″) long and 2–4 cm (¾–1½″) broad with keeled central rib behind; blade tapers to flattened stalk
STEM: Smooth, pale green, and flattened towards top
BLOOMING PERIOD: June–July
HABITAT: Sphagnum bogs
LOCATION: Mara Meadows. Rare

NORTHERN TWAYBLADE
Listera borealis

ORCHID FAMILY
Orchidaceae
Perennial

OTHER NAMES: Narrow Leaves, Big Ears
COLOUR: Pale green
HEIGHT: 7.5–25 cm (3–10″)
FLOWERS: Short, open, spike-like arrangement
EACH FLOWER: Lip 9 mm (⅜″) long, broad, flat, slightly wedge-shaped and stands out almost horizontally; notched at broad outer margin; tends to be translucent; petals and sepals narrow, lance-shaped, and a little shorter than lip and all curved backwards
LEAVES: About midway up stem is opposite pair of pointed oval, smooth stalkless leaves, 5–5.6 cm (2–2¼″) long and 4.5 cm (1¾″) broad; underside shows several darker green parallel veins
STEMS: Shiny and smooth below leaves and hairy above
BLOOMING PERIOD: May–July
HABITAT: Damp coniferous forests and mossy streambanks

**FRAGRANT WHITE
REIN ORCHID**
Platanthera dilatata
(Habenaria dilatata)

ORCHID FAMILY
Orchidaceae
Perennial

OTHER NAMES: Tall White Bog Orchid
COLOUR: White
HEIGHT: 16–100 cm (6–39¼″)
FLOWERS: Long, dense spike
EACH FLOWER: Sweet-scented, petals, sepals and lip all waxy white; upper sepal egg-shaped and up to 6 mm (¼″) long and together with slightly smaller lateral petals, forms hood; lateral sepals narrower and more pointed and outcurved; lip up to nearly 1.3 cm (½″) long, broad at base and abruptly narrowing to project outwards; spur cylindrical and same length as lip
LEAVES: Lance-shaped and up full length of stem; lower ones may be up to 20 cm (8″) long and are more rounded at tip while upper ones become more pointed and shorter until below flowers they are small and bract-like
STEMS: Slender, green, and smooth
BLOOMING PERIOD: June–September
HABITAT: Ditches along mountain roadsides, bogs, swampy areas and wet, marshy alpine meadows where it is usually smaller

GREEN-FLOWERED REIN ORCHID
Platanthera hyperboarea
(Habenaria hyperboarea)

ORCHID FAMILY
Orchidaceae
Perennial

OTHER NAMES: Tall Northern Green Orchid
COLOUR: Green to yellowish-green
HEIGHT: 20–40 cm (8–16″)
FLOWERS: Long thin spike on single stem
EACH FLOWER: Narrow, green lip up to 7 mm (¼″) long; top sepal curves over 2 lateral petals forming a hood; lower, side sepals wide and pointed and 5 mm (³⁄₁₆″) long; lip extends backwards into cylindrical spur shorter than lip; narrow, pointed bract at base of each flower
LEAVES: 2–3 basal, lance-shaped leaves 7.5–10 cm (3–4″) long and 2 cm (¾″) broad, sheathing stem; stem leaves become smaller up stem
STEMS: Succulent, green, smooth, and almost triangular at base
BLOOMING PERIOD: June–August
HABITAT: Mostly in wet sphagnum bogs, marshes, damp shady woods or open lush, grassy banks and lake edges

ELEGANT ALASKA REIN ORCHID

Platanthera unalascensis subsp. elata
(Habenaria unalascensis var. elata)

ORCHID FAMILY
Orchidaceae
Perennial

OTHER NAMES: Elegant Piperia, Long-spiked Piperia
COLOUR: Greenish-white to white
HEIGHT: 25–40 cm (10–16″)
FLOWERS: Dense spike of greenish-white "stars"
EACH FLOWER: 3 petals and 3 sepals all similar in colour; upper sepal and petals on either side have green central band; lower petal forms lip, bounded on either side by sepals, all 3 being greenish-white with no central green band; flower narrows into long spur at least twice as long as lip, the whole being borne on long, twisted ovary
LEAVES: 2 or 3 leaves at base, 10–20 cm (4–8″) long and usually withered by the time flowers are blooming
STEMS: Round, rigid, smooth, and green with several green bracts scattered up length
BLOOMING PERIOD: July and August
HABITAT: Dry or moist slopes in shady areas

ALASKA REIN ORCHID

ORCHID FAMILY
Orchidaceae
Perennial

Platanthera unalascensis subsp. unalascensis (Habenaria unalascensis subsp. unalascensis)

OTHER NAMES: Western Rein Orchid, Slender-spire Orchid
COLOUR: Pale green to whitish
HEIGHT: 36–46 cm (14–18″)
FLOWERS: Slender spike of sweet scented flowers
EACH FLOWER: 3 yellowish, triangular sepals 3–5 mm (⅛–³⁄₁₆″) long; middle upper sepal more rounded. 2 narrower petals almost same length as upper sepal and greener; lip more oblong and a little longer than petals; spur very thin and cylindrical about same length as lip; ovary green, 6–15 mm (¼–⅝″) long, with tiny bract at base
LEAVES: 2 or 3 basal leaves, 7.5–9 cm (3–3½″) long and 1.3 cm (½″) to over 2.5 cm (1″) broad, becoming narrower at tip
STEMS: Smooth and green with 2–6 bracts at intervals
BLOOMING PERIOD: June–August
HABITAT: More open grassy areas in dry or moist places up to middle elevations

HOODED LADIES'-TRESSES
Spiranthes romanzoffiana

ORCHID FAMILY
Orchidaceae
Perennial

OTHER NAMES: Pearltwist
COLOUR: Creamy-white to greenish-white
HEIGHT: 10–46 cm (4–18")
FLOWERS: Many flowers arranged in compact spirals forming a spike
EACH FLOWER: 9 mm (⅜") long; petals and sepals converge towards each other to form a hood while lip is curved downwards with an almost pointed tip; below each flower is a bract
LEAVES: Mostly basal, narrow, lance-shaped, 7.5–20 cm (3–8"); may be 1 or 2 leaf-like bracts up stem
STEMS: Round, green, and smooth
BLOOMING PERIOD: July–August
HABITAT: Open moist meadows, bogs, and open wooded areas

FRINGED GRASS-OF-PARNASSUS
Parnassia fimbriata

GRASS OF PARNASSUS FAMILY
Parnassiaceae (Saxifrage Family)
(Saxifragaceae)
Perennial

COLOUR: White to cream
HEIGHT: 15–46 cm (6–18″)
FLOWERS: Solitary on single stems
EACH FLOWER: 2–2.5 cm (¾–1″) across with 5 broad, oblong, round-ended, veined petals, fringed with thick hairs at base; oval sepals shorter than petals and may be finely toothed at tips; 5 stamens
LEAVES: The several 2.5–10 cm (1–4″) smooth leaf-stalks from base terminate in shiny, heart- or kidney-shaped blades; small, leaf-like bract halfway up stem
STEMS: Unbranched, smooth, and green
BLOOMING PERIOD: July–September
HABITAT: Bogs and swampy meadows in mountains up to timberline

GREATER PLANTAIN
Plantago major

PLANTAIN FAMILY
Plantaginaceae
Perennial

COLOUR: Brownish-green
HEIGHT: 5–30 cm (2–12″)
FLOWERS: Many tiny flowers in tight spike up to 15 cm (6″) long
EACH FLOWER: 2 mm (1/10″) long, almost round with 4 tiny, outcurved, pointed petals and 4 stamens
LEAVES: All from base with flat stalks and large rounded-oval, ribbed blades 6.5 cm (2½″) long and 5 cm (2″) broad
STEMS: 1 to several single, round, rigid, downy stems to each plant
BLOOMING PERIOD: May–August
HABITAT: Roadsides, lawns, and less grassy waste places

WOOLLY PLANTAIN
Plantago patagonica

PLANTAIN FAMILY
Plantaginaceae
Annual

COLOUR: Grey-green to brownish
HEIGHT: 12 5–20 cm (5–8″)
FLOWERS: Dense, woolly, cylindrical spike, 5–10 cm (2–4″) long
EACH FLOWER: Inconspicuous, tiny, and brownish with 4 papery petals and greenish, downy sepals; bracts narrow, pointed, and grey-green, with downy hairs
LEAVES: Several basal leaves, almost strap-like, tapering to a point above and flattened stalk below, thickly covered with white, woolly hairs
STEMS: Wiry and thin and slightly downy
BLOOMING PERIOD: May–June
HABITAT: Dry sagebrush flats and valleys

ANNUAL JACOB'S-LADDER
Polemonium micranthum

PHLOX FAMILY
Polemoniaceae
Annual

COLOUR: White to bluish-white
HEIGHT: 15 cm (6″)
FLOWERS: 1 to a few at ends of stems
EACH FLOWER: 5 mm (3/16″) across and deep saucer-shaped with 5 broadly pointed petals; 10 short stamens; 5 hairy, pointed sepals often longer than petals; opposite each flower is a small leaf divided into opposite, tiny segments
LEAVES: Have short hairy stalks before bearing several opposite pairs of hairy leaflets, resembling a ladder
STEMS: Simply branched and hairy
BLOOMING PERIOD: April–May
HABITAT: Moist fields and banks, frequently with sagebrush

PARSNIP-FLOWERED UMBRELLAPLANT
Eriogonum heracleoides var. angustifolium

BUCKWHEAT FAMILY
Polygonaceae
Perennial

COLOUR: White to pale yellow or pinkish
HEIGHT: Loose flattish clusters up to 7.5 cm (3") across on umbrella-stems which may be once- or twice-branched
EACH FLOWER: 3 mm (⅛") across, cup-shaped, 6 petal-like sepals; at base of each flower is 5-pointed, cup-shaped involucre; points reflexed; tiny whorl of bracts below each stem branch
LEAVES: Narrow, lance-shaped, and narrowing to brownish, downy stem at base; may be 1 or 2 whorls of stem-leaves; leaf blades may be 1.3–5 cm (½–2") long and 6–9 mm (¼–⅜") broad, upper surface greyish-green, lower surface grey due to soft downy hairs
STEMS: Flower-stem rigid, round, grey, and downy with 1 or 2 whorls of leaves
BLOOMING PERIOD: May–July
HABITAT: Dry to arid areas in desert-sagebrush slopes and banks
NOTE: Whorls of stem-leaves identify this from other Eriogonum species

SNOW UMBRELLAPLANT
Eriogonum niveum

BUCKWHEAT FAMILY
Polygonaceae
Perennial

COLOUR: White to pinkish or yellowish
HEIGHT: 15–46 cm (6–18")
FLOWERS: Many small papery flowers in small clusters at ends of branched stems
EACH FLOWER: 3–7 mm (⅛–¼") across, composed of 6 petal-like segments; inner 3 segments round, with greenish or pinkish central vein; outer 3 segments similar but may be broader or shorter; 9 stamens with reddish anthers and 3-branched style protrude beyond petal-like segments, giving fuzzy appearance; several flowers to small involucre which is bell-shaped and has 5 short, triangular points and small bracts below
LEAVES: Basal leaves spatula-shaped with 7–9 mm (¼–⅜") stalks, and blades about same length and 7 mm (¼") broad at base, greyish and velvety beneath and less so above
STEMS: Several, brittle, grey, velvety, round, thin stems from woody stock, usually branching halfway up, with tiny bracts at stem joints
BLOOMING PERIOD: June–August
HABITAT: Dry to arid sagebrush slopes in rocky or sandy soils

MOUNTAIN SORREL
Oxyria digyna

BUCKWHEAT FAMILY
Polygonaceae
Perennial

OTHER NAMES: Alpine Sorrel
COLOUR: Green to reddish-green
HEIGHT: 10–40 cm (4–16″)
FLOWERS: Many small flowers in dense, spike-like clusters
EACH FLOWER: Up to 2 mm (1/16″) long; with 4 lobes, 2 narrow and 2 broad; 6 stamens; several flowers form tiny clusters
LEAVES: Mostly basal with 4–5 cm (1½–2″) stalks and round to heart- or kidney-shaped, almost fleshy blades
STEMS: Branched from base, erect and reddish
BLOOMING PERIOD: June–August
HABITAT: Moist rock pockets and crevices at higher altitudes

SHEEP SORREL
Rumex acetosella

BUCKWHEAT FAMILY
Polygonaceae
Perennial

OTHER NAMES: Sour Grass, Sour Weed, Red Sorrel
COLOUR: Reddish to reddish-green
HEIGHT: 10–30 cm (4–12")
FLOWERS: Numerous tiny flowers in long, slender spikes from upper portion of stem; several stems to plant
EACH FLOWER: Less than 2 mm (1/16") long with 3 inner segments and 3 outer segments
LEAVES: Mostly basal, shiny, green with long, narrow blades, with some lobed near base and narrowing into stalks; blades up to 4 cm (1½") long
STEMS: Often spread out and unbranched below flowers
BLOOMING PERIOD: May–August
HABITAT: Acid soils on roadsides and waste ground up to moderate elevations

WESTERN DOCK
Rumex occidentalis

BUCKWHEAT FAMILY
Polygonaceae
Perennial

COLOUR: Pale green to reddish tinged
HEIGHT: 60 cm–1.8 m (2–6')
FLOWERS: Small flowers in many tight spikes up upper part of stem, forming plume
EACH FLOWER: 5 mm (3/16") long; 6 segments, outer 3 about 5 mm (1/16") long and inner 3, triangular and longer
LEAVES: Lower leaves have 5 cm (2") stalks and oblong blades up to 30 cm (1') long, with reddish midrib; leaves become smaller up stem
STEMS: Usually unbranched below, woody, ridged, and green or reddish
BLOOMING PERIOD: June–August
HABITAT: Roadsides, meadows, and streambanks

WESTERN SPRING BEAUTY
Claytonia lanceolata
var. lanceolata

PURSLANE FAMILY
Portulacaceae
Perennial

OTHER NAMES: Indian Potato, Ground Nut
COLOUR: White to pale pink
HEIGHT: 5–15 cm (2–6″)
FLOWERS: Very loose often one-sided cluster
EACH FLOWER: Up to 2.5 cm (1″) across with usually 5 petals, may be notched at outer margin and pink veined; 5 stamens on inside base of petals and 3-parted style; calyx composed of 2 sepals
LEAVES: Almost fleshy; 1 or 2 basal leaves, narrow to broad lance-shaped with stalks; on stem is pair of opposite, similar shaped stalkless leaves 5 cm–13 cm (2–5″) long and 1.9–4 cm (¾–1½″) broad
STEMS: Slender and smooth, reddish at base
BLOOMING PERIOD: April–July according to elevation
HABITAT: In early spring at lower elevations in sagebrush foothills and later up to alpine slopes

MINER'S LETTUCE
Claytonia perfoliata
(Montia perfoliata)

PURSLANE FAMILY
Portulacaceae
Annual

COLOUR: White to pinkish
HEIGHT: From 4–36 cm (1½–14″)
FLOWERS: Small flowers in clusters at tops of stems
EACH FLOWER: Up to 7 mm (¼″) across with 5, often pink veined petals about twice as long as 2 sepals; 5 stamens; below each flower cluster 2 joined leaves which vary in shape from almost circular and disk-like to rhomboid-shaped and quite variable in size and colour
LEAVES: All basal except for disk-like leaves below flower clusters; blades vary in shape from spatula-shaped to triangular or diamond-shaped, with stalks sometimes as long as flower-stems; foliage varies in colour from green through greyish to coppery colour
STEMS: Smooth and unbranched and varying in colour like leaves
BLOOMING PERIOD: March–July
HABITAT: From open sedimentary areas among cactus and sagebrush to shady, wooded areas at lower elevations

NARROW-LEAVED MONTIA
Montia linearis

PURSLANE FAMILY
Portulacaceae
Annual

COLOUR: White
HEIGHT: 5–20 cm (2–8″)
FLOWERS: Several, often in one-sided clusters
EACH FLOWER: 7 mm (¼″) across, shallow saucer-shaped when fully open with 5 petals and 3 stamens and 2 smooth, green sepals; stalks often drooping
LEAVES: Almost fleshy, narrow up to 4 cm (1½″) long, shallowly grooved and arranged more or less alternately up stem which they almost clasp
STEMS: Smooth, green, and single or branched
BLOOMING PERIOD: April–July
HABITAT: At low elevations in moist, sandy soil

OKANOGAN FAMEFLOWER
Talinum okanoganense

PURSLANE FAMILY
Portulacaceae
Perennial

OTHER NAMES: Rock Pink
COLOUR: White to pinkish
HEIGHT: 3–7 cm (1–2¾")
FLOWERS: On single reddish stems up to 1.5 cm (⅝") long with 2 tiny leaflets halfway up, from cushion-like clump of small leaves
EACH FLOWER: 1 cm (⁷⁄₁₆") across, saucer-shaped with pointed petals with pinkish midrib on outside; 2 tiny, red sepals; up to 30 stamens surround 3-lobed, fuzzy-looking pistil; flowers appear to open after mid-day
LEAVES: Small elongated, greenish-red, fleshy leaves up to 6 mm (¼") long in small tufts at ends of short, branched stems, giving cushion-like appearance
STEMS: Brown, woody, and rough; up to 6 cm (2⅜") long and many-branched from long taproot
BLOOMING PERIOD: Late May–June
HABITAT: Bare, arid, exposed rocky summits and slopes
LOCATION: Kamloops (Tranquille Range), Kelowna (McDougall Rim)–rare

NORTHERN STARFLOWER
Trientalis europaea
subsp. arctica (Trientalis arctica)

PRIMROSE FAMILY
Primulaceae
Perennial

COLOUR: White
HEIGHT: 7.5–20 cm (3–8″)
FLOWERS: 1 or 2 on long stems
EACH FLOWER: 1.3 cm (½″) across with 6–7 pointed petals and 6–7 stamens; calyx has 6 narrow sepals
LEAVES: Several scattered up stem; pointed, egg-shaped with broad end outermost
STEMS: Smooth, slender, and reddish; sometimes branched above
BLOOMING PERIOD: May–August
HABITAT: Sphagnum bogs and swamps

ONE-FLOWERED WINTERGREEN
Moneses uniflora

WINTERGREEN FAMILY
Pyrolaceae
(Heath Family)
(Ericaceae) Perennial

OTHER NAMES: Single Delight, Wood Nymph
COLOUR: White to pale pink
HEIGHT: 5–10 cm (2–4")
FLOWERS: Single nodding flower to single stem
EACH FLOWER: 2.5 cm (1") across with 5 triangular, crinkly, waxy petals with conspicuous, paired stamens which surround round, green, 5-segmented ovary with long style and 5-parted stigma; calyx composed of 5 very small greenish-white sepals; below flowerhead is small bract
LEAVES: Basal, round, finely toothed with short stalk; blades dull above and almost shiny below; may be 1 or 2 tiny cup-shaped bracts on stems
STEMS: Smooth, may be pinkish
BLOOMING PERIOD: June–July
HABITAT: Damp wooded areas at most elevations

FEW-FLOWERED ONE-SIDED WINTERGREEN
Orthilia secunda subsp. secunda
(Pyrola secunda)

WINTERGREEN FAMILY
Pyrolaceae
(Heath Family)
(Ericaceae) Perennial

OTHER NAMES: One-sided Pyrola
COLOUR: Greenish-white
HEIGHT: 15–23 cm (6–9″)
FLOWERS: One-sided usually drooping spike with 6 to 10 flowers to spike
EACH FLOWER: Up to 5 mm (³⁄₁₆″) long with 5 oval petals, pointed at tips and forming an urn shape; 5 sepals triangular and greenish; stamens as long as petals; pistil protrudes beyond petals as flower matures; flower-stems up to 5 mm (³⁄₁₆″) long, with small bract where they join main stem
LEAVES: Many oval, pointed, and almost shiny-green both sides, darker green above than below; almost crinkly with finely-toothed margins; blades 2.5–3.4 cm (1–1⅜″) long and 1.5 cm (⅝″) wide; leaf-stalks 2–3 cm (¾–1¼″) long
STEMS: Branched at base, creeping, reddish above and woody below
BLOOMING PERIOD: May–August according to elevation
HABITAT: Moist, open woods and coniferous forests and banks

RED BANEBERRY
Actaea rubra

BUTTERCUP FAMILY
Ranunculaceae
Perennial

OTHER NAMES: Chinaberry, Doll's Eyes
COLOUR: White
HEIGHT: 30–90 cm (1–3′)
FLOWERS: Dense, "bottle-brush-shaped" cluster at ends of long, branched stems
EACH FLOWER: 5–10 narrow petals up to 7 mm (¼″) long and 3–5 oval, petal-like sepals almost as long as petals; numerous stamens and 1 pistil
LEAVES: 1 or 2 long leaf-stalks branch into 2 or 3 opposite pairs, bearing 3-lobed blades, each lobe is again 3-lobed and sharply toothed; also a terminal blade
STEMS: 1 or more which may be branched; may be smooth or slightly hairy
BLOOMING PERIOD: May–July
HABITAT: Moist woods and streambanks from low to high elevations
NOTE: Poisonous. Berries may be red or white

PACIFIC ANEMONE
Anemone multifida
var. multifida

BUTTERCUP FAMILY
Ranunculaceae
Perennial

OTHER NAMES: Windflower
COLOUR: Cream to yellow or pinkish
HEIGHT: 15–50 cm (6–20")
FLOWERS: Single flowers at top of simply branched stems
EACH FLOWER: 2.5 cm (1") across and deep cup-shaped with 5 petal-like sepals; numerous stamens
LEAVES: Several basal leaves with hairy stalks 7.5–10 cm (3–4") long, hairy blades divide into 3 lobes, each lobe again divides into 3 smaller lobes; partway up stem is involucre; whorl of similar-shaped leaves with either very short stalks or stalkless
STEMS: Single below and often branching at involucre, at which point the stem appears to have swelling
BLOOMING PERIOD: May–August
HABITAT: Grassy meadows from the foothills up to high mountaintops
NOTE: Poisonous

NORTHERN ANEMONE
Anemone parviflora

BUTTERCUP FAMILY
Ranunculaceae
Perennial

COLOUR: White to bluish-tinged
HEIGHT: 5–36 cm (2–14″)
FLOWERS: Single terminal flower to single stem
EACH FLOWER: Saucer-shaped, up to 2 cm (¾″) across with 5–7 white sepals usually bluish-tinged at base; many golden stamens. Below flowers is the involucre, a whorl of 3-lobed leaves
LEAVES: Several basal with 1.3–2.5 cm (½–1″) stalks; blades 3-lobed and each lobe again 3-lobed
STEMS: Slightly downy and pinkish towards base
BLOOMING PERIOD: May–August
HABITAT: Moist meadows and streambanks, from lower to middle elevations
NOTE: Poisonous

ALPINE WHITE MARSH-MARIGOLD
Caltha leptosepala

BUTTERCUP FAMILY
Ranunculaceae
Perennial

OTHER NAMES: Mountain Marsh-marigold, Meadowbright
COLOUR: White
HEIGHT: 7.5–20 cm (3–8″)
FLOWERS: Single terminal flower
EACH FLOWER: 2.5–4 cm (1–1½″) across with 6 or more narrow, rounded, petal-like sepals forming shallow cup in centre of which are many yellow stamens
LEAVES: Several basal with varying length stalks, 4–10 cm (1½–4″) long; blades fleshy and almost circular, 5–7.5 (2–3″) broad and long
STEMS: Almost ribbed, succulent, and reddish
BLOOMING PERIOD: May–August
HABITAT: Wet places from sub-alpine to above timberline

WESTERN WHITE CLEMATIS
Clematis ligusticifolia

BUTTERCUP FAMILY
Ranunculaceae
Perennial Liana

OTHER NAMES: White Virgin's Bower, Traveller's Joy
COLOUR: White to cream
HEIGHT: Variable, with trailing or climbing stems
FLOWERS: Loose, opposite clusters
EACH FLOWER: Up to 2 cm (¾") across; male and female flowers are separate; 4 narrow petal-like sepals and in female flower many pistils and numerous sterile stamens; male flower has numerous stamens and no pistils
LEAVES: On long opposite stalks usually with 2 opposite pairs and 1 terminal leaflet, all egg-shaped and coarsely toothed
STEMS: 3–12 m (10–40')
BLOOMING PERIOD: June–July
HABITAT: Sagebrush and ponderosa pine areas
NOTE: Poisonous. May cause dermatitis

WESTERN PASQUEFLOWER
Pulsatilla occidentalis
(Anemone occidentalis)

BUTTERCUP FAMILY
Ranunculaceae
Perennial

OTHER NAMES: Tow-head Baby, Old Man of the Mountains
COLOUR: White to purplish-white
HEIGHT: 15–25 cm (6–10″)
FLOWERS: One to each stem; often in clumps
EACH FLOWER: Cup-shaped; 2.5–4 cm (1–1½″) across; 6 broad, white petal-like sepals, purple-tinged at base; many yellow stamens forming fluffy centre to cup; immediately below flower on stem is a whorl of finely dissected leaves, the involucre
LEAVES: 1 or 2 finely dissected, stalked leaves arising from base; softly downy
STEMS: Round, green, and softly downy
BLOOMING PERIOD: Late July–August, as snow melts
HABITAT: Alpine to sub-alpine meadows in moist ground

WHITE GLOBEFLOWER
Trollius laxus
subsp. albiflorus

BUTTERCUP FAMILY
Ranunculaceae
Perennial

COLOUR: Creamy-white
HEIGHT: 10–50 cm (4–20")
FLOWERS: Single flower to unbranched stem; may be several stems
EACH FLOWER: 2.5–4 cm (1–1½") across with 5–6 broad, petal-like sepals; many golden stamens encircling and almost concealing 15–25 tiny petals in middle
LEAVES: Basal leaves have stalks which sheathe main stem; blades deeply cleft into 3 lobes which in turn are shallowly cleft into 3 toothed lobes; 1 or 2 stem-leaves with shorter stalks, the top one usually stalkless; leaves dark green and shiny
STEMS: Stout and round
BLOOMING PERIOD: May–August as snow melts
HABITAT: Marshy areas and wet slopes at higher elevations
NOTE: Poisonous

SYLVAN GOAT'S-BEARD
Aruncus dioicus
(Aruncus sylvester)

ROSE FAMILY
Rosaceae
Perennial

COLOUR: White
HEIGHT: 90 cm–over 2 m (3–7′)
FLOWERS: Loose untidy spike at upper end of stems, composed of many, branched flower-stems, each branchlet forming tight spike of tiny white flowers with long, bristly-looking stamens, giving fluffy appearance
LEAVES: Alternate, with stiff, reddish stalks dividing into 3 shorter stalks each bearing opposite pairs of oval, pointed, finely-toothed leaflets and terminal leaflet; all leaves have deep herring-bone veins
STEMS: Rigid, woody, and pinkish
BLOOMING PERIOD: May–July
HABITAT: Moist woods and along streambanks

WHITE MOUNTAIN-AVENS
Dryas octopetala

ROSE FAMILY
Rosaceae
Perennial

OTHER NAMES: Alpine Avens, White Dryas, Alpine Rose
COLOUR: White to creamy-white
HEIGHT: 10–15 cm (4–6")
FLOWERS: Many terminal flowers from mat-forming plant
EACH FLOWER: 2.5 cm (1") or more across, saucer-shaped with usually 8 broad petals and numerous stamens; calyx has purplish pointed, hairy lobes
LEAVES: Many, simple oblong leaves with rounded ends; 1.3–2 cm (½–¾") long and 7 mm (¼") broad; edges serrated and slightly rolled under; upper surface hairy and pale
STEMS: 10–15 cm (4–6") long and hairy
BLOOMING PERIOD: July–mid-August
HABITAT: From middle elevations to above timberline on exposed, gravelly ridges and slopes

BLUE-LEAVED WILD STRAWBERRY
Fragaria virginiana subsp. glauca

ROSE FAMILY
Rosaceae
Perennial

COLOUR: White
HEIGHT: 5–15 cm (2–6″)
FLOWERS: Several on thin branches at upper ends of stems
EACH FLOWER: 1.3–2 cm (½–¾″) across; 5 broad, rounded petals and numerous yellow stamens; 5 green, pointed sepals
LEAVES: Leaf-stalks from base up to 15 cm (6″) long, terminating in 3 distinct oval, toothed leaflets, 2–6.5 cm (¾–2½″) long
STEMS: Flower-stems and leaf-stalks thin, reddish, and slightly hairy
BLOOMING PERIOD: May–August
HABITAT: Open wooded areas and dryish sandy or gravelly meadows

LUETKEA
Luetkea pectinata

Rose Family
Rosaceae
Perennial shrub

Other Names: Partridge Foot, Meadow Spirea
Colour: White to cream
Height: 5–15 cm (2–6″)
Flowers: Small, in dense, elongated, round-topped cluster on single stems. In low clumps
Each Flower: 5 tiny, spatula-shaped petals about 3 mm (⅛″) long; up to 20 stamens and 5 distinct pistils; 5 small, triangular sepals
Leaves: Alternate up full length of stem, with short stalks terminating in fan-shaped fringe formed by 3, 1.3 cm (½″) narrow, deeply cleft lobes which are again deeply cleft into 3; also tufts of leaves at base
Stems: Slender and often reddish
Blooming Period: June–August
Habitat: Moist open or shady, sandy or rocky mountain meadows from sub-alpine elevations to above timberline

WESTERN THIMBLEBERRY
Rubus parviflorus
subsp. parviflorus

ROSE FAMILY
Rosaceae
Perennial shrub

COLOUR: White
HEIGHT: 90 cm–2.5 m (3–8′)
FLOWERS: A few at top of stem
EACH FLOWER: 2.5–5 cm (1–2″) across with 5 broad, roundly pointed, thin rice-papery-looking petals; numerous brownish-yellow stamens; calyx has 5 long pointed sepals which stand out
LEAVES: Many large leaves with stalks and stipules; toothed blades large maple-leaf-shaped, 10–20 cm (4–8″) broad, soft, dull green and deeply-veined
STEMS: Woody, pale green, and smooth
BLOOMING PERIOD: May–July
HABITAT: Usually moist wooded areas but also in drier terrain to middle elevations

FIVE-LEAVED CREEPING RASPBERRY
Rubus pedatus

Rose Family
Rosaceae
Perennial

Colour: White
Height: 5–7.5 cm (2–3″)
Flowers: On single thread-like stems at intervals along mat-forming, trailing stem
Each Flower: Up to 2 cm (¾″) across; 5 white petals and numerous stamens surrounding several pistils; calyx has 5 pointed, reflexed sepals appearing fringed at tips
Leaves: 2 or 3 with 2.5–4 cm (1–1½″) stems arising from nodes on main stem; blades are deeply cleft into 5 oval, toothed lobes; veined and shiny; 2 stipules at base of leaf-stems
Stems: Trailing, thin and wiry, rooting at intervals
Blooming Period: May–July
Habitat: Moist woods and mossy banks up to just below timberline

BIRCH-LEAVED SPIREA
Spiraea betulifolia
subsp. lucida

Rose Family
Rosaceae
Perennial shrub

OTHER NAMES: Flat-top Spirea, White Meadowsweet
COLOUR: White
HEIGHT: 15–60 cm (6–24″)
FLOWERS: Tiny flowers in dense, flat-topped, fuzzy cluster, 4–15 cm (1½–6″) across at top of single stem
EACH FLOWER: Up to 3 mm (⅛″) across with 5 petals and many stamens
LEAVES: Alternate with short stalks and oval or egg-shaped dull, green blades toothed round upper border
STEMS: Rigid, round, smooth, and often pinkish
BLOOMING PERIOD: June–July
HABITAT: Dry to moist, open wooded areas from low to middle elevations

NORTHERN BEDSTRAW
Galium boreale

MADDER FAMILY
Rubiaceae
Perennial

COLOUR: White
HEIGHT: 30–60 cm (1–2′)
FLOWERS: Tightly clustered on opposite stems at upper end of main stem; in clumps
EACH FLOWER: Up to 7 mm (¼″) across with 4 pointed petals forming a cross; 4 stamens; below petals is small, round, green ovary
LEAVES: In whorls of 4, narrow and pointed with prominent midrib and covered with tiny bristly hairs giving rough feeling
STEMS: Square and green with tiny, bristly hairs
BLOOMING PERIOD: June–August
HABITAT: Grassy roadsides and meadows

PALE COMANDRA
Comandra umbellata subsp. pallida

SANDALWOOD FAMILY
Santalaceae
Perennial

OTHER NAMES: Bastard Toadflax
COLOUR: Creamy-white to pinkish
HEIGHT: 5–30 cm (2–12″)
FLOWERS: Many small flowers in tight clusters at tops of single stems, of which there are several to a clump
EACH FLOWER: 3 mm (⅛″) across; calyx green and tubular, 5 mm (³⁄₁₆″) long and opening into 5 pointed, creamy-white to pinkish petal-like sepals; 5 stamens each attached to a "petal" and surrounding single style; at base of each tiny flower is a green, pointed bract
LEAVES: Many stalkless, narrow, pointed, greyish-green, almost fleshy leaves arranged spirally up stem; up to 3 cm (¼″) long and 5–6 mm (³⁄₁₆″–¼″) wide; tips mostly pinkish; bottom leaves scale-like
STEMS: Rigid, smooth and purplish-tinged especially at top and base
BLOOMING PERIOD: March–July
HABITAT: Arid hillsides

ROUND-LEAVED ALUMROOT
Heuchera cylindrica

SAXIFRAGE FAMILY
Saxifragaceae
Perennial

COLOUR: Cream to greenish-yellow
HEIGHT: 15–75 cm (6–30″)
FLOWERS: Small compact flowers in round spikes on single stems; many stems to plant
EACH FLOWER: 7–9 mm (¼–⅜″) long, conspicuous by bell-shaped, 5-lobed cream to greenish-yellow calyx which obscures narrow, shorter petals which may be absent
LEAVES: All basal with stalks and oval blades which are lobed and scalloped round the edges, and 1.3–4 cm (½–1½″) long
STEMS: Unbranched and leafless except for 1 or 2 brownish bracts; may be hairy above and less hairy below
BLOOMING PERIOD: April–August
HABITAT: Rocky areas and dry, gravelly banks and slopes

BULBIFEROUS WOODLANDSTAR
Lithophragma glabrum
(Lithophragma bulbifera)

SAXIFRAGE FAMILY
Saxifragaceae
Perennial

OTHER NAMES: Starflower, Fringecup
COLOUR: White to pinkish
HEIGHT: 10–25 cm (4–10″)
FLOWERS: 2–5 flowers clustered at top of stem, sometimes replaced by purplish bulblets
EACH FLOWER: 5 petals about 9 mm (⅜″) long and deeply fringed into 3–5 lobes; calyx cup-shaped, 5-toothed
LEAVES: Finely short-haired; basal leaves up to 2.5 cm (1″) broad, deeply cleft into 3–5 lobes which are again cleft; 1 or 2 smaller stemless leaves on main stem with several small reddish-purple bulblets in axils
STEMS: Single, slender, reddish, softly hairy
BLOOMING PERIOD: March–May
HABITAT: Open grassland and sagebrush areas to ponderosa pine and Douglas fir forest

ALASKA SAXIFRAGE
Saxifraga ferruginea

SAXIFRAGE FAMILY
Saxifragaceae
Perennial

OTHER NAMES: Rusty Saxifrage
COLOUR: White to pinkish
HEIGHT: 10–47 cm (4–18″)
FLOWERS: Small white flowers at ends of branches on upper ⅓ of stem; among flowers are tiny bulbs
EACH FLOWER: Up to 8 mm (⅓″) across; 5 oval-pointed petals, 3 of which are broader and more spatula-shaped and constricted at base with 2 yellow spots where they broaden; 10 orange-red stamens; calyx 5-pointed, reddish, and recurved
LEAVES: In rosette at base, with short stalks, broadening into lance- or spatula-shaped blades, shallowly toothed round upper margins; hairy, especially beneath, older leaves becoming reddish
STEMS: Slender and reddish and simply branching above with small bract where they branch
BLOOMING PERIOD: June–August
HABITAT: Damp, mountainous areas

GRASSLAND SAXIFRAGE
Saxifraga integrifolia
var. leptopetala

SAXIFRAGE FAMILY
Saxifragaceae
Perennial

OTHER NAMES: Early Saxifrage
COLOUR: White
HEIGHT: 13–25 cm (5–10″)
FLOWERS: In tight clusters at top of single stem
EACH FLOWER: 5 mm (3/16″) across, 5 tiny, white, rounded petals and 10 orange stamens more conspicuous than petals; 5 outcurved green sepals
LEAVES: All basal, very short-stalked and paddle-shaped, 5–5.6 cm (2–2¼″) long and 1.5 cm (5/8″) broad, slightly hairy and sometimes pinkish at tips
STEMS: Green, round, and with short red hairs, slightly "sticky"
BLOOMING PERIOD: April–May
HABITAT: Open, moist, grassy places from low to sub-alpine elevations

BROOK SAXIFRAGE
Saxifraga odontoloma

SAXIFRAGE FAMILY
Saxifragaceae
Perennial

COLOUR: White
HEIGHT: 30–46 cm (1–1½')
FLOWERS: Sparse open cluster of small white flowers at upper portion of single long stem
EACH FLOWER: 3–7 mm (⅛–¼") across; 4 rounded petals and 4 stamens; calyx composed of 4 pointed sepals. Flower-stems 2.5 cm (1") long and hair-like
LEAVES: All basal with half-round stalks 10–15 cm (4–6") long; blades almost round, smooth, and sharply toothed, 4 cm (1½") long and 4.2 cm (1¾") broad
STEMS: Round, green, and smooth
BLOOMING PERIOD: July–September
HABITAT: Wet areas, streams, and meadows at high elevations

BUTTERCUP-LEAVED SAXIFRAGE
Suksdorfia ranuncifolia

Saxifrage Family
Saxifragaceae
Perennial

Colour: White
Height: 10–30 cm (4–12″)
Flowers: Many in upright, almost flat-topped cluster at top of single stem
Each Flower: 9 mm (⅜″) across; 5 petals and 10 stamens; calyx composed of 5 green, pointed sepals
Leaves: Several leaves from base with stalks up to 2.5 cm (1″) or more long; pale green, buttercup leaf blades 2.5–4 cm (1–1½″) across, smooth and deeply cleft into 3 fan-shaped lobes, usually with scalloped margins; several narrow, irregular shaped, tiny, stalkless, short-haired leaves up stem
Stems: Unbranched and hairy
Blooming Period: May–August
Habitat: Wet, mossy rocks and banks from foothills to high elevations

TALL FRINGECUP
Tellima grandiflora

SAXIFRAGE FAMILY
Saxifragaceae
Perennial

COLOUR: Greenish-white
HEIGHT: Up to 75 cm (30″)
FLOWERS: Thin spike-like arrangement
EACH FLOWER: 7 mm (¼″) across; cup-shaped with 5 outcurved petals with fringed tips; become pinkish with age; 10 stamens surrounding styles; green calyx cup-shaped with 5 points and alternating with petals
LEAVES: Basal leaves have long, coarsely-haired stalks and large blades with several toothed lobes; leaves become progressively smaller and shorter-stalked up stem
STEMS: Unbranched, rigid, and coarsely haired
BLOOMING PERIOD: April–July
HABITAT: Damp woods and streambanks

UNIFOLIATE-LEAVED FOAMFLOWER
Tiarella unifoliata

SAXIFRAGE FAMILY
Saxifragaceae
Perennial

OTHER NAMES: False Mitrewort, Lace Flower
COLOUR: White
HEIGHT: 13–25 cm (5–10″)
FLOWERS: Loose spray at ends of many flower-stems at upper end of main stem; several stems to root-stock
EACH FLOWER: Up to 7 mm (¼″) across; 5 tiny, narrow petals, forming star; 10 stamens; calyx has 5 lobes with upper lobe usually larger; many tiny flowers look like foam from a distance
LEAVES: Basal leaves have long stalks and blades are roughly triangular in outline but notched into 3 pointed, toothed lobes; blades up to 7.5 cm (3″) long and 9 cm (3½″) broad; stem-leaves smaller
STEMS: Thin, slender, and finely hairy
BLOOMING PERIOD: June–August
HABITAT: Moist woods above middle elevations

COIL-BEAKED LOUSEWORT
Pedicularis contorta

FIGWORT FAMILY
Scrohpulariaceae
Perennial

COLOUR: Cream to white
HEIGHT: 20–30 cm (8–12″)
FLOWERS: Loose spike
EACH FLOWER: Composed of 2 lips; upper one is hood-like, curved beak ending in curved spur enclosing style; lower lip 3-lobed, outer lobes wing-like; 4 stamens; calyx 5-toothed, deeply cleft at front and 7 mm (¼″) long; below each flower is ragged, green bract; beak very twisted
LEAVES: Up to 7.5 cm (3″) long, thin, many-toothed, alternate leaflets, giving ragged appearance; 4 or 5 diminishing in size up stem and many basal leaves, 7.5–10 cm (3–4″) long
STEMS: Rigid and reddish
BLOOMING PERIOD: Late July and August
HABITAT: Dry, open places on high slopes from just below to above timberline

SICKLE-TOP LOUSEWORT
Pedicularis racemosa

FIGWORT FAMILY
Scrophulariaceae
Perennial

OTHER NAMES: Leafy Lousewort
COLOUR: White to pinkish or yellowish-tinged
HEIGHT: 15–50 cm (6–20")
FLOWERS: Twisted-looking flowers in leaf-axils and sometimes on stem; several stems to root-stock
EACH FLOWER: 9 mm–1.5 cm (⅜–⅝") long; 2-lipped; upper lip compressed with "wings" either side and extended into arched, trunk-like beak, pushed off to one side and almost touching large lower lip; calyx cleft below and more toothed above
LEAVES: Almost alternate up length of stem and narrow, lance-shaped with serrated margins; smooth, somewhat leathery, and often reddish-tinged; middle ones longer
STEMS: Sturdy, smooth, and reddish
BLOOMING PERIOD: June–September
HABITAT: Mountainous, in open coniferous woods and slopes

COMMON CATTAIL
Typha latifolia

CATTAIL FAMILY
Typhaceae
Perennial

OTHER NAMES: Bullrush, Tule
COLOUR: Brown
HEIGHT: 1.2–2.5 m (4–8′)
FLOWERS: Male and female flowers separate on same plant; female flowers in dark brown, velvety, cylindrical, sausage-shaped mass up to 20 cm (8″) long, containing pistils; male flowers situated above in thinner, coarser, yellowish mass which contains stamens; after pollen has been shed on female flowers below, male flowers blown away
LEAVES: Several long, narrow, sword-shaped leaves, up to 2.5 cm (1″) broad, sheathe stems at base, often longer than flower-stem
STEMS: Round, stout, and pithy inside
BLOOMING PERIOD: June–July
HABITAT: Roadside ditches, lake edges, and marshes

LYALL'S AMERICAN STINGING NETTLE
Urtica dioica subsp. gracilis
(Urtica dioica var. lyallii)

NETTLE FAMILY
Urticaceae
Perennial

OTHER NAMES: Common Nettle, Western Nettle
COLOUR: Pale green
HEIGHT: 60 cm–1.2 m (2–4')
FLOWERS: Numerous tiny flowers in dense, long, drooping spikes from upper leaf-axils; male and female flowers separate on same plant
EACH FLOWER: Male flowers have 4 petal-like segments, 4 stamens and rudimentary pistil; while female flowers have 4 unequal petal-like segments and pistil
LEAVES: Opposite, with stipules at base; lower leaves have stalks and are coarse, pointed, heart-shaped, and coarsely toothed; upper leaves narrower and become gradually smaller up stem; blades covered with stinging hairs
STEMS: Unbranched, rigid, ribbed, and covered with stiff hairs
BLOOMING PERIOD: May–September
HABITAT: Mostly in open or shady areas up to subalpine elevations
NOTE: May cause dermatitis

LONGHORN PLECTRITIS
Plectritis macrocera

VALERIAN FAMILY
Valerianaceae
Annual

OTHER NAMES: Corn-salad
COLOUR: White to pinkish
HEIGHT: 10–60 cm (4–24″)
FLOWERS: Many tiny flowers in tight, almost globular cluster, at top of single stem with one to a few whorls of flowers below
EACH FLOWER: 4–7 mm (3/16–1/4″) long, apparently tubular opening into 5 rounded lobes, tube having short, thick spur; 3 stamens. There is no calyx
LEAVES: Opposite, lower ones may have short stalks and spatula-shaped blades; upper ones stalkless and blades more oblong, 9 mm–4 cm (3/8–1½″) long and 3 mm–1.5 cm (1/8–5/8″) broad, may have slightly indented margins; midrib is prominent
STEMS: Unbranched, smooth, green, and almost square
BLOOMING PERIOD: March–June
HABITAT: Moist banks and open grassy slopes

SITKA VALERIAN
Valeriana sitchensis

VALERIAN FAMILY
Valerianaceae
Perennial

COLOUR: White to pinkish
HEIGHT: 30 cm–1.2 m (1–4′)
FLOWERS: Round-topped, close cluster at upper end of stem 2.5–5 cm (1–2″) across and sweet scented
EACH FLOWER: 7 mm (¼″) across; 5 mm (³⁄₁₆″) tube opening into 5 white to pinkish-tinged lobes with long style terminating in 3-lobed stigma which protrudes almost 7 mm (¼″) beyond petals; calyx bright green with small bracts at base
LEAVES: Opposite, up lower half of stem; lower ones have 4 cm (1½″) stalks with opposite pairs of leaflets and 1 terminal leaflet; several pairs of similar opposite leaves with shorter stalks, at intervals up main stem
STEM: Smooth, green, finely ribbed, hollow, tough, and branched above
BLOOMING PERIOD: June–August, according to elevation
HABITAT: Moist open or wooded mountain areas from middle to upper elevations

CANADA VIOLET
Viola canadensis

VIOLET FAMILY
Violaceae
Perennial

COLOUR: White
HEIGHT: 10–40 cm (4–16")
FLOWERS: 1 to several on stems from upper leaf-axils; many branches from 1 root-stock
EACH FLOWER: 1.5–2 cm (⅝–¾") across; 5 petals 9 mm (⅜") long; middle, bottom petal broader and rounder than rest with several pencilled, purple lines like its neighbours on either side; broad lower petal develops into rounded spur at base; 5 pointed, green sepals, the ones either side of spur stand out like wings
LEAVES: 2 or 3 basal leaves 7.5–15 cm (3–6") stalks; smooth, green and half round; blades broadly heart-shaped abruptly becoming pointed, 5 cm (2") long and 7.5 cm (3") broad; edges irregular
STEMS: Green, smooth, and half round, branching towards top into flower-stems which are shorter than leaf-stalks
BLOOMING PERIOD: May–July
HABITAT: Loamy soil in moist, shady areas in woods and forests

PLANTS IN MORE THAN ONE COLOUR

BUCKBEAN *Menyanthes trifoliata* white to pink-tinged
CANADA VIOLET *Viola canadensis* white or yellow
CHOCOLATE LILY *Fritillaria lanceolata* chocolate brown with greenish-yellow mottle
COMMON CATNIP *Nepeta cataria* white and purple
COMMON CHICORY *Cichorium intybus* blue or white
COMMON FOXGLOVE *Digitalis purpurea* pinkish-purple to white
COMMON RED INDIAN PAINTBRUSH *Castilleja miniata* red to yellow
COMMON WESTERN PIPSISSEWA *Chimaphila umbellata* pink or white

DIFFUSE ASTER *Centaurea diffusa* pale purple to white
DRUMMOND'S ROCK CRESS *Arabis drummondii* pale purple or white

ELEGANT DEATH-CAMAS *Zigadenus elegans* subsp. *elegans* white and green

FAIRYSLIPPER *Calypso bulbosa* purplish-rose or white
FERN-LEAVED LOMATIUM *Lomatium dissectum* purple or yellow
FEW-FLOWERED SHOOTINGSTAR *Dodecatheon pulchellum* purplish-rose or yellow
FIELD BINDWEED *Convolvulus arvensis* white to pink
FIELD MINT *Mentha arvensis* purplish-blue, pink, and white

GIANT HELLEBORINE *Epipactis gigantea* green and purple
GLAUCUS GENTIAN *Gentiana glauca* green and blue
GRASS-LEAVED DEATH-CAMAS *Zigadenus venenosus* white to yellow

HOARY FALSE YARROW *Chaenactis douglasii* white to flesh-coloured
HOLBOELL'S ROCKCRESS *Arabis holboellii* white and purple

LARGE-FRUITED LOMATIUM *Lomatium macrocarpum* white or purple
LEWIS'S MONKEYFLOWER *Mimulus lewisii* red or white
LONG-LEAVED PHLOX *Phlox longifolia* pink to white

MARSH SKULLCAP *Scutellaria galericulata* pale blue and white
MOSS CAMPION *Silene acaulis* subsp. *subacaulescens* pale pink, purple, to white
MOUNTAIN LADY'S-SLIPPER *Cypripedium montanum* white and purple
MOUNTAIN SORREL *Oxyria digyna* green and reddish-green

NODDING ONION *Allium cernuum* mauve-pink or white
NORTHERN STARFLOWER *Trientalis europaea* subsp. *arctica* white to red

OLD MAN'S WHISKERS *Geum triflorum* purplish-pink and yellow

PACIFIC ANEMONE *Anemone multifida* var. *multifida* white to reddish-purple
PARRY'S CAMPION *Silene parryi* white to greenish or purplish
PARSNIP-FLOWERED UMBRELLAPLANT *Eriogonum heracleoides* var. *angustifolium* white to yellow or pinkish
PINEDROPS *Pterospora andromeda* yellow to white
PINK MICROSTERIS *Microsteris gracilis* subsp. *humilis* pink and yellow
PRAIRIE CROCUS *Pulsatilla patens* subsp. *multifida* blue
PRAIRIE GENTIAN *Gentiana affinis* bright deep blue and green
PURPLE-LEAVED WILLOWHERB *Epilobium ciliatum* deep pink to white
PURPLE-STEMMED MONKEYFLOWER *Mimulus floribundus* yellow and reddish-brown

RED EUROPEAN GLASSWORT *Salicornia europaea* subsp. *rubra* green (red fruit)
RICHARDSON'S CRANE'S-BILL *Geranium richardsonii* white to pinkish

ROUND-LEAVED ORCHIS *Amerorchis rotundifolia* purplish-pink to white
RUSSIAN THISTLE *Salsola kali var. tenuifolia* purple and green
SAGEBRUSH MARIPOSA LILY *Calochortus macrocarpus* purple to white
SCARLET SKYROCKET *Ipomopsis aggregata subsp. aggregata* red and white
SHAGGY FLEABANE *Erigeron pumilus* pale purple to white
SHEEP SORREL *Rumex acetosella* green and red
SILKY LUPINE *Lupinus sericeus* pale blue, pinkish-blue, or yellow
SILVERLEAF PHACELIA *Phacelia hastata subsp. hastata* white to purple
SMALL-FLOWERED BLUE-EYED MARY *Collinsia parviflora* blue and white
SPOTTED TOUCH-ME-NOT *Impatiens capensis* orange and brownish-red
STICKY PURPLE CRANE'S-BILL *Geranium viscosissimum* white or deep rose-pink
STRAWBERRY-BLITE GOOSEFOOT *Chenopodium capitatum* green (red fruit)

THREAD-LEAVED PHACELIA *Phacelia linearis* pale lavender-blue to white
TUFTED LOOSESTRIFE *Lysimachia thyrsiflora* yellow and purple
TUFTED PHLOX *Phlox caespitosa* blue to purplish or white

WESTERN DOCK *Rumex occidentalis* green and red
WESTERN MEADOW-RUE *Thalictrum occidentale* greenish-white to greenish-purple
WESTERN SPRING BEAUTY *Claytonia lanceolata var. lanceolata* white to pink
WESTERN WHITE TRILLIUM *Trillium ovatum* white to pinkish-purple

GLOSSARY

ALTERNATE: Leaves or flower-stems may be arranged on opposite sides of the stems but are not opposite to each other
ANTHER: The top part of the stamen that carries the pollen
ANNUAL: A plant which dies after completing its life cycle in one year
AXIL: The upper acute angle formed by the junction of a leaf with the main stem or stem-branch

BARB: A short bristle with hooked end
BASAL: At the base of a plant
BIENNIAL: A plant which germinates in the first year and dies after blooming in the second year
BLADE: The flat, thin part of a leaf, as distinct from the stalk
BLOOM: The whitish appearance of some stems and leaves, similar to that on a freshly picked plum
BRACT: Similar to a very small leaf and often scale-like, situated below some flowers or flowerheads or on some stems such as orchids
BUR: When the involucre is covered with many barbs

CALYX: That part of a flower below and outside the petals and consisting either of separate sepals, or of joined sepals forming a toothed cup or tube
CLASPING: When the base of a leaf is partly wrapped around the plant stem or stem-branches
CLEFT: A leaf blade may be almost divided into segments when it is cut or cleft halfway or almost to the midrib
CLUSTER: Flowers or fruits grouped together
CONIFEROUS: Cone-bearing, usually evergreen trees, such as fir and pine
COROLLA: Collective term for the petals which are inside the sepals

DECIDUOUS: Trees or shrubs whose leaves fall
DISK-FLOWER: One of many flowers forming the central disk of a daisy family flowerhead
DISSECTED: Finely cut into narrow segments, usually pertaining to leaves

ENTIRE: Not toothed, lobed, or divided

FLOWERHEAD: A tight cluster of small flowers as in the daisy family
FRUIT: The ripened ovary containing seeds, such as a berry or pod

GLOBULAR: Round and ball-like, globe-shaped

HAIRY: Visible hairs on a leaf, stem, or calyx
HERBACEOUS: Plants with soft, green stems as opposed to woody
HOOD: When petals arch or curve to form a hood, as in the mint family

INSECTIVORUS: A plant such as Butterwort that is capable of digesting the juices of insects by secretions from the leaves
INVOLUCRE: A circle or circles of bracts beneath a flowerhead as in the daisy family
IRREGULAR: A flower in which the petals and or sepals are not all alike

KEEL: Pertaining to a leaf such as that of an iris, which is folded at the edges to form a longitudinal ridge down the back

LANCE-SHAPED: A leaf that is longer than broad and tapers slightly at the base and gradually tapers upwards to a point
LATERAL: At the sides
LEAF-AXIL: The upper acute angle formed by the junction of a leaf with the main stem or stem-branch

LIANA: Climbing plant with woody stems
LIP: The lower petal forming a lip as in the orchid and mint families
LOBE: The rounded segment of a leaf or petal

MARGIN: The edge of a leaf or petal
MIDRIB: The central and main vein of a leaf

NODE: The point on a stem where a leaf is attached

OPPOSITE: When 2 leaves are arranged on opposite sides of the stem and are opposite each other
OVARY: The swollen part of the pistil, below the style, containing the seeds and later becoming the fruit

PALATE: The raised part of the lower lip of the corolla, which may close or partly close the throat, as in Toadflax
PARASITE: A plant that obtains its food from another living plant
PENANTH: Combined petals and sepals (corolla and calyx)
PERENNIAL: A plant that lives and reproduces for several years; the stems and leaves may die each year, but portions close to or below the ground remain perennial
PETAL: The usually coloured, conspicuous inner circle of flat blades just inside the calyx of a flower. Petals may be all the same as in a Buttercup or of different shapes and sizes as in a Lupine or joined to form a tube as in a Penstemon
PISTIL: The female part of a flower, comprising the ovary, style an stigma
POLLEN: The fine powder carried by the anthers of the stamens

RAY-FLOWER: One of the several outer flowers of the daisy family, strap-like and often called a petal. The ray-flowers may surround the disk-flowers

RECEPTACLE: The broadened upper end of a flower stem which bears the flower parts

RECURVED: Curved backwards or outwards such as the upper petal of a Lupine

REFLEXED: Bent backwards or outwards

REGULAR: A flower in which the petals and sepals are all alike

ROOT-STOCK: An underground stem from which stems above ground arise

ROSETTE: A circular cluster of leaves usually at the base of a plant

SAPROPHYTE: A plant that obtains its food from dead organic matter

SEPAL: One of two or more parts of the calyx, usually green and pointed but may be petal-like and of any colour

SERRATED: Finely and regularly-toothed, like the teeth of a saw; pertaining to leaves

SHEATH: The lowest part of some leaves which are wrapped around the main stem as in the Cattail

SHEATHING: Wrapping completely around the stem; pertaining to leaves

SPADIX: A thick, fleshy stem bearing small flowers as in the Skunk Cabbage

SPATHE: A large pointed bract enclosing the spadix as in the Skunk Cabbage

SPIKE: Elongated cluster of small stalkless or very short stalked flowers at the upper end of stem

SPUR: An elongated horn-like extension of a petal or petals as in the Violet

STALK: The narrow part of a leaf joining the blade to the plant-stem

STAMEN: The male, pollen-bearing part of a flower consisting of a filament and an anther
STANDARD: The upper, usually erect and recurved petal in pea family flowers, also called the banner
STERILE: Infertile, as a stamen without an anther cannot produce pollen
STIGMA: The sticky, uppermost part of the pistil and terminating the style
STIPULES: Small leaf-like structures at the junction of some leaf-stalks with the stem, as in some vetches
STYLE: That part of the pistil which joins the ovary and stigma
SUCCULENT: Juicy

TENDRIL: The slender, coiling thread-like extension of a modified leaf or stem, used for climbing, as in Clematis
TEPALS: When petals and sepals are all alike, as in Death Camas and some other members of the Lily family
TERMINAL: At the top of a stem or end of a leaf
TOOTHED: Pointed, tooth-like projections on margins of leaves, coarser than serrations
TRAILING: Lying on the ground but not rooting; pertaining to stems as in Morning Glory
TUBULAR: Tube or funnel-shaped, when petals or sepals are joined, as in Scarlet Gilia

UMBRELLA-LIKE: Flat-topped flower cluster with stalks radiating from a central point like ribs of an umbrella (also known as umbel)

WHORL: A circle of leaves round the stem, as in Bunchberry
WINGS: The two side petals in flowers of the pea family

FLOWER PARTS AND LEAF TERMINOLOGY

PARTS OF A TYPICAL FLOWER

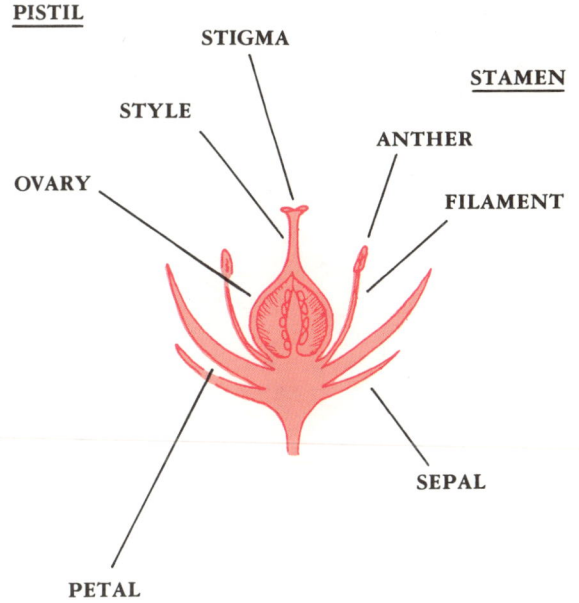

Corolla: collectively all the petals of a flower

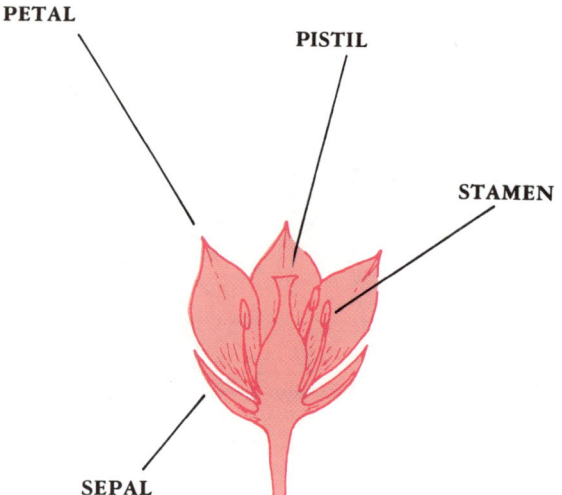

Calyx: collectively all the sepals of a flower

PARTS OF AN ASTER FLOWER
(ASTERACEAE)

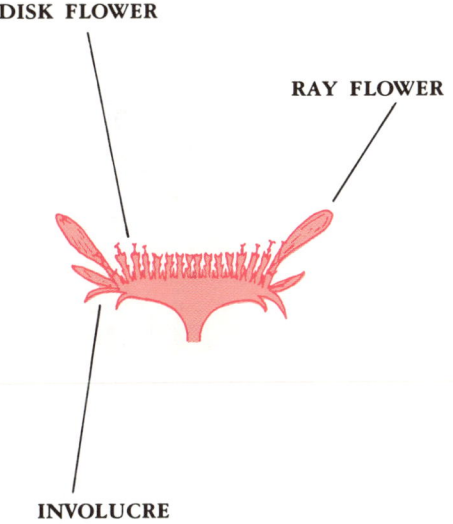

PARTS OF AN ORCHID FLOWER
(ORCHIDACEAE)

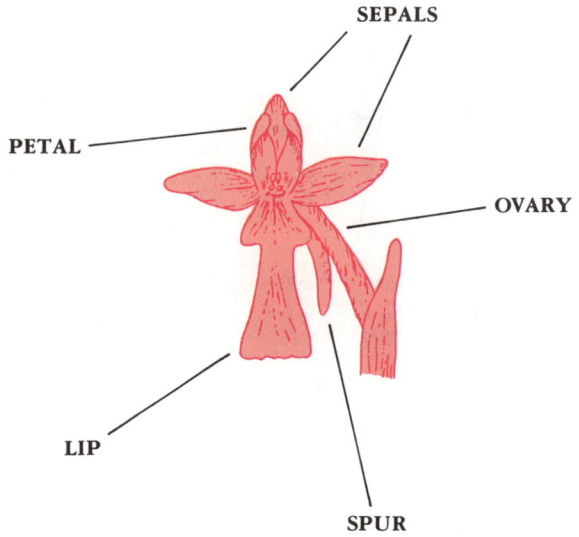

PARTS OF A PEA FLOWER
(FABACEAE)

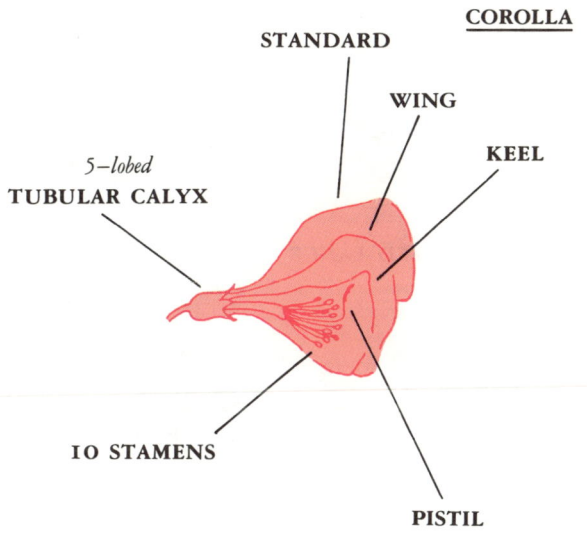

LEAF SHAPES

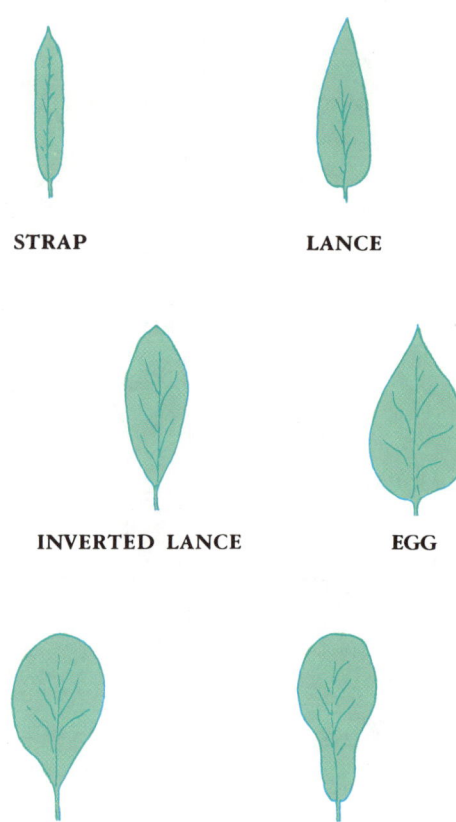

ELLIPTICAL

ROUND

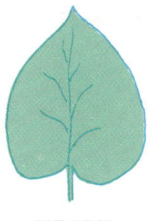
HEART

KIDNEY

TRIANGULAR

ARROWHEAD

LEAF ARRANGEMENTS

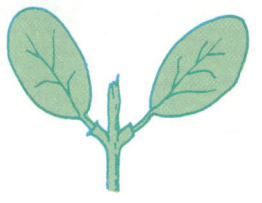

LEAVES OPPOSITE

LEAVES ALTERNATE

LEAVES WHORLED: 3 OR MORE LEAVES ARRANGED IN A CIRCLE AROUND THE STEM

REFERENCES

ANGOVE, K. AND BANCROFT, B. *A Guide to Some Common Plants of the Southern Interior of British Columbia.* Land Management Handbook, No. 7. Victoria: Information Services Branch. British Columbia Ministry of Forests and Lands 1983

BENTHAM, G. REVISED BY SIR J.D. HOOKER. *Handbook of British Flora,* 7th ed. Kent: L. Reeve & Co. 1930

CLARK, G.H. AND FLETCHER, J.K. *Farm Weeds of Canada* 2nd ed. Ottawa: Dominion of Canada, Department of Agriculture 1909

CLARK, L.J. *Wild Flowers of British Columbia.* Sidney, B.C.: Gray's Publishing Ltd. 1973

CORMACK, R.G.H. *Wild Flowers of Alberta.* Edmonton: Department of Industry and Development 1967

CRAIGHEAD, J.J., CRAIGHEAD, F.C., AND DAVIS, R.J. *A Field Guide to Rocky Mountain Wild Flowers.* Boston: Houghton Mifflin 1963

HASKIN, L.L. *Wild Flowers of the Pacific Coast.* Portland: Binfords and Mort 1959

HENRY, J.K. *Flora of the Southern Interior of British Columbia and Vancouver Island.* W.J. Gage 1915

HITCHCOCK, C.L., CRONQUIST, A., OWNBY, M., AND THOMPSON, J.W. *Vascular Plants of the Pacific Northwest.* 5 volumes. Seattle: University of Washington Press 1969

HYLANDER, C.J. *The Macmillan Wild Flower Book.* Toronto: Macmillan 1954

LARRISON, E.J., PATRICK, G.W., BAKER, W.H., AND

YAICH, J.A. *Washington Wildflowers.* Seattle: Seattle Audubon Society 1974

LEMMON, R.S. AND JOHNSON, C.C. *Wild Flowers of North America in Full Color.* New York: Nelson Doubleday 1961

LYONS, C.P. *Trees, Shrubs and Flowers to Know in British Columbia.* 2nd ed. Toronto: J.M. Dent 1959

MEIDINGER, D. *Recommended Vernacular Names for Common Plants of British Columbia.* Victoria: British Columbia Ministry of Forests and Lands Research Report RR 87002-HQ 1987

RICKETT, H.W. *Wild Flowers of the United States. Volume 5, The Northwestern States.* New York: McGraw-Hill 1966

SCOTTER, G.W. AND FLYGARE, H. *Wildflowers of the Canadian Rockies.* Edmonton: Hurtig Publishers 1986

SPELLENBERG, R. *The Audubon Society Field Guide to North American Wildflowers, Western Region.* New York: Knopf 1979

SZCZAWINSKI, A.F. *The Orchids of British Columbia.* Handbook No. 16, 2nd ed. Victoria: British Columbia Provincial Museum, Dept. of Recreation and Conservation 1969
The Heather Family (Ericaceae) of British Columbia. Handbook No. 19, 2nd ed. Victoria: British Columbia Provincial Museum, Dept. of Recreation and Conservation 1970

TAYLOR, R.L. AND MACBRYDE, B. *Vascular Plants of British Columbia: A Descriptive Resource Inventory.* Vancouver: University of British Columbia Press 1977

TAYLOR, T.M.C. *The Lily Family (Liliaceae) of British Columbia.* Handbook No. 25. Victoria: British Columbia Provincial Museum: Dept. of Recreation and Conservation 1966

PHOTO CREDITS

PROVINCE OF BRITISH COLUMBIA: Idaho Lookout, 6. STEVE CANNINGS: Ballhead Waterleaf (*Hydrophyllum capitatum*), 111. ANNE HAU: Golden Fleabane (*Erigeron aureus*), 167; Western Meadow-rue (*Thalictrum occidentale*), 136. JOAN HERRIOT: Blue-bead Clintonia (*Clintonia uniflora*), 287; Red European Glasswort (*Salicornia europaea* subsp. *rubra*), 31; Large-leaved Rattlesnake Orchid (*Goodyera oblongifolia*), 304; Western Swamp Kalmia (*Kalmia microphylla* subsp. *occidentalis*), 33. LES HILL: Greater Bladderwort (*Utricularia vulgaris*), 197. SHARON LOUGHLIN: Columbian Monkshood (*Aconitum columbianum*), 132; Yellow Pond-lily (*Nuphar lutea* subsp. *polysepala*), 204. JIM POJAR: Buttercup-leaved Saxifrage (*Suksdorfia ranuncifolia*), 349; Great Northern Aster (*Aster modestus*), 80; Small-leaved Montia (*Montia parvifolia*), 61. MARY LOU TAPSON-JONES: Alpine White-Marsh Marigold (*Caltha leptosepala*), 331; Drummond's Rock Cress (*Arabis drummondii*), 99; Fern-leaved Lomatium (*Lomatium dissectum*), 76; Marsh Skullcap (*Scutellaria galericulata*), 119; Narrow-leaved Skeletonweed (*Stephanomeria tenuifolia*), 23; Red Sand Spurrey (*Spergularia rubra*), 29; Spotted Coralroot (*Corallorhiza maculata* subsp. *maculata*) 126; Swamp Hedge Nettle (*Stachys palustris* subsp. *pilosa*), 120; Water Smartweed (*Polygonum amphibium*), 58. All other pictures by JOAN BURBRIDGE.

INDEX

Achillea millefolium, 252
Aconitum columbianum, 132
Actaea rubra, 328
Agoseris glauca, 154
Agoseris, False, 175
Alaska Rein Orchid, 310
    Rein Orchid, Elegant, 309
    Saxifrage, 346
Albany Beechdrop, 203
Alkanet, 93
Allium cernuum, 43
Alpine Avens, 336
    Beauty, 287
    Lewisia, 59
    Rose, 336
    Sorrel, 318
    White Marsh-Marigold, 331
Alumroot, Round-leaved, 344
Alyssum, Hoary False, 264
Amaranthus retroflexus, 241
American Brooklime, 142
    Cowslip, 62
    Skunk Cabbage, 153
    Speedwell, 143
    Stinging Nettle, Lyall's, 355
    Twinflower, 26
Amerorchis rotundifolia, 51
Anaphalis margaritacea, 253
Anchusa officinalis, 93
Anemone, Northern, 330
    Pacific, 329
Anemone multifida var. *multifida,* 329
    occidentalis, 333
    parviflora, 330
    patens, 135
Annual Jacob's Ladder, 315
Antelopebush, 223
Antennaria, dimorpha, 254
    lanata, 255
    microphylla, 20
    rosea, 20
Apocynum androsaemifolium, 18
    cannabinum, 249
Aquilegia flavescens, 211
    formosa, 212

Arabis drummondii, 99
    holboellii, 263
    lyallii, 100
Aralia nudicaulis, 250
Arctic Lupine, 105
Arctium lappa, 78
Arctostaphylos uva-ursi, 32
Arnica, Broad-leaved, 158
    Brown-haired Orange-flowered, 157
    Chamisso's, 155
    Hairy, 159
    Heart-leaved, 156
Arnica chamissonis, 155
    cordifolia, 156
    fulgens, 157
    latifolia, 158
    mollis, 159
Arrowhead, Arum-leaved, 240
Arrow-leaved Balsamroot, 163
    Ragwort, 177
Artemisia biennis, 256
    dracunculus, 257
    frigida, 160
    ludoviciana, 161
    tridentata, 162
Arum, Yellow, 153
Arum-leaved Arrowhead, 240
Aruncus dioicus, 335
    sylvester, 335
Asarum caudatum, 77
Asclepias speciosa, 19
Aster, Great Northern, 80
    Hairy Golden, 162
    Large Purple, 79
    Showy, 79
    Tufted, White Prairie, 258
    Western, 81
Aster conspicuus, 79
    modestus, 80
    occidentalis, 81
    pansus, 258
Astragalus miser, 104
Avens, Alpine, 336
    Plumed, 66

Baby's-Breath, 269
Baby, Tow-head, 333
Ballhead Waterleaf, 111
Balsamorhiza sagittata, 163
Balsamroot, Arrow-leaved, 163
Baneberry, Red, 328
Barren Strawberry, 224
Basin Sagebrush, Big, 162
Basket Grass, 296
Bastard Toadflax, 343
Bearberry, 32
Beard, Lion's, 66
Beardtongue, Shrubby, 140
  Small Purple, 141
Bear-grass, 296
Beauty, Alpine, 287
  Western Spring, 321
Bedstraw, Northern, 342
Bee Plant, Rocky Mountain, 25
  Spiderflower, 25
Beechdrop, Albany, 203
Beggar's Blanket, 234
Beggarticks, Nodding, 164
Bell Rue, 133
Bells, Bronze, 292
  Mission, 289
  Rock, 211
Ben, White, 273
Bergamot, Wild, 42
Berry, Pigeon, 278
Berteroa incana, 264
Betony, Wood, 231
Bidens cernua, 164
Biennial Sagewort, 256
  Wormwood, 256
Big Basin Sagebrush, 162
Big Ears, 306
Bigelow's Coralroot, 128
Bindweed, Field, 277
Birch-leaved Spirea, 341
Birdbills, 62
Birthroot, 294
Biscuit-root, 245
Biscuitroot, Nineleaf, 151
  Wyeth, 150

Bishop's Cap, 225
Bitter Brush, 223
Bitterroot Lewisia, 60
Bladder Campion, 273
Bladderwort, Greater, 197
Blanket, Beggar's, 234
Blanket Flower, 170
Blazing-star, 202
Blazing-star, White-stemmed, 201
Bleedingheart, Pacific, 38
Blue Clematis, Western, 133
  Flax, Western, 124
  Iris, Western, 114
  Lettuce, 91
  Penstemon, Slender, 141
  Sailors, 84
  Skunkleaf, 131
  Vervain, 145
  Violet, Early, 146
Blue-bead Clintonia, 287
Bluebell, Mountain, 96
  Scotch, 101
Bluebells of Scotland, 101
Blue-devil, 95
Blue-eyed Grass, Idaho, 115
  Purple, 41
Blue-eyed Mary, Small-flowered, 138
Blue-eyes, 138
Blue-flowered Lettuce, 91
Blue-leaved Wild Strawberry, 337
Blue-lips, 138
Blue-weed, 95
Bog Orchid, Tall White, 307
Bog Pyrola, 65
  Violet, Northern, 147
Bonnet, Brides, 287
Bower, Virgin's, 133
  White Virgin's, 332
Bracted Lousewort, 231
Brewer's Mitrewort, 225
  Monkey-flower, 70
Bride's Bonnet, 287
Brittle Prickly-pear Cactus, 187
Broad-leaved Arnica, 158
  Fireweed, 50

Brodiaea douglasii, 123
Bronze Bells, 292
Brooklime, American, 142
Brook Lobelia, 102
    Saxifrage, 348
Broomrape, Naked, 129
    One-flowered, 129
Brown-eyed Susan, 170
Brown-haired Orange-flowered Arnica, 157
Brown Knapweed, 83
Brush, Bitter, 223
Buckbean, 299
Buglossoides arvensis, 262
Bulbiferous Woodlandstar, 345
Bullrush, 354
Bull Thistle, 87
Bunchberry, Canadian, 278
Burdock, Great, 78
Bur Marigold, 164
    Thistle, 87
Bush, Steeple, 68
Butter-and-Eggs, 228
Buttercup, Celery-leaved, 218
    Early, 216
    Sagebrush, 216
    Shore, 212
    Spring, 216
    Subalpine, 214
    Western, 217
    Yellow, Water, 215
Buttercup-leaved Saxifrage, 349
Butterwort, Common, 121

Cactus, Brittle Prickly-pear, 187
Calochortus apiculatus, 286
    macrocarpus, 122
Caltha leptosepala, 331
Calypso bulbosa, 52
Campanula rotundifolia, 101
Campion, Bladder, 272
    Menzies, 270
    Moss, 28
    Parry's, 271
    White, 269

Canada Goldenrod, 178
    Mint, 116
    Thistle, 85
    Violet, 358
Canadian Bunchberry, 278
    Fleabane, 260
Cap, Bishop's, 225
Cardaria draba, 265
Carpenter Weed, 118
Carrotleaf, 76
Cassiope, Four-angled, 280
    Lapland, 280
Cassiope tetragona, 280
Castilleja miniata, 69
Catchfly, Small-flowered, 271
Catmint, 117
Catnip, Common, 117
Cat's-paws, 20
Cattail, Common, 354
Celery-leaved Buttercup, 218
Centaurea diffusa, 82
    jacea, 83
Chaenactis, Hoary, 259
Chaenactis douglasii, 259
Chalice-cup Lily, 44
Chamisso's Arnica, 155
Chamomilla suaveolens, 165
Chatterbox, 53
Checker Lily, 289
Chelan Penstemon, 142
Chenopodium album, 274
    botrys, 275
    capitatum, 30
Chicory, Common, 84
    Lettuce, 91
Chimaphila umbellata ssp. *occidentalis,* 64
Chinaberry, 328
Chocolate Lily, 289
    Tips, 76
Chrysanthemum leucanthemum, 261
Chrysopsis villosa, 172
Chrysothamnus nauseosus, 166
Cichorium intybus, 84
Cinquefoil, Drummond's, 221

Five Finger, 222
Graceful, 222
Marsh, 67
Cirsium arvense, 85
  edule, 86
  undulatum, 21
  vulgare, 87
Clarkia pulchella, 47
Clasping-leaved Pepper-grass, 186
Claytonia lanceolata var. lanceolata, 321
  perfoliata, 322
Clematis, Western, 133
  Western White, 332
Clematis columbiana, 133
  ligusticifolia, 332
  occidentalis ssp. grosseserrata, 133
Cleome, Pink, 25
Cleome serrulata, 25
Clintonia, Blue-bead, 287
Clintonia uniflora, 287
Clocks, 39
Clover, Holy, 36
  Red, 37
  Yellow, 194
Cluster Lily, 123
Coil-beaked Lousewort, 352
Collinsia parviflora, 138
Collomia, Large-flowered, 54
  Salmon-coloured, 54
Collomia grandiflora, 54
Columbia Gromwell, 185
  Lily, 200
Columbian Monkshood, 132
Columbine, Sitka, 210
  Western, 210
  Yellow, 211
Comandra, Pale, 343
Comandra umbellata ssp. pallida, 343
Common Butterwort, 121
  Catnip, 117
  Cattail, 354
  Chicory, 84
  Cow-parsnip, 244
  Fleabane, 22

Foxglove, 139
Gromwell, 262
Harebell, 101
Hound's-tongue, 94
Milkweed, 19
Monkeyflower, 230
Mullein, 234
Nettle, 355
Pearly Everlasting, 253
Pink Pyrola, 65
Poison Hemlock, 243
Rabbitbrush, 166
Red Indian Paintbrush, 69
Sainfoin, 36
Salsify, 92
Self-heal, 118
Silverweed, 220
St. John's-wort, 188
Stork's-bill, 39
Tansy, 182
Thistle, 87
Toadflax, 228
Water cress, 267
Western Pipsissewa, 64
Whitlow-grass, 266
Yarrow, 252
Compass Plant, 174
Conium maculatum, 243
Convolvulus arvensis, 277
Conyza canadensis, 260
Corallorhiza maculata ssp. maculata, 126
  maculata ssp. mertensiana, 127
  mertensiana, 127
  striata, 128
  trifida, 206
Coralroot, Bigelow's, 128
  Early, 206
  Large, 126
  Merten's, 127
  Mottled, 126
  Northern, 206
  Pale, 206
  Spotted, 126
  Striped, 128

Western, 127
Yellow, 206
Corn Lily, 295
Corn-salad, 356
Cornus canadensis, 278
Corpse-plant, 300
Corydalis, Golden, 195
Corydalis aurea, 195
Cowlily, 204
Cow-parsnip, Common, 244
Cowslip, American, 62
Cranberry, Hog, 32
Crane's-bill, 39
   Richardson's, 284
   Sticky Purple, 40
Cream Mountain-heather, 281
Creeping Raspberry, Five-leaved, 340
   Sibbaldia, 224
   Thistle, 85
Cress, Drummond's Rock, 99
   Hoary, 265
   Holboell's Rock, 263
   Lyall's Rock, 100
Crocus, Prairie, 135
Crowfoot, 216
Cucumberroot Twistedstalk, 293
Cup, Painted, 69
   Queen's, 287
Curlycup Gumweed, 171
Cursed Thistle, 85
Cushion Pink, 28
Cusick's Speedwell, 146
Cynoglossum officinale, 94
Cypripedium calceolus ssp. *parviflorum,* 207
   montanum, 302
   passerinum, 303

Daisy Fleabane, 22
Daisy, Mountain, 88
   Oxeye, 261
   Showy, 90
Dalmation Toadflax, 227
Dandelion, Short-beaked False, 154
Death-camas, Elegant, 297

   Grass-leaved, 298
Deer-head Orchid, 52
Delight, Single, 326
Delphinium, Upland, 134
Delphinium nuttallianum, 134
Deptford Pink, 27
Desert Parsley, 150
Devil's-club, 251
Devil's Paintbrush, 173
Dianthus armeria, 27
Dicentra formosa, 38
Diffuse Knapweed, 82
Digitalis purpurea, 139
Disporum hookeri var. *oreganum,* 288
Dock, Western, 320
Dodecatheon pauciflorum, 62
   pulchellum ssp. *pulchellum,* 62
Dogbane Indian-hemp, 249
   Spreading, 18
Dogbur, 94
Dog-tooth Violet, 198
Dogwood, Dwarf, 278
Doll's Eyes, 328
Draba verna, 266
Dragon Sagewort, 257
Drosera anglica, 279
Drummond's Cinquefoil, 221
   Rock Cress, 99
Dryas, White, 336
   Yellow, 219
Dryas drummondii var. *drummondii,* 219
   octopetala, 336
Duck Potato, 240
Dwarf Dogwood, 278
   Lewisia, 59
   Mountain Lupine, 106
   Silene, 28

Early Blue Violet, 146
   Buttercup, 216
   Coralroot, 206
   Saxifrage, 347
Ears, Big, 306
Echium vulgare, 95
Edible Thistle, 86

Elegant Alaska Rein Orchid, 309
   Death-camas, 297
   Piperia, 309
Elephant, Little Red, 72
Elephant's-head Lousewort, 72
Epilobium, Watson's, 49
Epilobium angustifolium, 48
   ciliatum, 49
   latifolium, 50
   watsonii, 49
Epipactis gigantea, 53
Erigeron aureus, 167
   linearis, 168
   perigrinus, 88
   philadelphicus, 22
   pumilus, 89
   speciosus, 90
Eriogonum heracleoides var.
   angustifolium, 316
   niveum, 317
   umbellatum, 208
Erodium cicutarium, 39
Erophila verna ssp. spathulata, 266
Erythronium grandiflorum, 198
European Glasswort, Green, 276
   Red, 31
Euthamia occidentalis, 169
Evening Primrose, Pale, 301
   Yellow, 205
Evergreen Yellow Violet, 237
Eyes, Doll's, 328

Fairies, Pink, 47
Fairybell, Small-flowered, 288
Fairybells, Hooker's, 288
   Smooth, 288
Fairyslipper, 52
False Agoseris, 175
   Alyssum, Hoary, 264
   Dandelion, Short-beaked, 154
   Goldenrod, 166
   Heather, 34
   Hellebore, Green, 295
   Mitrewort, 351
   Solomon's-seal, 290

   Spikenard, 290
   Vervain, 145
   Yarrow, Hoary, 259
Fameflower, Okanogan, 324
Fat Hen, 274
Fawn Lily, 198
Feltwort, 110
Fen Orchis, 305
Fern Leaf, 231
Fern-leaved Lomatium, 76
Few-flowered One-sided Wintergreen, 327
   Shootingstar, 62
Field Bindweed, 277
   Locoweed, 193
   Mint, 116
   Thistle, Soft, 85
Filaree, 39
Fine-leaved Fleabane, 168
Fireweed, 48
Fireweed, Broad-leaved, 50
Fivefinger, Marsh, 67
Five Finger Cinquefoil, 222
Five-leaved Creeping Raspberry, 340
Five-stamened Mitrewort, 226
Flag, Water, 196
Flannel-plant, 234
Flat-top Spirea, 341
Flax, Lewis, 124
   Prairie, 124
   Western Blue, 124
Fleabane, Canadian, 260
   Common, 22
   Daisy, 22
   Fine-leaved, 168
   Golden, 167
   Oregon, 90
   Philadelphia, 22
   Shaggy, 89
   Showy, 88
   Subalpine, 90
   Tall Purple, 88
Fleur-de-lis, 114
Flower, Gipsy, 94
   Lace, 351

Moccasin, 302
Pasque, 135
Foamflower, Unifoliate-leaved, 351
Foot, Partridge, 338
Forget-me-not, Mountain, 98
   Small-leaved, 99
Four-angled Cassiope, 280
Foxfire, 55
Foxglove, Common, 139
Fragaria virginiana ssp. glauca, 337
Fragile Opuntia, 187
Fragrant White Rein Orchid, 307
Franklin's Lady's-slipper, 303
Fringecup, 345
   Tall, 350
Fringe, Purple, 113
Fringed, Grass-of-Parnassus, 312
   Loosestrife, 209
   Sagebrush, 160
Fritillaria lanceolata, 289
   pudica, 199
Fritillary, Yellowbell, 199

Gaillardia aristata, 170
Gairdner's Yampah, 247
Galium boreale, 342
Garlic, Wild, 43
Gentiana affinis, 108
   glauca, 109
Gentianella armarella, 110
Gentian, Glaucus, 109
   Large, 108
   Northern, 110
   Oblong-leaved, 108
   Pale, 109
   Prairie, 108
Geranium, Pink, 40
Geranium richardsonii, 284
   viscosissimum, 40
Geum triflorum, 66
Geyer's Lomatium, 245
Ghost-pipe, 300
Giant Helleborine, 53
   Ragwort, 177
Gilia, Scarlet, 55

Gilia aggregata, 55
Ginger, Indian, 77
   Western Wild, 77
Gipsy Flower, 94
Glacier Lily, Yellow, 198
Glasswort, Green European, 276
   Red European, 31
Glaucus Gentian, 109
Globeflower, White, 334
Globe Mallow, 46
Glory, Morning, 277
Goat's-beard, 183
   Sylvan, 335
Golden Aster, Hairy, 172
   Corydalis, 195
   Fleabane, 167
Goldenbush, 166
Goldenrod, Canada, 178
   False, 166
   Northern, 179
   Spike-like, 180
   Western, 169
Golden Slipper, 207
Goodyera oblongifolia, 304
Goosefoot, 274
   Jerusalem-oak, 275
   Strawberry-blite, 30
Graceful Cinquefoil, 222
Granny's Nightcap, 211
Grass, Basket, 297
   Idaho, Blue-eyed, 115
   Purple Blue-eyed, 41
   Sour, 296
   Squaw, 296
Grass Pink, 27
   Widows, 41
Grassland Saxifrage, 347
Grass-leaved Death-camas, 298
Grass-of-Parnassus, Fringed, 312
Greasewood, 223
Great Burdock, 78
   Mullein, 234
   Northern Aster, 80
   Sundew, 279
   Willowherb, 48

Greater Bladderwort, 197
　Plantain, 313
Green European Glasswort, 276
　False Hellebore, 295
　Lily, 297
　Orchid, Tall Northern, 308
Green-banded Mariposa Lily, 122
Green-flowered Rein Orchid, 308
Green-leaved Rattlesnake Orchid, 304
Grindelia squarrosa, 171
Gromwell, Columbia, 185
　Common, 262
Ground Nut, 321
Gumweed, Curlycup, 171
Gypsophila paniculata, 269
Gypsy Flower, 94

Habenaria dilatata, 307
　hyperborea, 308
　unalescensis var. elata, 309
　unalascensis ssp. unalascensis, 310
Hairy Arnica, 159
　Golden Aster, 172
Hardhack, 68
Harebell, Common, 101
Hawkweed, Orange, 173
Heal-all, 118
Heart-leaved Arnica, 156
Heather, False, 34
　Moss, 280
Hedge-nettle, Swamp, 120
Hedysarum, Northern, 35
　Sulphur, 191
Hedysarum boreale, 35
　sulphurescens, 191
Hellebore, Green False, 295
　Indian, 295
Helleborine, Giant, 53
Helmet, Policeman's, 24
Hemlock Water Parsnip, 248
Hen, Fat, 274
Heracleum lanatum, 244
　Sphondylium ssp. montanum, 244
Heterotheca villosa, 172
Heuchera cylindrica, 344

Hieracium aurantiacum, 173
Hoary Chaenactis, 259
　Cress, 265
　False Alyssum, 264
　False Yarrow, 259
Hog Cranberry, 32
Holboell's Rock Cress, 263
Hollyhock, Mountain, 46
　Wild, 46
Holy Clover, 36
Hooded Ladies'-tresses, 311
　Skullcap, 119
Hooker's Fairybells, 288
Horse Mint, 42
Horseweed, 260
Hound's-tongue, Common, 94
Hyacinth, Wild, 123
Hydrophyllum capitatum, 111
Hypericum perforatum, 188

Idaho Blue-eyed-Grass, 115
Iliamna rivularis, 46
Impatiens capensis, 184
　grandulifera, 24
Indian Ginger, 77
　Hellebore, 295
　Paintbrush, Red, 69
　Poke, 295
　Potato, 321
　Tobacco, 253
Indian-hemp Dogbane, 249
Indian-pipe, 300
Indian-shoe, Yellow, 207
Innocence, 138
Ipomopsis aggregata ssp. aggregata, 55
Iris missouriensis, 114
　pseudacorus, 196
Iris, Rocky Mountain, 114
　Western Blue, 114
　Yellow, 196

Jacob's-ladder, 131
Jacob's-ladder, Annual, 315
Jerusalem-oak Goosefoot, 275

Jewelweed, 184
Joy, Traveller's, 332

Kalmia, Western Swamp, 33
Kalmia microphylla ssp. *occidentalis*, 33
  polifolia, 33
Kalm's Lobelia, 102
Kinnikinnik, 32
Kirtle-pink, Spotted, 51
Knapweed, Brown, 83
  Diffuse, 82

Lace Flower, 351
Lactuca pulchella, 91
  serriola, 174
  tatarica ssp. *pulchella*, 91
Ladies, Languid, 96
Ladies-tobacco, 20
Ladies'-tresses, Hooded, 311
Lady's-slipper, Franklin's, 303
  Mountain, 302
  Small White Northern, 303
  Small Yellow, 207
  Sparrow's-egg, 303
  White, 302
Lady's Thumb, 58
Lamb's-quarters, 274
Lance-leaved Stonecrop, 189
Languid Ladies, 96
Lantern, Swamp, 153
Lapland Cassiope, 280
Large Coralroot, 126
  Gentian, 108
  Purple Aster, 79
  Touch-me-not, 24
  Twisted-stalk, 293
Large-flowered Collomia, 54
  Triteleia, 123
Large-fruited Lomatium, 246
Large-leaved Rattlesnake Orchid, 304
Larkspur, 134
Laurel, Mountain, 33
  Pale, 33
Leaf, Fern, 231
Leafy Lousewort, 353

Leaves, Narrow, 305
Leek, 43
Lemonweed, 185
Lepidium perfoliatum, 186
Lettuce, Blue, 91
  Blue-flowered, 91
  Chicory, 92
  Miner's, 322
  Prickly, 174
Leucanthemum vulgare, 261
Lewis Flax, 124
Lewisia, Alpine, 59
  Bitterroot, 60
  Dwarf, 59
Lewisia pygmaea var. *pygmaea*, 59
  rediviva, 60
Lewis's Monkeyflower, 71
Lilium columbianum, 200
  philadelficum var. *andinum*, 44
Lily, Chalice-cup, 44
  Checker, 289
  Chocolate, 289
  Cluster, 123
  Columbia, 200
  Corn, 295
  Fawn, 198
  Green, 297
  Green-banded Mariposa, 122
  Mariposa, Green-banded, 122
  Oregon, 200
  Philadelphia, 44
  Red, 44
  Sagebrush Mariposa, 122
  Snake, 114
  Snow, 198
  Three-spot Mariposa, 283
  Tiger, 200
  Wand, 297
  Wood, 44
  Yellow Glacier, 198
Linaria dalmatica, 227
  vulgaris, 228
Linnaea borealis, 26
Linum lewisii ssp. *lewisii*, 124
  perenne var. *lewisii*, 124

387

Lion's Beard, 66
Liparis, Loesel's, 305
Liparis loeselii, 305
Listera borealis, 306
Lithophragma bulbifera, 345
  glabrum, 345
Lithospermum arvense, 262
  ruderale, 185
Little Red Elephant, 72
Liverberry, 293
Lobelia, Brook, 102
  Kalm's, 102
Lobelia kalmii, 102
Locoweed, Field, 193
Loesel's Liparis, 305
  Twayblade, 305
Lomatium, Fern-leaved, 76
  Geyer's, 245
  Large-fruited, 246
Lomatium ambiguum, 150
  dissectum, 76
  geyeri, 245
  macrocarpum, 246
  triternatum, 151
Loments, Yellow, 191
Long-flowered Mertensia, 96
Longhorn Plectritis, 356
Long-leaved Phlox, 57
  Sundew, 279
Long-spiked Piperia, 309
Loosestrife, Fringed, 209
  Purple, 125
  Tufted, 210
Lousewort, Bracted, 231
  Coil-beaked, 352
  Elephant's-head, 72
  Leafy, 33
  Sickle-top, 353
Low Mountain Lupine, 106
  Pussytoes, 254
Luetkea, 338
Luetkea pectinata, 338
Lupine, Arctic, 105
  Dwarf Mountain, 106
  Low Mountain, 106
  Silky, 107
  Sulphur, 282
Lupinus arcticus ssp. *canadensis*, 105
  latifolius, 105
  lyallii, 106
  sericeus, 107
  sulphureus, 282
Lyall's American Stinging Nettle, 355
  Rock Cress, 100
Lychnis alba, 270
Lysichiton americanum, 153
Lysichitum americanum, 153
Lysimachia ciliata, 209
  thyrsiflora, 210
Lythrum salicaria, 125

Madder-stripes, 128
Mallow, Globe, 46
Mandarin, Pink, 45
  White, 293
Marigold, Bur, 164
Mariposa Lily, Green-banded, 122
  Sagebrush, 122
  Three-spot, 287
Marsh Cinquefoil, 67
  Fivefinger, 67
  Skullcap, 119
Marsh-marigold, Alpine White, 331
  Mountain, 331
Mary, Small-flowered Blue-eyed, 138
Matricaria matricarioides, 165
Meadowbright, 331
Meadow-rue, Western, 136
Meadow Spirea, 338
Meadowsweet, White, 341
Mealy Primrose, 63
Melilotus alba, 283
  officinalis, 192
Mentha arvensis, 116
Mentzelia albicaulis, 201
  laevicaulis, 202
Menyanthes trifoliata, 299
Menzies' Campion, 271
Merten's Coralroot, 127
Mertensia, Long-flowered, 96

Mertensia longiflora, 96
Microseris troximoides, 175
Microsteris, Pink, 56
Microsteris gracilis ssp. humilis, 56
Milfoil, 252
Milk Thistle, Weed, 174
Milk-vetch, Timber, 104
Milkweed, Common, 19
   Showy, 19
Mimulus breweri, 70
   floribundus, 229
   guttatus, 230
   lewisii, 71
Miner's Lettuce, 322
Mint, Canada, 116
   Field, 116
   Horse, 42
Mission Bells, 289
Mitella breweri, 225, 226
   pentandra, 226
Mitrewort, Brewer's, 225
   False, 351
   Five-stamened, 226
Moccasin-flower, 302
   Yellow, 207
Monarda fistulosa, 42
Moneses uniflora, 326
Monkeyflower, Brewer's, 70
   Common, 230
   Lewis's, 71
   Purple-stemmed, 229
   Red, 71
Monkshood, Columbian, 132
Monotropa uniflora, 300
Montia, Narrow-leaved, 323
   Small-leaved, 61
Montia linearis, 323
   parvifolia, 61
   perfoliata, 322
Moonshine, 253
Morning Glory, 277
Moss Campion, 28
   Heather, 280
   Pink, 28
Mottled Coralroot, 126

Mountain-avens, White, 336
   Yellow, 219
Mountain Bluebell, 96
   Daisy, 88
   Forget-me-not, 98
   Hollyhock, 46
   Lady's-slipper, 302
   Laurel, 33
   Lupine, Dwarf, 106
   Lupine, Low, 106
   Marsh marigold, 331
   Phacelia, 113
   Sorrel, 318
   Veronica, 144
Mountainbells, Western, 292
Mountain-heather, Cream, 281
   Pink, 34
   Red, 34
Mountains, Old Man of the, 333
Mugwort, Western, 161
Mullein, Common, 234
   Great, 234
Myosotis asiatica, 97
   laxa, 98
   sylvatica, var. alpestris, 97

Naked Broomrape, 129
Narrow-leaved Montia, 323
   Parsley, 151
   Skeletonweed, 23
Narrow-leaves, 306
Narrow-petaled Stonecrop, 190
Nasturtium officinale, 267
Nepeta cataria, 117
Nettle, Common, 355
   Lyall's American Stinging, 355
   Western, 355
Nightcap, Granny's, 212
Nineleaf Biscuitroot, 151
Nodding Beggarticks, 164
   Onion, 43
Northern Anemone, 330
   Aster, Great, 80
   Bedstraw, 142
   Bog Violet, 147

Coralroot, 206
Gentian, 110
Goldenrod, 179
Green Orchid, Tall, 308
Hedysarum, 35
Lady's-slipper, Small White, 303
Starflower, 325
Twayblade, 306
Twinflower, 26
Nothocalais troximoides, 175
Nuphar lutea ssp. *polysepala,* 204
 polysepala, 204
Nut, Ground, 321
Nuttall's Prairie Yellow Violet, 236
Nymph, Wood, 326

Oblong-leaved Gentian, 108
Oenothera biennis, 205
 depressa ssp. *strigosa,* 205
 pallida, 301
Okanogan Fameflower, 324
Old Man of the Mountains, 333
Old Man's Whiskers, 66
One-flowered Broomrape, 129
 Wintergreen, 326
One-sided Pyrola, 327
 Wintergreen, Few-flowered, 327
One-stemmed Ragwort, 176
Onion, Nodding, 43
Onobrychis viciifolia, 36
Oplopanax horridus, 251
Opuntia, Fragile, 187
Opuntia fragilis, 187
Orange-flowered Arnica, Brown-haired, 157
Orange Hawkweed, 173
Orchid, Alaska Rein, 310
 Deer-head, 52
 Elegant Alaska Rein, 309
 Fragrant White Rein, 307
 Green-flowered Rein, 308
 Green-leaved Rattlesnake, 304
 Large-leaved Rattlesnake, 304
 Slender-spire, 310
 Tall Northern Green, 308

Tall White Bog, 307
Western Rein, 310
Orchis, Fen, 305
 Round-leaved, 51
 Stream, 53
Orchis rotundifolia, 51
Oregon Fleabane, 90
 Lily, 200
 Wintergreen, 65
Orobanche uniflora, 129
Orthilia secunda ssp. *secunda,* 327
Oxeye Daisy, 261
Oxyria digyna, 318
Oxytropis campestris, 193
Oyster, Vegetable, 92
Oyster Plant, 183

Pacific Anemone, 329
 Bleedingheart, 38
Paddle-leaf Sundew, 279
Paintbrush, Common Red Indian, 69
 Devil's, 173
Painted Cup, 69
Pale Comandra, 343
 Coralroot, 206
 Evening Primrose, 301
 Gentian, 109
 Laurel, 33
Parnassia fimbriata, 312
Parry's Campion, 272
Parsley Desert, 150
 Narrow-leaved, 151
Parsnip-flowered Umbrellaplant, 316
Partridge Foot, 338
Pasqueflower, 135
Pasqueflower, Western, 333
Pasture Sage, 160
Peacock, 62
Pearltwist, 311
Pearly-everlasting, Common, 253
Pedicularis bracteosa, 231
 contorta, 352
 groenlandica, 72
 racemosa, 353
Penstemon, Chelan, 142

Richardson's, 73
Slender Blue, 141
Tall, 141
Yellow, 232
Penstemon confertus, 232
fruticosus var. scouleri, 140
procerus, 141
pruinosus, 142
richardsonii, 73
Pepper and Salt, 233
Pepper-grass, Clasping-leaved, 186
Perennial Sow-thistle, Rough, 181
Perideridia gairdneri ssp. borealis, 247
Phacelia, Mountain, 113
Silky, 113
Silverleaf, 285
Thread-leaved, 112
Phacelia hastata ssp. hastata, 285
hastata var. leucophylla, 285
linearis, 112
sericea ssp. sericea, 113
Philadelphia Fleabane, 22
Lily, 44
Phlox, Long-leaved, 57
Tufted, 130
Phlox caespitosa, 130
longifolia, 57
Phyllodoce empetriformis, 34
glanduliflora, 281
Pigeon Berry, 278
Pigmy-tuna, 187
Pigweed, Redroot, 241
Pineappleweed, 165
Pinedrops, 203
Pine, Prince's, 64
Pinguicula vulgaris, 121
Pink Cleome, 25
Fairies, 47
Geranium, 40
Mandarin, 45
Microsteris, 56
Mountain-heather, 34
Pussytoes, 20
Pyrola, Common, 65
Pink, Cushion, 28

Deptford, 27
Grass, 27
Moss, 28
Rock, 324
Piperia, Elegant, 309
Long-spiked, 309
Pipsissewa, Common Western, 64
Plant, Compass, 174
Oyster, 183
Polecat, 55
Rocky Mountain Bee, 25
Plantago major, 313
patagonica, 314
Plantain, Greater, 313
Woolly, 314
Platanthera dilatata, 307
hyperborea, 308
unalascensis ssp. elata, 309
unalascensis ssp. unalascensis, 310
Plectritis, Longhorn, 356
Plectritis macrocera, 356
Plumed Avens, 66
Poison-hemlock, Common, 243
Poison-ivy, 242
Poison Sego, 297
Poke, Indian, 295
Polecat Plant, 55
Polemonium, Showy, 131
Polemonium micranthum, 315
pulcherrimum, 131
Policeman's Helmet, 24
Polygonum amphibium, 58
Pond-lily, Yellow, 204
Potato, Duck, 240
Indian, 321
Swamp, 240
Potentilla anserina, 220
drummondii ssp. drummondii, 221
gracilis, 222
palustris, 67
Prairie Aster, White Tufted, 258
Crocus, 135
Flax, 124
Gentian, 108
Sagebrush, 160

391

Thistle, 21
  Yellow Violet, Nuttall's, 236
Prickly Lettuce, 174
Prickly-pear Cactus, Brittle, 187
Primrose, Mealy, 62
  Pale Evening, 301
  Yellow Evening, 204
Primula incana, 63
Prince's Pine, 64
Prunella vulgaris, 118
Pterospora andromedea, 203
Puccoon, 185
Pulsatilla occidentalis, 333
  patens ssp. multifida, 135
Purple Aster, Large, 79
  Beardtongue, Small, 141
  Blue-eyed Grass, 41
  Crane's-bill, Sticky, 40
  Fleabane, Tall, 88
  Fringe, 113
  Loosestrife, 125
  Salsify, 92
Purple-leaved Willowherb, 49
Purple-spot White Slipper, 303
Purple-stemmed Monkeyflower, 229
Purshia tridentata, 223
Pussytoes, Low, 254
  Pink, 20
  Rosy, 20
  Woolly, 255
Pyrola asarifolia, 65
  secunda, 327
Pyrola, Bog, 65
  Common Pink, 65
  One-sided, 327

Queen's Cup, 287

Rabbitbrush, Common, 166
Ragged Robin, 47
Ragwort, Arrow-leaved, 177
  Giant, 177
  One-stemmed, 176
Ranunculus cymbalaria var. saximontanus, 213
  eschscholtzii, 214
  flabellaris, 215
  glaberrimus, 216
  occidentalis ssp. occidentalis, 217
  sceleratus ssp. multifidus, 218
Raspberry, Five-leaved Creeping, 340
Rattle, Yellow, 233
Rattlesnake Orchid, Green-leaved, 304
  Large-leaved, 304
Red Baneberry, 328
  Clover, 37
  Elephant, Little, 72
  European Glasswort, 31
  Indian Paintbrush, Common, 69
  Lily, 44
  Monkeyflower, 71
  Mountain-heather, 34
  Sand Spurrey, 29
  Sorrel, 319
Redroot Pigweed, 241
Rein Orchid, Alaska, 310
  Elegant Alaska, 309
  Fragrant White, 307
  Green-flowered, 308
  Western, 310
Resinweed, 171
Rhinanthus crista galli, 233
  minor, 233
Rhus radicans, 240
Rice-root, 289
Richardson's Crane's-bill, 284
  Penstemon, 73
Robin, Ragged, 47
  Wake, 294
Rock Bells, 211
  Pink, 324
  Rose, 60
Rock Cress, Drummond's, 99
  Holboell's, 263
  Lyall's, 100
Rock Rose, 60
Rocky Mountain Bee Plant, 25
  Iris, 114
Rorippa nasturtium aquaticum, 267

Rose, Alpine, 336
   Rock, 60
   Sandhill, 60
Rosy Pussytoes, 20
Rough Perennial Sow-thistle, 181
Round-leaved Alumroot, 344
   Orchis, 51
Rubus parviflorus ssp. *parviflorus*, 339
   pedatus, 340
Rumex acetosella, 319
   occidentalis, 320
Russian Thistle, 103
Rusty Saxifrage, 346

Sage, Pasture, 160
Sagebrush Buttercup, 216
   Mariposa Lily, 122
Sagebrush, Big Basin, 162
   Fringed, 160
   Prairie, 160
Sagewort, Biennial, 256
   Dragon, 257
Sagittaria cuneata, 240
Sailors, Blue, 84
Sainfoin, Common, 36
Salicornia europaea, 31, 276
   europaea ssp. *rubra*, 31
   rubra, 31
Salmon-coloured Collomia, 54
Salsify, Common, 92
   Purple, 92
   Yellow, 183
Salsola kali ssp. *ruthenica*, 103
   var. *tenuifolia*, 103
Saltwort, 31, 276
Samphire, 31, 276
Sandberry, 32
Sandfain, 36
Sandhill Rose, 60
Sand Spurrey, Red, 29
Sanicle, Sierra, 152
Sanicula graveolens, 152
Sarsaparilla, Wild, 250
Satinflower, 40
Saxifraga ferruginea, 346

   integrifolia var. *leptopetala*, 347
   odontoloma, 348
Saxifrage, Alaska, 346
   Brook, 348
   Buttercup-leaved, 349
   Early, 347
   Grassland, 347
   Rusty, 346
   Violet, 137
Scarlet Gilia, 55
   Skyrocket, 55
Scorpionweed, 113
Scotch Bluebell, 101
Scutellaria galericulata, 119
Sedum lanceolatum, 189
   stenopetalum, 189, 190
Sego, Poison, 297
Self-heal, Common, 118
Senecio integerrimus var. *exaltatus*, 176
   triangularis, 177
Shaggy Fleabane, 89
Sheep Sorrel, 319
Shootingstar, Few-flowered, 62
Shore Buttercup, 213
Short-beaked False Dandelion, 154
Showy Aster, 79
   Daisy, 90
   Fleabane, 90
   Milkweed, 19
   Polemonium, 131
Shrubby Beardtongue, 140
Sibbaldia, Creeping, 224
Sibbaldia procumbens, 224
Sickle-top Lousewort, 353
Sierra Sanicle, 150
Silene, Dwarf, 28
Silene acaulis var. *subacaulescens*, 28
   alba ssp. *alba*, 270
   cucubalus, 273
   menziesii, 271
   parryi, 272
   vulgaris, 273
Silene, Dwarf, 28
Silkweed, 19
Silky Lupine, 107

Phacelia, 113
Silverleaf Phacelia, 285
Silverweed, Common, 220
Simple-stemmed Twistedstalk, 45
Single Delight, 326
Sisyrinchium angustifolium, 115
   idahoense, 115
   inflatum, 41
Sitka Columbine, 212
   Valerian, 357
Sium suave, 248
Skeletonweed, Narrow-leaved, 23
Skevish, 22
Skullcap, Hooded, 119
   Marsh, 119
Skunk-cabbage, American, 153
Skunkleaf, Blue, 131
Skyrocket, Scarlet, 55
Slender Blue Penstemon, 141
Slender-spire Orchid, 310
Slipper, Golden, 186
   Purple-spot White, 303
Small Purple Beardtongue, 141
   White Northern Lady's-slipper, 303
   Yellow Lady's-slipper, 207
Small-flowered Blue-eyed Mary, 138
   Catchfly, 271
   Fairybell, 288
Small-leaved Forget-me-not, 98
   Montia, 61
Smartweed, Water, 58
Smilacina racemosa, 290
   stellata, 291
Smooth Fairybells, 288
   Violet, 235
Snake Lily, 114
Snakeroot, Western, 152
Snapdragon, 228
Snowdrop, Yellow, 199
Snow Lily, 198
   Umbrellaplant, 317
Soft Field Thistle, 85
Solidago canadensis, 178
   multiradiata, 179
   occidentalis, 169

   spathulata, 180
Sonchus arvensis, 181
Sorrel, Alpine, 318
   Mountain, 318
   Red, 319
   Sheep, 319
Solomon's-seal, False, 290
   Star-flowered, 291
Sour Grass, 319
   Weed, 319
Sow-thistle, Rough Perennial, 181
Sparrow's-egg Lady's-slipper, 303
Spatlum, 60
Spatterdock, 204
Spear Thistle, 87
Speedwell, American, 142
   Cusick's, 143
Spergularia rubra, 29
Spiderflower, Bee, 25
Spike-like Goldenrod, 180
Spikenard, False, 290
   Wild, 291
Spiraea betulifolia ssp. lucida, 341
   douglasii, 68
Spiranthes romanzoffiana, 311
Spirea, Birch-leaved, 341
   Flat-top, 341
   Meadow, 338
Spotted Coralroot, 126
   Kirtle-pink, 51
   Touch-me-not, 184
Spreading Dogbane, 18
Spring Beauty, Western, 321
   Buttercup, 216
   Sunflower, 163
Spurrey, Red Sand, 29
Squaw Grass, 296
Stachys palustris ssp. *pilosa,* 120
Starflower, 345
   Northern, 325
Star-flowered Solomon's-seal, 291
Star-thistle, 82
Star Tulip, 122
Steeple Bush, 68
Steironema ciliata, 209

Stenanthium, Western, 292
Stenanthium occidentale, 292
Stephanomeria tenuifolia, 23
Stick-leaf, 202
Sticktight, 164
Sticky Purple Crane's-bill, 40
Stinging Nettle, Lyall's American, 355
St. John's-wort, Common, 188
Stonecrop, Lance-leaved, 189
   Narrow-petaled, 190
Stork's-bill, Common, 39
Strawberry, Barren, 224
   Blue-leaved, Wild, 337
Strawberry-blite Goosefoot, 30
Stream Orchis, 53
Streptopus amplexifolius, 293
   roseus var. *curvipes,* 45
Striped Coralroot, 128
Subalpine Buttercup, 214
   Fleabane, 88
Succory, Wild, 84
Suksdorfia ranuncifolia, 349
   violacea, 137
Sulphur-flowered Umbrellaplant, 208
Sulphur Hedysarum, 191
   Lupine, 282
Sundew, Great, 279
   Long-leaved, 279
   Paddle-leaf, 279
Sunflower, Spring, 163
Susan, Brown-eyed, 170
Swamp Hedge Nettle, 120
   Kalmia, Western, 33
   Lantern, 153
   Potato, 240
   Violet, 147
Swamplaurel, 33
Sweet Vetch, 35
Sweet-clover, White, 283
   Yellow, 192
Sylvan Goat's-beard, 335

Talinum okanoganense, 324
Tall Fringecup, 350

Northern Green Orchid, 308
Penstemon, 141
Purple Fleabane, 88
White Bog Orchid, 307
Tanacetum vulgare, 182
Tansy, Common, 182
Tarragon, 257
Tarweed, 171
Tellima grandiflora, 350
Thalictrum occidentale, 136
Thelypodium laciniatum, 268
Thelypody, Thick-leaved, 268
Thick-leaved Thelypody, 268
Thimbleberry, Western, 339
Thistle, Bull, 87
   Bur, 87
   Canada, 85
   Common, 87
   Creeping, 85
   Cursed, 85
   Edible, 86
   Prairie, 21
   Russian, 103
   Soft Field, 85
   Spear, 87
   Wavy-leaved, 21
   Weed Milk, 174
   Woolly, 21
Thread-leaved Phacelia, 112
Three-spot Mariposa Lily, 286
Thumb, Lady's, 58
Tiarella unifoliata, 351
Tiger Lily, 200
Timber Milk-vetch, 104
Tips, Chocolate, 76
Toadflax, Bastard, 343
   Common, 228
   Dalmation, 227
Tobacco, Indian, 253
Touch-me-not, Large, 24
   Spotted, 184
Tow-head Baby, 333
Toxicodendron rydbergii, 242
Tragopogon dubius, 183
   porrifolius, 92

Traveller's Joy, 332
Trientalis arctica, 325
   europaea ssp. *arctica,* 325
Trifolium agrarium, 194
   aureum, 194
   pratense, 37
Trillium, Western White, 294
Trillium ovatum, 294
Triteleia grandiflora, 123
Triteleia, Large-flowered, 123
Trollius laxa ssp. *albiflorus,* 334
Tufted Loosestrife, 210
   Phlox, 130
   White Prairie Aster, 258
Tule, 354
Tulip, Star, 122
Tumbleweed, 103
Twayblade, Loesel's, 305
   Northern, 306
Twinflower, American, 26
   Northern, 26
Twistedstalk, Cucumberroot, 293
   Large, 293
   Simple-stemmed, 45
Typha latifolia, 354

Umbrellaplant, Parsnip-flowered, 316
   Snow, 317
   Sulphur-flowered, 208
Unifoliate-leaved Foamflower, 351
Upland Delphinium, 134
Urtica dioica ssp. *gracilis,* 355
   var. *lyallii,* 355
Utricularia vulgaris, 197

Valeriana sitchensis, 357
Valerian, Sitka, 357
Vegetable Oyster, 92
Venus-slipper, 52
Veratrum viride ssp. *eschscholtzii,* 295
Verbascum thapsus, 234
Verbena hastata, 145
Veronica, Mountain, 144

Veronica americana, 143
   cusickii, 144
Vervain, Blue, 145
   False, 145
Vetch, Sweet, 35
Viola adunca, 146
   canadensis, 358
   glabella, 235
   nephrophylla, 146, 147
   nuttallii, 236
   orbiculata, 237
Violet, Canada, 358
   Dog-tooth, 198
   Early Blue, 146
   Evergreen, Yellow, 237
   Northern Bog, 147
   Nuttall's Prairie Yellow, 236
   Smooth, 235
   Swamp, 147
   Yellow Wood, 235
Violet Saxifrage, 137
Viper's Bugloss, 95
Virgin's Bower, 133
   White, 332

Wake Robin, 294
Wand Lily, 297
Wapato, 240
Water Buttercup, Yellow, 215
   Flag, 196
   Smartweed, 58
Water cress, Common, 267
Waterleaf, Ballhead, 111
Water-parsnip, Hemlock, 248
Watson's Epilobium, 49
Wavy-leaved Thistle, 21
Waxflower, 64
Weed Milk Thistle, 174
Weed, Carpenter, 118
   Sour, 319
   Willow, 48
Western Aster, 81
   Blue Clematis, 133
   Blue Flax, 124
   Blue Iris, 114

Buttercup, 217
Columbine, 212
Coralroot, 127
Dock, 320
Goldenrod, 169
Meadow-rue, 136
Mountainbells, 292
Mugwort, 161
Nettle, 355
Pasqueflower, 333
Pipsissewa, Common, 64
Rein Orchid, 310
Snakeroot, 152
Spring Beauty, 321
Stenanthium, 292
Swamp Kalmia, 33
Swamplaurel, 33
Thimbleberry, 339
White Clematis, 332
White Trillium, 294
Wild Ginger, 77
Whisker's, Old Man's, 66
White Ben, 273
Bog Orchid, Tall, 307
Campion, 270
Clematis, Western, 332
Dryas, 336
Globeflower, 334
Lady's-slipper, 302
Mandarin, 293
Marsh Marigold, Alpine, 331
Meadowsweet, 345
Mountain Avens, 336
Northern Lady's-slipper, Small, 303
Prairie Aster, Tufted, 258
Rein Orchid, Fragrant, 307
Slipper, Purple-spot, 303
Sweet Clover, 283
Trillium, Western, 294
Virgin's Bower, 332
White-stemmed Blazing-star, 201
Whitlow-grass, Common, 266
Widows, Grass, 41
Wild Bergamot, 42
Garlic, 43

Ginger, Western, 77
Hollyhock, 46
Hyacinth, 123
Sarsaparilla, 250
Spikenard, 291
Strawberry, Blue-leaved, 337
Succory, 84
Willowherb, Great, 48
Purple-leaved, 49
Willow Weed, 48
Windflower, 135, 329
Wind Witch, 103
Wintergreen, Few-flowered One-sided, 327
One-flowered, 326
Oregon, 65
Witch, Wind, 103
Wokas, 204
Wolfbane, 132
Wood Betony, 231
Lily, 44
Nymph, 326
Violet, Yellow, 336
Woodlandstar, Bulbiferous, 345
Woolly Plantain, 314
Pussytoes, 255
Thistle, 21
Woolmat, 94
Wormwood, Biennial, 256
Wyeth Biscuitroot, 150

Xerophyllum tenax, 296

Yampah, Gairdner's, 247
Yarrow, Common, 252
Hoary False, 259
Yellow Arum, 153
Clover, 194
Columbine, 211
Coralroot, 206
Dryas, 219
Evening Primrose, 205
Glacier Lily, 198
Indian-shoe, 207
Iris, 196

Lady's-slipper, Small, 207
Loments, 191
Moccasin-flower, 207
Mountain Avens, 219
Penstemon, 232
Pond-lily, 204
Rattle, 233
Salsify, 183
Snowdrop, 199
Sweet-clover, 192
Violet, Evergreen, 237
Violet, Nuttall's Prairie, 236
Water Buttercup, 215
Wood Violet, 235
Yellowbell Fritillary, 199

Zigadenus elegans ssp. elegans, 297
venenosus, 298

CENTIMETERS

INCHES